T0326911

"Woodrow Wilson said, 'A nation which does not know what it was yesterday, does not know what it is today, nor what it is trying to do.' The same can be said of the church. In this powerful collection of essays and interviews by and with Christian leaders, fifty years of American evangelical thinking about the gospel and creation is laid out for our inspection. Here we are reintroduced to ourselves—yesterday and today. And in the midst we are challenged to think better about what it is we are trying to do—for ourselves, our planet, and our children. Perspective is a powerful thing. Read the book."

SANDRA RICHTER
Robert H. Gundry Chair of Biblical Studies, Westmont College;
author of *Stewards of Eden:*
What Scripture Says about the Environment

"*Stewards of the Earth* provides a unique historical perspective on the shifting and often uncomfortable relationship between evangelicals and environmental issues. As environmental challenges become more acute and this conversation intensifies, it is tempting to forget our history. Although I have been involved in the creation care movement for nearly thirty years, there is much here that I had never seen and much that gives context for where we are today. The book also includes some classic articles, such as Dr. Paul Brand's amazing 'A Handful of Mud,' which was one of my inspirations for getting involved in issues of soil and water. Environmental stewardship has been a topic of discussion within the evangelical church for far longer than I knew and has always been an issue of both passion and pushback. This book helps to fill in much of that history."

SCOTT SABIN
chief executive officer, Plant With Purpose

"This poignant edited volume, complete with a powerful introduction by evangelical luminary Loren Wilkinson, is hands-down one of the best one-stop-shop volumes on evangelical thinking about creation care over the last few decades. The fruit of this volume will grow for a time to come. As an evangelical myself who has struggled to walk faithfully with Christ in our polarized world, books such as this give me abounding hope. The way of Jesus is so needed in our moment of crisis. This book dares to ask: are we ready to follow?"

A. J. SWOBODA

assistant professor of Bible, theology, and
world Christianity, Bushnell University;
coauthor of *Introducing Evangelical Ecotheology:
Foundations in Scripture, Theology, History, and Praxis*

"This is an extraordinarily useful collection of essays that will be an important resource for anyone interested in how evangelical Christians over the last fifty years have thought about their responsibilities for God's creation and the diverse ways they have responded to the environmental movement and related cultural trends. There is much in these essays to celebrate and also much to disagree with and even lament. I pray that Christians may learn from both the insights and the mistakes preserved here to become all the more faithful in the next fifty years in how we witness to Christ, love our neighbors, and care for God's good creation."

JONATHAN A. MOO

Edward B. Lindaman Endowed Chair, professor of New Testament
and environmental studies, Whitworth University;
coauthor of *Creation Care: A Biblical Theology of the Natural World*

"Stewardship of creation is central to the image of God, and in the modern world one of our toughest ethical dilemmas is how to manage humanity's environmental impact. *Stewards of the Earth* is both a fascinating window into fifty years of evangelicalism groping with this problem and an invitation to fresh thinking about this important dilemma."

GREG FORSTER

director, Oikonomia Network; visiting assistant professor of
faith and culture, Trinity Evangelical Divinity School; author of
Economics: A Student's Guide and coeditor of *Human Flourishing:
Economic Wisdom for a Fruitful Christian Vision of the Good Life*

STEWARDS OF THE EARTH

Christianity and Creation Care

STEWARDS OF THE EARTH

—

Christianity and Creation Care

Stewards of the Earth: Christianity and Creation Care
Best of Christianity Today

Copyright 2022 Christianity Today International

Lexham Press, 1313 Commercial St., Bellingham, WA 98225
LexhamPress.com

Print ISBN 9781683595816
Digital ISBN 9781683595823
Library of Congress Control Number 2021947077

Lexham Editorial: Elliot Ritzema, Abigail Stocker, Kelsey Matthews
Cover Design: Lydia Dahl, Brittany Schrock
Typesetting: Fanny Palacios

CONTENTS

Introduction

———

FIFTY YEARS OF AMERICAN EVANGELICAL THINKING ABOUT THE GOSPEL AND CREATION

Loren Wilkinson

O ver the last half century we humans have become gradually aware that our presence is damaging the overall health of the planet. The articles, interviews, and editorials in this book provide an overview of the way evangelical Christians in America have responded to that awareness. They reflect attitudes which are variously insightful, inspiring, and obtuse. Together they reveal both complex tragedies and deep reasons for hope.

One can read them in several ways. One way is to see them mainly as a good sampling of the whole culture's response. At first, they are both alarmist and superficial. The first, a 1970 editorial warning that we have failed in our "cultural mandate" to exercise proper dominion, takes seriously a speculation that life on the planet could be over in thirty-five years (that was over fifty years ago!), and suggests that environmental destruction may be God's way of bringing about the end times. That editorial stresses things like litter, dirty rivers, and crowded campgrounds, but only after a couple of decades does the real seriousness of the problem begin to sink in. The first mention of climate change is Bill McKibben's 1995 article about Christmas, TV, and consumerism. Subsequent articles, while backing off from predictions about the end of the world, reflect the realization that the environmental movement is no passing fad but an unavoidable warning that our civilization must change.

Another way to read the articles is as a portrait of the particular concerns of American evangelical culture. While the first editorial sounds an alarm, the second, published just before the first Earth Day in 1970, sounds a warning. Titled "Ecologism: A New Paganism?" it (like many of the early articles) strongly disagrees with historian Lynn White's influential 1967 case that Christianity bears a "huge burden of guilt" for environmental problems. And it points out that the ranks of environmentalists are filled with pagans, pantheists, and other heretics.

Evangelical preoccupations show up in other ways as well. A 1971 editorial, "Terracide," calls—wisely—for Christian values to resist excessive consumption but uses the need to establish that "objective ethic" as a way of revisiting one of the theological disputes of the time: "Neo-orthodoxy grew out of existentialism, and contextual ethics was a consequence of the theological priority given to subjective, personal encounter. This, in turn, has encouraged exploitation." The subtext implies a direct line from Kierkegaard to Barth to consumerism.

Other distinctly evangelical concerns are evident. A 1990 article by Kim Lawton asks, "Is There Room for Pro-Life Environmentalists?" It points out that the environmental organizations some evangelicals support are, almost without exception, in favor of abortion as a way of limiting population control. The article points out the ironic tension, still unacknowledged by the larger environmental movement, between supporting the casual destruction of pre-natal human life, on the one hand, and a passionate concern for non-human life on the other.

Several of the other articles also defend the unique value of human life against a movement that sometimes suggests that humans are only a problem for the planet. For example, a 2009 editorial objects to favoring animal needs over human needs, and argues that "we can be 'speciesists' and [still] show compassion for animals." Valid as these concerns are, they do show a tendency to regard abortion as the only absolute evil, and to minimize environmental damage.

That early article on abortion points to one of the tragedies evident in the collection, second only to the planetary tragedy the articles respond to: the growing polarization in American culture. That dichotomy puts evangelical Christians, united in their suspicion of science and their opposition to abortion, on one side of a great divide, and on the other side are environmentalists, pagans, new-agers, and most scientists.

It's clear that *CT* is trying to bridge that divide. Andy Crouch (in "Environmental Wager," 2007) points out, critically, that a main reason evangelicals have a hard time taking climate change seriously is because they distrust scientists, who also tend to believe in evolution. And in the same year, an editorial titled "One-Size Politics Doesn't Fit All" responds to a letter signed by a number of prominent evangelical leaders (including James Dobson of Focus on the Family). The letter is highly critical of the stance taken by the National Association of Evangelicals on the seriousness of climate change, arguing that such a stance "detracts from the serious moral issues of the time." But the *CT* editors, while acknowledging lack of evangelical consensus on climate change, as on many other issues, conclude, "let's stop questioning each other's evangelical credentials and just do the work we believe God has called us to." They make clear that part of that work—another crucial "moral issue"—is the care of creation.

Nevertheless, that 2007 editorial is an ominous anticipation of a divide that has become much more pronounced. The very term "evangelical" has become so politicized that some Christians refuse to use it. Andrew Spencer describes that divide in a 2017 article, "Three Reasons Why Evangelicals Stopped Advocating for the Environment." It was written in response to the newly elected president Trump's withdrawal from the Paris climate agreement, and the overwhelming evangelical support of both Trump and his anti-environmental policies. He identifies three reasons for that evangelical opposition: (1) the widespread acceptance of the Lynn White thesis, which sees Western Christianity as a major source of the crisis; (2) the environmentalist/abortion link; and (3) a perceived leftward theological drift in environmentally involved Christians. And though Spencer makes it clear there are powerful biblical reasons for Christians to care for the earth, he doesn't hold out much hope for a reversal of the situation.

———

But there *are* strong reasons for hope, and though I have begun this introduction with the darker side of this collection, I want to end with the light it provides. Almost all of the articles make plain—with growing depth and insight—the strong biblical basis for the care of creation. They recover biblical truths that cultural controversies have obscured: that God delights in a creation he sees as good; that creation (however human sin has marked it) is still "very good"; that in the incarnation God reaffirms that goodness; that in Christ (whom Mary Magdalene profoundly mistook for a gardener) the Creator gives back to redeemed image-bearers the gardener's task to till, keep, and care; that whatever our understanding of eschatology, God's ultimate purpose for creation is its renewal, not its destruction. David Neff's 2007 article "Second Coming Ecology" makes that point clearly.

These theological principles are embodied in the lives of many people we meet in these articles. The work and influence of Wendell Berry appears often. Though he is admired by the secular environmental movement, he does not conceal the biblical core of his work. His thoughtful agrarianism is the focus of Ragan Sutterfield's 2006 article, "Imagining a Different Way to Live."

The recovered importance of food and agriculture in the Christian vision is another prominent theme. Leslie Leyland Fields's "A Feast Fit for a King" (2010) is critical of both junk food and factory farming, on the one hand, and its ideological opposite, "orthorexia" (a neurotic concern with eating correctly) on the other. But she ends with biblical praise for the goodness of food. Another influential farmer is the irrepressible Joel Salatin, whose thoughtful way of raising meat and eggs, respecting the created goodness of the animals, is a rebuke both to the whole meat industry and to doctrinaire vegetarians. Rob Moll quotes him in his 2007 article, "The Good Shepherd," on the increasing interest by Christians in his work: "Thirty years ago, 80 percent of all visitors to our farm were hippie, cosmic-worshiping, nirvana earth muffins. ... Today, 80 percent are Christian homeschoolers."

One of the finest of these personal stories is Paul Brand's "A Handful of Mud." Brand describes growing up as the son of missionaries in a remote village in India. He and his friends were catching frogs in a rice paddy when an old man, the keeper of the paddies whom they knew as "Tata," Grandfather, confronted them. They knew what he would say: their playing in the paddy was bad for the rice crop. But he continued, contrasting a stream of inflowing pure water with the muddy outflow from the paddy where they were playing:

> That mud flowing over the dam has given my family food since before I was born, and before my grandfather was born. It would have given my grandchildren and their grandchildren food forever. Now it will never feed us again. When you see mud in the channels of water, you know that life is flowing away from the mountains.

Brand describes sharing that piece of Indian folk wisdom with his own grandson at his home by the Mississippi River, where he daily watched the soil from upriver American farms flow out to sea. And he eloquently connects that folk wisdom to deep biblical roots.

A third way in which these essays can be read is as a way of recalling one's own life and thought at the time these pieces were written. Here I must be a bit autobiographical, for I have been involved as an "evangelical environmentalist" with the subject of these essays over the whole span of their composition. In fact, I wrote four of them (including a report to *CT* from the Rio Earth Summit in 1992). As a graduate student I was involved (quixotically) in the first Earth Day in 1970; my wife and I began one of the first Christian Environmental Studies programs at Seattle Pacific College in 1974 (read more about the proliferation of such programs in the "Higher Education" part of Randy Frame's 1996 article, "The Greening of the Gospel"); and I was part of Calvin College's first "Center for Christian Scholarship" project in 1977–78, which produced the book *Earthkeeping*. The topic we were given (and the subtitle of the first edition of that book) was "Stewardship of Natural Resources." When we updated it ten years later, we noticed the unbiblical anthropocentrism of that title. So the 1990 edition had the wiser subtitle, "Stewardship of

Creation." On that project I joined a physicist, an economist, a philosopher, and the biologist Cal DeWitt.

Since 1981 I have taught at Regent College, a Canadian graduate school of theological studies, where it has been my privilege to teach evangelical students from all over the world, many with deep environmental concerns—and in that process to meet or have as colleagues several of the authors in this collection. We are now dual citizens of both the United States and Canada, and that perspective, plus my international students and colleagues, has kept me from giving up on the word "evangelical." The gospel is not a political label, but it is "glad tidings" for the whole earth.

One of those people I met at Regent is Peter Harris, who with his wife Miranda founded A Rocha, an international Christian conservation organization now working in over twenty countries. He came as a "missionary in residence" to Regent in 1996, where he met Eugene Peterson. The interview with Harris and Peterson by Andy Crouch in 2011 ("The Joyful Environmentalists") gives a good picture of the truth that is being recovered in this collection of essays: that the work of "environmentalism" is part of the gospel. It's caught biblically in Peterson's translation of Philippians 2:15: "Go into the world uncorrupted, a breath of fresh air in this squalid and polluted society. Provide people with a glimpse of good living and of the living God" (Message). Harris (in Crouch's interview) agrees:

> I think the Christian vision of conservation is exactly as Eugene framed it. It's a wider one that has to do with human flourishing. … Ecological consequences of the broken relationship with God [appear] all the way through Scripture. But at the same time, there's the phenomenal hope that as people are restored in Christ to a right

relationship with God, there will be a restoration of our relationship to creation and healing for the creation.

———————

The language of healing and restoration takes us back to the essay by Paul Brand. Paul was a doctor who pioneered the understanding of leprosy as the result of a disease which destroyed the ability to feel pain, resulting in destruction of extremities. (He and Philip Yancey co-authored an important book called *The Gift of Pain.*) One of Paul's close colleagues in India was Ernest Fritschi; together they worked out both the relationship between leprosy and pain, and techniques for reconstructive surgery which restored to people the use of their hands. Toward the end of "A Handful of Mud," Brand describes Fritschi and the leprosy hospital he helped build on eroded land near Karigiri in southern India. Like Brand, Fritschi grew up in India and lamented its vanishing diversity of life. "Ernest," writes Brand, "had faith in the land and was determined to prove that it could be productive of more than buildings and a hospital." So as part of his work at the hospital, he started to heal the land: controlling erosion, reintroducing native plants and animals, fencing out the goats. Brand describes what Karigiri eventually became:

> I remember the hospital and its surrounding staff houses and chapel as they grew. They were grey and white and stood out on the skyline. They could be seen for miles as the only structures breaking the monotony of the gravel slopes. Today, as I approach that hospital, it is hidden in a forest with trees higher than the tallest buildings. The place has been declared a sanctuary by the environmental

department of the state government in recognition of what already exists. The whole area is full of birds.

I visited Karigiri in 1983 and remember the excitement with which Fritschi showed us its new life, describing the work that had enabled it. A few years later, I visited again with my family. This time we accompanied him on rounds to visit the patients. When one complained of pain, he said "Good!—that shows you are getting better." Later, as we sat in the Christian chapel he had designed—modeled on a Dravidian temple and open to the cooling trees—I realized that he been a kind of pain sensor for that whole eroded region, and that his ability to feel pain as a prelude to healing and restoration came directly from his worship of "the wounded surgeon" at the heart of Christian faith.

In their various ways, the essays in this collection describe the slow process of a whole Christian culture, following their Creator and Redeemer, learning to feel pain on behalf of creation.

Chapter 1

———

FULFILLING GOD'S CULTURAL MANDATE

Editorial | 1970

Ａnd God said, as he blessed man and woman: "Be fruitful, and multiply, and replenish the earth, and subdue it ..." (Gen. 1:28).[1] Mankind has prospered, and filled the earth. But now, as he is loosing the bonds that hold him to this planet, there is serious concern that he also has abused the legacy of God's goodness bestowed at the Creation.

Among the alarmed are scientists, many of whom, speaking from a non-biblical view, assert that runaway technology, population, pollution, and consumption, if left uncontrolled, could spell the extinction of the human race. Soon.

"I suppose we have between thirty-five and one hundred years before the end of life on earth," said a leading European biologist in answer to a question about how seriously we should take the

---

[1] Scripture quotations in this article are from the King James Version.

new public concern about environment. "It's not too late—but almost," declares Dr. Barry Commoner, director of the Center for the Biology of Natural Systems at Washington University in St. Louis and author of *Science and Survival*. He believes the United States is approaching the point of no return in its disruption of nature's chemical balances and has about one generation left in which to reverse its suicidal course.

Other experts are even less optimistic. The United States now has six to twelve months to "make it" in the field of managing its environment, insists Dr. John B. Sheaffer, research associate at the University of Chicago's Center for Urban Studies. Otherwise, he feels, public opinion to muster drastic measures to counteract the environmental crisis will lose momentum.

Clatter, clutter, and the signs of death already are upon us. Even as a suit was filed in Chicago recently to force twelve national and international airlines that fly in and out of the city to equip their planes with antipollution devices, eleven Chicagoans—nine of them infants—died of tracheal bronchitis in the seven-day period after sulphur dioxide pollution in the city's air rose to critical levels.

One day, suddenly, billions of creatures may literally be struggling for a last breath. People and engines are using up oxygen at an alarming rate: one trans-Atlantic jet burns thirty-five tons. And some scientists are predicting that competition for food and raw materials will grow ever more savage as populations grow and natural resources shrink. The age of affluence has very much been an age of waste. The National Research Council warns that the planet Earth is running out of gas—natural gas. Already some substances essential to society—mercury, tin, tungsten—are short. In another fifty years petroleum and natural gas may be 90 percent depleted, forebodes the council's report.

Then there is the problem of disposing of mankind's waste products. The National Academy of Sciences disclosed that American motorists drop an average of 1,304 pieces of litter each month for every mile in the vast network of US highways. It is a sobering thought to realize that many young people today have never known unpolluted rivers or smogless skies. Water and air contamination are matched by another threat—"noise pollution." Sonic booms, traffic noise, and rock music are credited with causing numerous ailments. Dr. Lester W. Sontag, director of the Fels Research Institute in Yellow Springs, Ohio, thinks noise even disturbs unborn children.

Consider the vitiating effect of encroaching civilization on recreation and wilderness areas. Campgrounds become more crowded annually, even as the Bureau of Outdoor Recreation and other agencies strain to set aside and purchase more recreation land. Naturalists warn that eighty-nine species of wildlife and fish are on the brink of extinction. Men who killed passenger pigeons, bison herds, or whooping cranes a century or so ago might be excused; today those who thoughtlessly destroy the God-ordained balance of nature are guilty of sin.

Beyond its scientific, biological, and political ramifications, our environmental problem is basically theological and religious. Religious groups such as the National Council of Churches' new Environmental Stewardship Action Team are coming to grips with the moral and ethical aspects of ecology. Dale Francis of the Catholic magazine *Twin Circle* has coined a word, *theoecology*, which he uses to refer to the responsibilities given to man by God to have dominion over the earth.

A panel of scientists and theologians under the auspices of a national ecological organization last fall called for use of "the deepest religious and ethical insight and the most advanced scientific studies" in solving ecological problems. Specifically, they said:

Population size and consumption levels must be proportional to the carrying capacity of the environment. ... Social policies [should include] the price of preventing pollution in the cost of production. ... A world community [should be developed] in which the conservation of natural resources, the systems of production and consumption, and the aims of economic activity are directed toward real human needs and are pursued in manners which support man's continuing survival and well-being.

We agree with their statement, but for the evangelical Christian, the issue is at root biblical. The "cultural mandate" in Genesis 1:26 is often quoted as the justification for man's subjugation of the earth and everything in it: "And God said, Let us make man in our image, after our likeness: and let them have dominion over the fish of the sea, and over the fowl of the air, and over the cattle, and over all the earth, and over every creeping thing that creepeth upon the earth."

God does admonish man in this text to multiply and to subdue the earth. As the doughty David Brower, former head of the Sierra Club and now president of the Friends of the Earth, puts it: "We have now done that, and the question is what do we do for an encore?"

There is another text in Isaiah: "Woe unto them that build house to house, that lay field to field, till there be no place, that they may be placed alone in the midst of the earth" (Isa. 5:8). That's where we are now.

It should be noted that the Scripture tells man to subdue the earth—not exploit it. And to "be fruitful" means more than perpetrating an endless round of reproduction. Nothing can be fruitful unless there is a livable environment. The word "replenish" (Hebrew *male*) means not only to "fill with persons or animals"; it means to "perfect," "to make good," and to "fill with a source of inspiration or power."

The Christian must remember that he is entrusted with the stewardship of all God's earthly creation (Ps. 8:6–8), but that it remains God's: "For every beast of the forest is mine, and the cattle upon a thousand hills. I know all the fowls of the mountains: and the wild beasts of the field are mine" (Ps. 50:10–11).

Recently a new business called Ecology, Incorporated, announced the sale of 300,000 shares of common stock. The new venture proposes to convert urban solid wastes into fertilizer. "These shares involve a high degree of risk," the prospectus says. But think of the peril to mankind if we fail to do everything possible to secure a poison-free environment. As God's stewards, we can do no less than to work for that goal.

President Nixon is to be commended for his announced determination to salvage our environment. The task will require many billions of dollars, and public funds should be appropriated for this cause. Let us not deceive ourselves, however, as we have done so many times before, into thinking that money alone will solve the problem. Partisan politics should be kept out of it. We face many hard decisions in the fight against pollution, and to win we may have to sacrifice more than a few conveniences.

When God looked upon what he had made, he called it very good. The physical world *is* good. And even though we believe Christ will return before man can utterly destroy himself, future generations have as much right to enjoy this world—and make it fruitful—as we. Christians must ensure this right and so fulfill the biblical commission to subdue and replenish the earth.

Chapter 2

ECOLOGISM: A NEW PAGANISM?

Editorial | 1970

On April 22 America will have its first national environmental teach-in. Pollution will be protested; population growth will be deplored; politicians will pillory and be pilloried; and privileged industries will be pommeled. In the midst of it all, informative presentations will be made.

We like clean air, water, streets, and spaces as much as the next person (see the lead editorial in our February 27 issue). But we don't propose to worship nature, any more than we take part in the worship of science, which is called scientism. Unfortunately, at least a few persons appear to have gone beyond legitimate concern for our environment to pervert the science of ecology into what might be called *ecologism*. These people are uninhibited in their opposition to orthodox Christianity (as well as to such derivatives as humanism and Communism), and to replace it they urge what is essentially old-fashioned paganism.

The Environmental Handbook, specially published for the teach-in by Friends of the Earth, a leading activist anti-pollution organization, was quickly sold out in its first edition. In it Keith Murray of the Berkeley Ecology Center says:

> It seems evident that there are throughout the world certain social and religious forces which have worked through history toward an ecologically and culturally enlightened state of affairs. Let these be encouraged: Gnostics, hip Marxists, Teilhard de Chardin Catholics, Druids, Taoists, Biologists, Zens, Shamans, Bushmen, American Indians, Polynesians, Anarchists, Alchemists ... the list is long. All primitive cultures, all communal and ashram movements [p. 331].

Because of the need to limit population growth, Murray urges us to "explore other social structures and marriage forms, such as group marriage and polyandrous marriage, which provide family life but may produce less children" (p. 324).

Another eco-activist, Keith Lampe, manages in two pages to urge the elimination of nationalism, capitalism, socialism, Communism, humanism, faith in technology, as well as Judaism and Christianity.

The first major article in the teach-in text is by Lynn White, Jr., a history professor at UCLA. He deplores the "victory of Christianity over paganism," condemns it for being "the most anthropocentric religion the world has seen," and is incensed that "by destroying pagan animism, Christianity made it possible to exploit nature in a mood of indifference to the feelings of natural objects." White argues that "more science and more technology are not going to get us out of the present ecologic crisis until we find a new religion, or rethink our old one." He concludes that "orthodox Christian arrogance" is the culprit and that "since the roots of our trouble are so largely religious, the remedy must also be essentially religious, whether we call it that or not."

Most of the handbook deals with specific wrongs that Christians can oppose within their own framework of belief. But it seems apparent that they should guard against identifying themselves too closely with persons and ideologies that are hostile to divine revelation. We too want to clean up pollution in nature, but not by polluting men's souls with a revived paganism.

Chapter 3

——

TERRACIDE

Editorial | 1971

M any supposedly crucial social issues are really medium size problems blown up by opportunists. Concern for our environment is not just one of these inflated issues. Though it, too, may represent ego investment for some, the issue itself is real and great. There can be no mistaking that our planet is dying. It is a matter not of if but of when. Everyone suffers from the problem, and everyone shares the blame.

From a Christian perspective, we might ask: So what? It isn't God's plan that man inhabit the earth indefinitely anyway. Let's satisfy ourselves with preaching the Gospel of redemption, which will save people from the wrath to come. There is no hope for the good green earth created by God, so why bother? Forget it. This fatalism, coupled with something of a resurgence of "easy believism," now crops up in the Jesus-people movement.

God in his ultimate judgment upon the earth may indeed use the instrument of environmental disaster of one kind or another. But we are not certain from his Word that he will take this route.

Even if he were to do so, he would hardly ask us to help by being indifferent. The wrath of God will be visited upon earth in his own time and in his own way, and it will come in spite of man's efforts rather than because of them.

In the meantime, our mandate is to preserve life. This was of the very essence of the Incarnation. Jesus said, "The thief comes only to steal, to kill, to destroy; I have come that men may have life, and may have it in all its fullness" (John 10:10 NEB). To fail to respect life and all other environmental resources is to demean creation and to violate biblical principles of stewardship.

What is the basic problem in the environmental crisis? We agree with Dr. Carl Reidel of the Center of Environmental Studies when he says in the interview beginning page 4 of this issue that values are at the heart of the issue. Our unwritten national goal is an ever higher standard of living. It stems from our bent for acquiring material things to compensate for lack of spiritual fulfillment. The result is exploitation. The only answer to despoliation lies in lifting men above sinful inclinations to a new plane of life and thought—and biblical Christianity does this best of all. (See also "Ecology and Apocalypse," lead book review, page 20.)

The attempt to make Christianity the ecological scapegoat is without foundation. To "have dominion" over God's creation no more requires mankind to exploit it than having charge of a secretary requires a man to seduce her. The values system that is at the root of our environmental troubles does not come from the Judeo-Christian tradition. The Bible does not promote affluence. The fault lies not with revealed religion but with those who insist on a lifestyle that is at odds with it. The greatest damage to our environment by far has been done *since* the Bible ceased to be the cultural norm of the Western world.

The despoliation of our environment is neither a capitalistic nor a communistic problem. It is a human problem, and as such involves the fall of man and his depraved nature that overemphasizes self-interest.

Can something be done to arrest our increasing ecological imbalance? Surely doomsday is not inevitable. However, some of the directions in which modern man is looking will yield only disappointments. Technology, for example, is being appealed to. It can and should be used as an intermediate stop-gap, but experts say it eventually becomes self-defeating and therefore stops short of providing an ultimate answer.

The technological problem is further complicated by the growing population and the urgent problem of seeing that people on earth who can and will work can and will eat. It is problematical whether we can produce enough food to go around through non-pollutional technology.

If the problem is seen as one of values, which it is, then it will become apparent that there is no solution in presently prevailing views of man and his ethics. Ever changing values are an extension of the philosophical thesis that there are no fixed principles or categories. Darwinian theory has invaded so many disciplines that process itself is sometimes regarded as the only ultimate reality. But in this there is no hope for earth. Only as men recognize universally valid principles will we have a basis for controlling pollution and restricting exploitation. Biological evolutionary theory is itself challenged by ecological evidence: man cannot be but another step on the totem pole of nature, and yet be among all other living things the only being capable of disturbing the ecological balance irretrievably. The fact is that in the will of God any form of life can disturb the balance irretrievably, but only man has thus far been divinely bestowed with the capacity of conscious restoration.

Neo-orthodoxy grew out of existentialism, and contextual ethics was a consequence of the theological priority given to subjective, personal encounter. This, in turn, has encouraged exploitation. To make decisions solely on the basis of immediate situations is the height of ecological irresponsibility. And only a return to a pervasive, objective ethic will provide the philosophical tool for averting disaster. The world simply cannot afford to have everyone doing his own thing.

But who is to initiate a reversal? Our inclination in recent decades has been to look to government or to education to solve our problems. But in various areas these "saviours" have let us down. People in our own day seem to be looking for a new dynamic.

Some feel that if only we could restrain commercial interests we would be on our way to ecological recovery. But as long as consumers and stockholders maintain an exploitive value system, there is really no environmental hope. No amount of boycotting and lobbying will work.

If, on the other hand, an influential percentage of rank-and-file citizens were to repudiate an ever progressive affluence, we would then have the foundation for an effective social rollback. And who alone can change the value system? The followers of Jesus Christ! Only a believer in Scripture has other than pragmatic reasons for respecting nature/creation.

The task is staggering. We are talking here of terracide, the stupid, senseless murder of the earth, man's killing himself by killing the environment on which he depends for physical life. Were Christians of today to take on the challenge of persuading men to change, they would be performing the greatest feat in the Church's history. And Jesus' prophecy that his followers would accomplish "greater works" (John 14:12) makes it a distinct possibility.

Chapter 4

———

CHRISTIANITY AND THE ENVIRONMENTAL CRISIS

Carl H. Reidel | 1971

To many minds the environmental crisis is the foremost issue of our times. They see it as having displaced the race problem, and even the question of war and peace and the threat of nuclear annihilation. For the latter is "merely" a threat, whereas extermination of human life because of environmental deterioration seems certain unless there is a dramatic turnabout in our way of life.

Feeling that the environment should be a prime concern of Christians, Christianity Today *presents this interview with Dr. Carl Reidel, assistant director of the Center for Environmental Studies at Williams College. Dr. Reidel holds a master's degree from Harvard and a PhD from Minnesota. He is a member of the First Baptist Church of Williamstown, Massachusetts.*

Question. Dr. Reidel, is the environmental crisis as serious as so many make it out to be?

Answer. Put it this way: Things are much, much worse than most people think.

Q. But how reliable are all the dire predictions? Haven't so-called experts been wrong before?

A. I can only say that there is an almost unanimous consensus on the gravity of the problem among the scientific community. Most issues are just that, with informed people lined up on both sides. But in ecology there is no significant difference of opinion on the truth that we are headed toward the obliteration of life.

Q. And you are among those who are very concerned, right?

A. Let me give you just two examples. A recent study showed that raw energy consumed in the world now exceeds by 10 percent the input to the world's biosphere through photosynthesis—the conversion of sunlight to energy by green plants. We are living on stored energy, namely that in fossil fuels like coal and gas. Or take these statistics: In the United States it took us from 1918 to the present to double our population. But we have doubled our food production since 1940. We have doubled our output of manufactured goods since 1954. We have doubled our use of electric power since 1960.

Q. What do you feel is responsible for the ecological crisis? Has science led us to defile our environment?

A. There is nothing wrong with our science. Science in essence is nothing more than sustained inquiry.

Q. Is technology to blame?

A. Only in a sense. Technological applications of science do not necessarily entail environmental pollution.

Q. So what is really at the heart of the problem?

A. Values, the values we have chosen as individuals and as a society. Sometimes we call it growth. Sometimes progress. What it amounts to is ever-increasing affluence. Not merely a high quality of life but an always climbing standard.

Q. How do you mean that?

A. Charles Reich put his finger on it in *The Greening of America*. He said, "Technology and production can be great benefactors of man, but they are mindless instruments, and if undirected they careen along with a momentum of their own. In our country, they pulverize everything in their path—the landscape, the natural environment, history and tradition, the amenities and civilities, the privacy and spaciousness of life, much beauty, and the fragile, slow-growing social structures that bind us together." Reich argues that our society has but one value—"the value of technology as represented by organization, efficiency, growth, progress. No value is allowed to interfere with this one."

Q. So what you are really saying is that environmental evil springs not from technology itself but from love of the affluence technology has spawned and sustains?

A. Yes. Our relentless pursuit of material affluence sustained by a social system that seems to value technological progress above all else.

Q. Is there still the possibility of a turnabout?

A. Only if we can change from a society that insists on crude and destructive attempts to conquer nature to one that learns instead to live in harmony with her.

Q. Can you explain that?

A. Francis Bacon warned us nearly four hundred years ago that we "cannot command nature except by obeying her." His advice would seem to argue that the solution lies in mankind's ability to understand and respect the immutable laws of nature. And he is right in a sense. The science of ecology clearly shows that man is inextricably linked to the entire web of life on this planet. Every technological innovation that disrupts the delicate processes of nature threatens the very life-support systems on which we depend. For too long we have been reaping the benefits of exploiting nature without counting the inevitable cost. Worldwide pollution is just one indication that we have violated the laws of nature, and have lost command.

Q. But man is not driven solely by the knowledge he possesses, is he?

A. No. We are captives of our culture and tradition. Our ethics are seldom shaped by sheer reason or scientific evidence. We know far more already about the ecological consequences of our technology than we employ in making decisions, simply because we are unable to turn from the affluence that technology provides. Pollution is an inevitable consequence of an affluent society that values material progress above all else. We would rather blame "technology" for pollution than admit it is the result of our love of affluence. But the fact remains that we could control most technological pollution if we would be willing to pay the price, controlling pollution where feasible and reducing consumption generally. It seems we would rather reap short-term benefits and leave the debt to be paid in the future, either by our children or by less fortunate people in other parts of the world.

Q. That seems a bit judgmental, but you would say, then, that some fundamental changes are in order?

A. If we are to do even what we already know how to do, much less respond to new ecological imperatives, there must be a transformation of our society, its culture and values. Such a transformation will be possible only when we are able to understand the bases of our culture and the motivation it fosters in us. From a Christian perspective this demands a re-examination of our convictions and commitments.

Q. Dare we try to introduce Christian truth, considering that in some quarters biblical faith is itself accused of being responsible for our ecological dilemma?

A. You are asking about the now famous essay by the historian Lynn White?

Q. That's it. The essay first appeared in "Science" magazine, dated March 10, 1967. It was reprinted in "The Environmental Handbook," published by Friends of the Earth for last year's teach-in. Other contributors to the "Handbook" also got in some digs about Christianity. What are their grounds for these allegations?

A. White places the blame for the Western world's exploitation of nature squarely on our Judeo-Christian tradition. The crisis, so the argument goes, has its origin in Genesis 1:28, where man is commanded to "fill the earth and subdue it; and have dominion ... over every living thing" (NRSV). This, White says, "not only established a dualism of man and nature but also insisted that it is God's will that man exploit nature for his proper ends."

Q. And doesn't he argue that modern science is an extrapolation of natural theology?

A. Not only that; White asserts that modern technology, as he puts it, "is at least partially to be explained as an occidental, voluntarist realization of the Christian dogma of man's transcendence of, and rightful mastery over, nature. But, as we now recognize, somewhat over a century ago science and technology—hitherto quite separate activities—joined to give mankind powers which, to judge by many of the ecologic effects, are out of control. If so, Christianity bears a huge burden of guilt."

Q. Dr. Reidel, is there a rebuttal to this line of argument?

A. The noted scientist and social philosopher René Dubos has argued very persuasively that "Judeo-Christian civilization has been no worse and no better than others in its relation to nature."

Q. And that throughout human history men have disturbed the ecological equilibrium, right?

A. Right. Dubos declares that the ecological crisis in our time has nothing to do with the Judeo-Christian tradition but rather comes from the tendency now prevalent all over the world to use land and waters, mountains and estuaries for short-range economic benefits. But this doesn't really take us off the hook as Christians.

Q. What do you mean?

A. I mean that evangelicals must face up to their own measure of guilt. Affluent countries are well on their way to depleting the natural resources of many underdeveloped countries to sustain their affluence. We are still preoccupied with immediate advantages rather than long-range consequences. As one example, we harvest fish from South American waters equivalent to the protein deficits in the diets of South Americans. And most of that fish harvest is used to feed American cats. We in the United States are but 6 percent of the world's population, but we account for 40 percent of the world's resource depletion.

Q. This fish-for-cats business, isn't that a somewhat isolated example?

A. It may seem so, only because we don't realize that many of the things that have become part of our daily lives contribute to the deterioration of the quality of life of others. But starving South Americans do suffer and our cats eat well. Take another example. We are told we are less than American if our families don't have the latest gadgetry of modern technology. And our economic system encourages us by making the unit price of electricity less as we use more, even though deterioration of the environment is accelerated through power production.

Q. Some observers contend that such talk is mere rhetoric or overkill, don't they?

A. See for yourself. The projected need for power generation to satisfy our demands is staggering, doubling every ten years, much of which will be consumed to fuel air conditioners in moderate climates and to drive appliances that will make life easier. This will mean more fossil fuel and nuclear generators that create thermal and nuclear pollution, plus a host of other consequences. We are already using world oil reserves at rates that make exhaustion of those resources likely in the foreseeable future.

Q. But aren't governments intervening in a significant way?

A. Not very much. As one glaring example, more than a billion dollars has already been spent to build an SST [Supersonic Transport] that we don't need and that scientists tell us will have a global impact on the upper atmosphere.

Q. Aren't you getting carried away here? We're only talking about a few dozen airplanes at the most for the rest of the century. Isn't it better to airlift several hundred people across the country in one jet than to have them drive a hundred cars?

A. Those few jets may alter the global climate. What is more, thousands will be subjected to sonic booms and far more pollution than that generated by a hundred cars. But that's not the issue. A billion dollars spent on local rapid transit could mean better transportation for thousands rather than for an elite few who can afford transcontinental travel. This is just one prime example of national priorities gone astray.

Q. In this connection, wouldn't it be well to try to induce suburbanites—Christian and otherwise—to use public transportation in getting to and from their jobs? What, specifically, should be done here?

A. We should provide attractive and efficient mass transportation. For the past few decades most efforts have been toward building bigger and faster automobiles, and constructing freeways. In the same period our public transportation systems have been neglected to the point that few people are willing to use them. But here again we get back to values: many commuters, for example, insist on driving to work for the sake of personal convenience.

Q. What else?

A. One agency, the Army Corps of Engineers, has plans for every major waterway in this nation that will profoundly upset the ecological relationships of these rivers. Governmental policies for the use of pesticides, inorganic fertilizers, irrigation, mining, oil exploitation, highway construction, water and air pollution abatement, forest management, and estuary protection all put expansion of the Gross National Product ahead of long-term values.

Q. But isn't it true, Dr. Reidel, that unless there is a healthy growth economy there will be unemployment and consequently a whole raft of social problems? And isn't it also true that although the United States uses the basic resources of foreign countries, it returns those resources in the form of manufactured goods that those countries would not otherwise have?

A. There will clearly be major problems in shifting from an economy based on growth as we now define it to one recognizing the ecological consequences of present trends. The task is to build an economy that calculates GNP on a new value system. We must recognize that a failure to do so may bring a collapse of life-support systems on a global scale that will dwarf the social consequences of unemployment and poor living standards locally. Why can't the technology that builds an SST be turned to rebuilding a nation's rapid-transit system? Or to building needed water-treatment plants, or reclaiming our decaying cities? GNP is just a measure of the rate at which we are achieving the values we cherish as a nation. Again, we need a fresh look at those values.

Q. Won't people starve without pesticides? Indeed, won't people die unless we continue to use a myriad of pollution-producing technological processes to produce and deliver?

A. Much agricultural production is dependent on pesticide use, but there are other alternatives to pest control. Furthermore, there is growing evidence that pesticides are losing their effectiveness as pests develop resistance. More important, however, is the fact that pesticide residues building up in natural systems—the ocean, soils, and in living organisms—may constitute a far more serious threat to human life than any temporary losses in agricultural production. As for "pollution-producing technological processes," the most damaging environmentally are producing luxuries, not basic necessities.

Q. Coming back to the biblical perspective ...

A. Yes. Dubos points out that the command in Genesis to have dominion over the earth is more than balanced in the second chapter of Genesis by the Lord's instruction "to till and keep" the Garden of Eden. Stewardship is a clear theme of the Bible, and one that recognizes the ecological fact that man does occupy a superior place in nature. If, as White argues, our superiority has led us astray, it is because some have misinterpreted this position as transcendence rather than as a niche fulfilled through stewardship.

Q. Is White to be taken seriously?

A. Well, again quoting Dubos, White's thesis has its real impact in that it "threatens to distract attention from the real problems of the relationship between the earth and mankind."

Q. What should that relationship be? White picks up some thoughts from Francis of Assisi and urges so-called equality or spiritual autonomy of all creatures. Would that help?

A. Hardly. This amounts to pantheism, which does away with categories and distinctions essential to the ecological perspective I have been defending. It raises more problems than answers.

Q. Like what?

A. The science of ecology defines the interrelationships between living organisms and their environment that have given us our emerging environmental understanding. Ecology depends on our ability to define the subtle distinctions that exist in the natural world. We gain a new appreciation for the worth of every individual organism in the creation, from the smallest microorganism to the largest mammal. Pantheism, whether scientific reductionism or White's new religion, is unable to affirm such distinctions.

Q. Francis Schaeffer addresses himself to this in his book, *Pollution and the Death of Man: The Christian View of Ecology*. He says that out of respect for God's creation we should, for example, "honor the ant." Do you agree?

A. Yes, in the way Schaeffer intends. We can honor the ant in that he was created with a unique place in nature, or "niche," as the ecologist would say. We honor the ant by understanding and respecting his place, not by romanticizing his place in human terms nor by seeking a common essence that destroys the distinctions between us.

Q. How is the New Testament relevant to our environmental problems?

A. Perhaps the most important way the New Testament speaks to this issue is in the simple fact that there is no Christian justification for the accumulation of material wealth at the expense of others. The rich young man was not willing to give up his affluence in exchange for the right to call Jesus "Lord." You cannot rationalize that you are willing "if someone can *prove* the need." Jesus said, "You cannot serve God and mammon." And his parables are rich with references to stewardship. His own lifestyle and that of his disciples demonstrated more than a simple willingness to live in material modesty or as good stewards. Moreover, the

Christian's view of creation rests on the belief that all of nature is God's creation, and that we hold it as stewards for him. We simply are not free to exploit nature for our own benefit if in so doing we destroy its life-giving ability. We now know that every disruption of the complex ecological system in nature affects the lives of men everywhere and even into the future.

Q. Dr. Reidel, where ought evangelicals to begin to combat the environmental tragedy? Would it really make any great difference if we were to give up a few cars and detergents?

A. The ultimate answer does not lie in making a few minor changes in our lifestyle, though what you suggest would make considerable difference if adopted on a large scale. But the Christian ought to know better than to offer a few token sacrifices. Jesus did not suggest that a few "good deeds" made the difference between a Christian and everyone else. Only when individual Christians make a *radical* reassessment of their personal values concerning material affluence, and start expressing that commitment collectively through the Church, will we see the beginning of world-wide action.

Q. But what are some concrete things that have the potential of initiating globally coordinated action?

A. I wish I could suggest a few "best" first steps. I suppose limiting ourselves to one small car using nonleaded gas and using a non-phosphate detergent are good ones. But we must not fool ourselves that this kind of change is the final answer. Sometimes the substitutes turn out to be worse than the original pollutants. Ultimately there are no technological solutions.

Only a change in values that makes a significant reduction in our consumption and in the global consumption of energy will be sufficient. And that *must* be accompanied with a significant reduction in birth rates.

Q. Can you be more specific?

A. I would offer one simple step, and this, mind you, is for Christians. Begin to tithe. I realize that is a rather shop-worn reply, but I know of no better way to face up to the personal question of one's own attitude toward material affluence. Learning to give up a tenth of his income will tell a person more about his willingness to make sacrifices for the good of others than any academic discussion. If a really committed Christian can't share a tenth of his income for the work he claims is *most* important to him, I don't think I can convince him to worry about "the ant," or starving South Americans, or Lake Erie. Furthermore, we can link the tithe to environmental concern by making that reduction in our own consumption count environmentally: supporting those industries that are ecology-conscious, getting a smaller car, and generally consuming less. This would have a major impact nationally and make our tithe count twice—for the Lord and for the environment. A fully tithing church would also be in a position not only to launch direct environmental efforts but also to tell a world about a lifestyle that gets at the root of the problem. Christianity has a lot to say about the effects of materialism on man's relation to nature and to his fellow man, and how those relations can be changed by a relationship with God through Jesus Christ. Indeed, in terms of value systems, the Christian ideal holds the ultimate answer to the environmental crisis.

Q. And if we don't take heed?

A. Christianity is becoming a major target of environmental activists, but not because we are worse offenders than anyone else or because we are the contemporary link to the Judeo-Christian heritage some hold responsible for technological pollution. We are criticized, I believe, because we claim the highest values and show little outward evidence of practicing what we preach. And we are back to the tithe. Taking a tenth of our income and time and talent from excess consumption, and putting it into a collective effort to teach the values that motivated the tithe, would say more to a troubled world than any pious defense.

Q. Do we have to behave as if man is going to be here forever?

A. For the Christian I would suggest the opposite. Living as the Bible teaches, that the Lord's return is imminent, might lead to the immediate reassessment of the meaning of Christian stewardship that I am advocating.

Chapter 5

—

THE ENVIRONMENTAL MOVEMENT—FIVE CAUSES OF CONFUSION

James M. Houston | 1972

Is there an environmental crisis? The accumulative impact of recent disasters and the publication of stirring books have created a general sense of crisis since 1969, but there remains considerable confusion about the problem and how to solve it.

Some experts say there is no problem. These "cornucopia economists" assure us there is still standing room available on earth, even though the global population will double by the end of this century to about seven billion people. Some over-specialized scientists who have eyes only for their own highly developed disciplines don't entirely deny the crisis but cling to the assertion that we have a lot to learn about our environment. They ask, for example, how we can fight air pollution when we are still ignorant of the nature of 70 percent of the pollutants in the atmosphere.

And of course there are businessmen with vested interests as resource-users who assume environmental deterioration is only a technical issue anyway, one that other techniques can solve.

On the other hand, politicians generally affirm that there is a crisis, as evidenced by new legislation enacted in many countries, by the United Nations environmental conference held in Stockholm in June, by the several UNESCO conferences already held, and by the support of celebrations like Conservation Year and Earth Day. Environmentalists have been alarmed for some time. Now moralists of many persuasions are beginning to think of the crisis as one not just of the physical environment but also of society.

Beyond these technical controversies, however, there are five basic causes of confusion that Christians should be warned against. After all, Jesus himself admonished his disciples, "Take care that no one misleads you" (Matt. 24:4 WNT).

1. Beware of panaceas and fads

It seems inherent in man to look for simple answers to complex problems. He seems to symbolize his needs in this manner and to confuse the symbols with the actual remedies. Is this true of the present environmental issue? Is it a gimmick of our day, born yesterday and gone tomorrow? Is it just a symptom of change, a simplistic symbol of man's unease concerning his whole destiny?

Some suspect the ecology issue because it has appeared so suddenly. Before 1969 the general public was scarcely aware of it. True, George Perkins Marsh had given dire warnings in his book *Man and the Land*, published in 1874. But Rachel Carson's *Silent Spring* didn't appear until 1962. Between these two events only professional groups such as conservationists and geographers were really awake to the issue. A few years ago ecologists were considered to be primarily bird-watchers! Now the ecologist is on the topmost pedestal of our society as philosopher, theologian, planner, and general statesman of the welfare of mankind. If it has arisen so suddenly, might the issue not be as suddenly bypassed in the public mind by other, newly relevant issues? This is the danger: if something else replaces the environment as the object of public concern, will a genuine crisis then confront an apathetic public?

While it has its faddish aspects, ecology is more than a fad. We should view our times as a "crisis of crises," as John Platt has suggested. The deeper we go into it, the more poignantly we realize the vast series of problems we are up against. It is not one major issue that now faces us but a whole galaxy of shattering problems, all of them coming to a point of crisis that threatens the entire human enterprise within the next fifteen to thirty years. Very few sober-minded scientists believe it is possible for the human race to survive far into the third millennium.

2. Beware of false emphases

In 1930, as Irving Babbit looked back to the previous century, he noted the irony of American history: "No age ever grew so ecstatic over natural beauty as the nineteenth century; at the same time no age ever did so much to deface nature" (*Rousseau and Romanticism*, p. 301). The age of Audubon, Thoreau, and Muir was also the age of the dust-bowls, deforestation, and urban sprawl. The new wilderness dwellers were concerned not about the oppressive social realities of Boston, New York, or Chicago but about escape to nature. This cult of the simple, rustic life as an escape from the metropolitan realities is still with us:

When despair for the world grows in me
and I wake in the night at the least sound
in fear of what my life and my children's lives may be,
I go and lie down where the wood drake
rests in his beauty on the water, and the great heron feeds.
I come into the peace of wild things
who do not tax their lives with forethought
of grief. I come into the presence of still water.
And I feel above me the day-blind stars
waiting with their light. For a time
I rest in the grace of the world, and am free.

Some environmental enthusiasts today may be seeking in nature solace from both the social issues of our day and the individual pressures of contemporary life.

Militant blacks in American ghettos tend to consider ecology a false and diversionary issue, irrelevant to the needs of the masses. Does the environmental issue distract attention from the points of social vulnerability where real and radical changes ought to be made? Should not our primary concern be people rather than things—even the environmental thing?

We must also be sure that pollution is not turned into big business. Man in his duplicity is quite capable of making one branch of a corporation an environmental offender while another branch of the same company turns out anti-pollution products. James Ridgeway's *The Politics of Pollution* (1970) shows that some leaders of capitalist enterprise are on the bandwagon too. Often the worst sinners are the greatest preachers, as current advertising of some companies reveals. This method of neutralizing an issue has been called "desublimation." When the chief polluters lead an anti-pollution crusade, they control protest by desublimating

it, by bringing it out into the open, and even appearing to identify with it. It is the old adage: "If you can't lick 'em, join 'em." We
need to avoid the trap of duplicity by dealing with environmental
deterioration at its source instead of making a new and separate
industry out of depollution.

3. Beware of false judgments

Since 1966 Lynn White, Richard Means, Ian McHarg, and others
have argued that it is the biblical view of man's attitude to nature
that has made man the manipulator and destroyer of the environment. Such a charge cannot be dismissed lightly; it has been
taken up by Nobel prize-winning biologists such as René Dubos
and Joshua Lederberg, as well as by some theologians.

It is of course true that the implicit belief-structure in the
rationality and harmony of the universe, which made science
possible, is a derivation of Christian theology. It is also true that
Christian societies have been destructive of the environment,
though it could certainly be argued that they have not been the
only destroyers. But we challenge White and his followers on
their biblical exegesis, or rather their lack of it.

Does the Bible, notably in the Genesis passages cited by
White, provide a warrant for man's exploitive and arrogant attitude toward nature? On the contrary, man is viewed as a steward
over nature. To "subdue" it (Gen. 1:28) also means to be responsible for it. The Bible clearly distinguishes the utilization of nature
from the wanton destruction of nature, as Deuteronomy 20:19–20
makes clear:

> When you besiege a city for a long time, making war
> against it in order to take it, you shall not destroy its trees
> by wielding an axe against them; for you may eat of them,
> but you shall not cut them down. Are the trees in the field

men that they should be besieged by you? Only the trees which you know are not trees for food may you destroy and cut down that you may build siege-works against the city that makes war with you, until it falls.[1]

Moreover, the urban experiences of man outside the garden (Gen. 4–11) provide a graphic reminder of the ambiguity of man's increasing power. These episodes show that each stage of civilization's growth (represented in Gen. 5:17 f.; 9:18; 11:32) is reflected in an increased capacity for violence, injustice, exploitation, themselves all products of that civilization. Today's environmental threat simply reflects the increased powers of ambiguities within our civilization. The immense increase of retaliatory power available in modern thermonuclear, chemical, and biological technology demands a correspondingly increased moral and spiritual commitment to principles of global concern, both ecological and social. White and his followers are too simplistic in their identification of the source of the trouble.

4. Beware of false analogies

If the Bible does not support the exploitation of nature, neither does it engender the worship of nature. Yet analogies have been used to make it do so. In the seventeenth century, the analogy of the clock and the clockmaker to explain the universe and the Creator led to a mechanistic view of the universe that still hangs on. In the nineteenth century, "evolution" became the analogue of biological theory that was applied to all the social behavior of man. Now it looks as if "ecology" will become a new analogue, applicable to late twentieth-century secularism.

---

[1] Unless otherwise noted, scripture quotations in this article are from the Revised Standard Verson.

An indication of what to expect has been given by Richard A. Underwood in "Ecological and Psychedelic Approaches to Theology" (*Soundings*, 1969). Ecology, he says, seeks the restoration of nature. It is therefore the contemporary scientific expression of cosmic redemption, the possibility of a realized eschatology. As a transcendental science it focuses attention upon the totality of life, calling for a reinterpretation of the man-nature relation. But ecology itself cannot bring about this reinterpretation, and Underwood concludes: "If ecology cannot succeed without a reorientation which is at base religious, and if religion of the culture itself is anti-ecological, then what is the way out?"

The answer Underwood suggests is psychedelic experience, a new kind of revealed religion, as ecology is a new kind of natural theology. Both thrust man into the interconnectedness of things, felt bodily and engendering new visions of reality. Both unite understanding and action, so that while ecology seeks an understanding of nature, which in turn involves a *metanoia* by scientific man to new efforts to save nature, the psychedelic experience seeks a restoration of the self in the midst of a nature corrupted by rationality.

This kind of analogical reasoning is of course nonsense, but dangerous nonsense that many swallow even though it suffers from A. N. Whitehead's "fallacy of misplaced concreteness" and G. E. Moore's "naturalistic fallacy" that values can be derived from facts. These leaps from one dimension to another are the cause of much contemporary heresy. Associated then with the gulf between the material and the personal, the natural and the supernatural, is dualism. Dualism, in turn, is the root cause of man's alienation from his physical environment, as well as from his fellow men. It is this that engenders man's manipulation of nature as well as the social engineering of his fellow.

5. Beware of false solutions

Ecology Action East, which publishes a radical journal, has argued that do-good ecological liberals cannot do more than delay the final catastrophe because they fail to make the connection between violence on the environment and the society that perpetrates that violence. They attack only the effects, not the causes, and technology becomes a convenient scapegoat while the deep-seated social conditions that make machines and technical processes harmful are bypassed. So far this is powerful stuff, but then such radicalism whimpers out with feeble suggestions for spontaneous self-development of the young, freedom to eroticize experience in all its forms, the promotion of joyous artfulness in life and work. But if all restraints are released from society to engender anarchy, how then will the earth fare?

Nor will a reinforcement of conventional religion help us, even if it is dished up in a new guise called "ecological theology." Reshaping religion with ecological perspectives may be of religious interest. Reshaping religion with psychedelic experimentation may produce new mystical experiences. But biblical faith stands opposed to such "religion"; such efforts of man to reach God by human efforts are idolatry. The biblical God is the Creator of nature and man. The heavens declare the glory of God, but the heavens are not God. Man will not find God in ecology, for God speaks directly to man.

However, the ecological issue is indeed challenging Christians to a radical lifestyle that may bring us closer to the Christianity of the early Church and instill more realism in Christian living.

In the first place, the ecological crisis challenges our attitudes to both the physical environment and our fellow men. It requires us to consider more deeply what and who man is, since matters of environmental quality depend ultimately upon our appraisals of man himself. Perhaps the environmental issue can provide new and meaningful symbols of man's needs. Perhaps too it can unify his aspirations and give them content.

In the second place, the environmental issue challenges us to go beyond knowledge, to do something, and that quickly. This sense of both realism and urgency should also permeate our Christian calling, for we are being summoned to new and deep senses of responsibility. Man is not just the thinker or the maker; he is the responsible agent. He is able to harness his thought and his technology to make the fitting response to what is happening. As John Black points out in his book, *The Dominion of Man: The Search For Ecological Responsibility* (1970), "If western civilization has failed, it has failed because it has been unable to find a concept which would engender a feeling of responsibility, for the use to which we put our control over nature."

In critical periods of Israel's history this emphasis on man as responsive was heightened by the challenge: "What does the LORD require of thee?" For us Christ is the paradigm of responsibility, the cure for the mass-mindedness of our day. He gives us the motive for right attitudes toward our environment and toward the needs of the underprivileged.

In the third place, the ecological crisis reminds us forcibly of the interdependence of life, the "web" of life. Because the earth's environment is no respecter of nationalism, provincialism, racism, or individualism, there may be in eco-politics common ground for international understanding and cooperation. At the same time the ecological sense of interdependence may also help curb the gigantic sense of individualism bred by our affluence, inside as well as outside the Church.

In the fourth place, ecology provides an awareness of limits by making it clear that the resources of the earth are limited, and subject to delicate balances. There can be no sense of responsibility, no response to the interrelatedness of life, if we continue to push the GNP. That contemporary disease of *pleonexema*, the itch for "more," so stimulated by the advertising and industrial powers of our society, must be contained. We must impose ceilings on our wants and luxuries. Likewise we must curtail our procreative freedom to bring more babies into an overpopulated world. To impose limits on human activity will, however, create enormous new problems for government, legislation, and authority.

In the fifth and final place, the Christian must lead in a new lifestyle that encompasses all these needs. Where does he begin? Perhaps in the regular practice of tithing his income. Learning to give first a tenth and then even more of it will tell the world more about his responsible stewardship on behalf of the earth and his fellow men than any academic discussion. This reduction in income can begin to count environmentally when he runs his car as long as the body and engine hold together and runs his house within a simple economy. This is one way Christians can start to control the environmental crisis now upon us.

Chapter 6

——

A MESSAGE TO POLLUTERS
FROM THE BIBLE

And "we are all polluters,"
says this scientist.

Martin La Bar | 1974

*E*cology is a word that is often used and less often understood. Ecology deals with the relationships of living things (organisms), including man, to their surroundings. It is a young science, dealing with a broad and complex subject, and has yet to reach the sophistication or predictive ability of anatomy or physics.

However, some conclusions seem clear. Among the most important are these:

1. Resources are limited. Therefore, they are passed from organism to organism. For example, the energy content (calories) of plant food matter is passed on to other living things, such as from grass to a cow to a man to bacteria, maggots, and fungi. Another way of putting this is to say that we are traveling together on "spaceship earth," or that the earth is a closed system.

2. All organisms are absolutely dependent on other organisms. This follows naturally from conclusion 1. Most animals depend directly on green plants for food. Green plants depend on animals to pollinate them, disperse their seeds, and eliminate competitors. Animals and green plants depend on fungi and bacteria for the recycling of important materials. This interdependence is expressed in terms such as *community*, a word used to designate all the organisms coexisting in a particular place.

3. A community repairs itself slowly if damaged. For example, forests will reappear in abandoned fields in most parts of the United States, but only after many years.

4. Pollution simplifies communities. A pollutant is abnormal by definition. Many organisms (man, rats, and most weeds are exceptions) will survive only under a narrow range of conditions normal to them. Spilling oil, changing the temperature, or altering some other condition usually eliminates some species from any community.

5. A simplified community is less able to repair itself than a complex community. This conclusion seems beyond common sense, and is somewhat controversial even among ecologists. However, most of them would say that a simple community, like a government with a strong legislature but little executive or judicial power, has fewer checks and balances.

6. An organism newly introduced into a community may cause great changes because there are few checks and balances on that organism. Hong Kong flu, Japanese beetles, English sparrows, the Kudzu vine (from Japan), Dutch elm disease, and chestnut blight (also from Japan) are examples, but the prime example is man.

7. "Spaceship earth" has entered the beginnings of a man-made ecological crisis.

Many people do not perceive a crisis. They seem to think that oil spills, bottles by the roadside, and perhaps some polluted water now and then are all there is to it. Some prophets of doom have cried "wolf" too often and fostered a belief that there is no need for alarm.

What is this crisis?

It is a crisis of *dwindling resources*. Energy, as fuel, as a power source, and as food, is the most critical, in part because energy generally cannot be recycled. The United States is already beginning to feel this, and the point has become quite clear during the oil shortage. Power companies are paying for advertising space to tell us *not* to use electricity unless we need to! Can you imagine an auto dealer telling us to think twice before buying his cars? Food and fuel shortages and high prices are no longer news.

It is a crisis of *pollution*. Man's body wastes, insecticides, oil spills, automobiles, and industries are choking some communities of organisms to the point of nearly complete destruction. Some rivers are open sewers with few or no fish. The pollution burden is increasing, and communities that might have recovered in a few years are often hit with a fresh wave of pollution before they have begun to recover.

It is a crisis of *extinction*. Between 1967 and 1970 the number of endangered species of animals increased from 78 to 101. Even such a relatively common animal as the alligator is in danger of vanishing forever. The American bald eagle may be doomed.

It is a crisis of *a single type of organism multiplying almost beyond precedent*, with bad effects on almost all others. Man, especially in the so-called developed countries, is fouling beaches with spilled oil, littering the countryside with bottles and cans, pouring poisons into the atmosphere, paving over land for sprawling suburbs and highways, destroying deserts with motorcycle races, ruining oyster beds with his sewage, and so on. And all at an increasing rate, for two reasons. First, there are constantly more of us, and second, each of us is demanding *more* every year. The meek may inherit the earth, but the rich pollute it.

Not only do some people not perceive a crisis, but many who do are misled as to its solution. Some feel it has already been solved: there has been so much talk, so many laws passed, that surely everything must be under control. This is not true. Probably more of us feel that the solution does not involve us, or are more concerned with "image" than reality. Some industries spend more money on advertising that tells us how clean they are than on actual cleanup efforts. The auto industry is telling us that pollution-control devices are responsible for decreased gas mileage. This is partly true, but a cop-out. Air conditioning, power steering, increased weight, and other fads are responsible also. Some politicians spend more effort in telling us they are against pollution than in really doing anything about it. Most of the rest of us feel that it isn't *our* fault, and it is up to the government to make industry clean up. But let's not forget Prohibition. Without wide support, laws may be unenforceable. Individual citizens and municipalities pollute more than industries do. It *is* our fault. Even publishing *Christianity Today* contributes to pollution! You and I are polluters.

8. No organism can survive in its own waste. We will poison ourselves, we will run out of resources, and we will destroy the plants and animals around us, which we absolutely depend on, even in these 1970s, unless drastic changes are made. We, too, are passengers on "spaceship earth." (For further information, consult *Ecology Crisis* by John Klotz [Concordia, 1971], which is written from a scriptural viewpoint, or any high school biology book.)

Heading Off the Crisis

Heading off this crisis is an immense task, involving all of us. It will probably demand some drastic rethinking. We will need to have fewer children. We will have to adjust to a lower standard of living. We will need to separate our wastes for recycling operations. We will have to do without some disposables and other conveniences. We may need to lower our standards of personal hygiene somewhat. We may need to buy economy cars and use bicycles and mass transit systems. We shall have to pay for better sewage treatment (our waste water will have to be used again before it reaches the ocean). We may have to air condition less. We should eat less. Our magnificent technology will have to be asked to do more about cleaning up the environment and recycling what we have already used than about satisfying our demands for frills (electric toothbrushes, color TV, superfluous clothes). Physically, we need to practice *thrift*. Every Christian ought to be an example of careful consumption.

That's quite a drastic solution, you say? Yes—but the alternatives are so much worse that there's really no choice. Besides, there will be health, aesthetic, and economic benefits (air pollution alone now costs the average American about eighty dollars per year).

Not only individuals but also nations must change their habits. To feed their pets and raise their meat, rich nations buy protein that poor ones need and cannot afford. It has been calculated that an agricultural program to feed everyone on earth for the next fifty years, even at present growth rates, could be financed for what the United States and the Soviet Union have spent over the last four years for defense.

Many nations have exploited fish stocks to the point of extinction. (The United States is less guilty than most.) Probably all countries have spent more on circuses than they should have, and less on bread. Recent developments in Africa and elsewhere suggest that a time of famine is beginning (see *CT*, April 12 issue, page 48). The United States and the Soviet Union are beginning to face up to the crisis in energy sources, pollution, and food supply, but not with the urgency these problems demand.

Ecology and the Bible

What does the Bible say about ecology? The Bible teaches:

1. Individual responsibility (e.g., Rom. 14:12; Ezek. 18:20). We cannot view this crisis without assessing our personal duty. We are *all* polluters. We all consume resources and produce waste. We often are negligent in both processes, and condone negligence on the part of others.

2. That the earth, as created, was good (Gen. 1:31). Psalm 19:1–6; Psalm 104; and Romans 1:20 imply strongly that it is *still* good, although perhaps not as glorious as it once was (Rom. 8:19–22).

3. That the earth and its creatures belong to God (Ps. 24:1; 50:10–13; 104:31; Matt. 10:29). If God is aware of the death of one sparrow, what about the extinction of entire species?

4. That God is concerned with how we act toward his creation. Genesis 1:28 gives us responsibility for *God's* creation. Think of it! (Incidentally, the Genesis 1:28 command to "be fruitful and multiply" appears to be one of the few we have obeyed). Just as we are responsible for our own immortal soul, *we are responsible for God's handiwork*. The Pentateuch has many statements directing the Jews in matters of this type. For instance, they were to be careful in depositing body wastes (Deut. 23:12, 13), and they were to let the land lie fallow every seventh year (Lev. 25:2–4).

5. That the cause of the crisis is *sin*. Some have argued that Christianity is responsible! (The best-known argument of this

type is Lynn White's, published in *Science* [Vol. 155, pp. 1203–7] and reprinted in Schaeffer's *Pollution and the Death of Man* and other compilations.)

On the other hand, Christopher Derrick in *The Delicate Creation* (Devin-Adair, 1973) says that mankind needs to repent of a heresy. He calls this heresy Manichaeanism, tracing its roots to ancient Manichaeanism and Gnosticism. According to Derrick, this Manichaeanism is dualist; it treats all matter, including man's body, as evil, and all spirit as good (though it relegates God to the periphery of the universe). Symptoms are the drug culture and mysticism (the spiritual is exalted) and the perversion of sex (matter is evil).

The same theme is presented in C. S. Lewis's works, especially in *The Abolition of Man* and *That Hideous Strength*. This is not surprising, because Lewis tutored Derrick. Filostrato in *That Hideous Strength* speaks for modern man, according to Lewis:

> In us organic life has produced Mind. It has done its work. After that we want no more of it. We do not want the world any longer furred over with organic life, like what you call the blue mould—all sprouting and budding and breeding and decaying. We must get rid of it. By little and little, of course. Slowly we learn how. Learn to make our brains live with less and less body: learn to build our bodies directly with chemicals, no longer have to stuff them full of dead brutes and weeds. Learn how to reproduce ourselves without copulation [Collier Books edition, 1962, p. 173].

Both Lewis and Derrick link population control to this heresy. This is unpopular thinking, but perhaps they are right. At any rate, man certainly does need to repent of his attitude toward creation, and much of the problem is not too many people but too much used by a few of them.

Selfishness is responsible (Luke 16:13). Many have greedily wasted a precious resource, belonging not to them but to God, for a quick profit. God teaches that land (and by implication what is on and in it) is a trust for future generations (Num. 36:5–9; Lev. 25:13–17).

Laziness and ignorance are responsible. It is easier to throw a can out a car window than to take it to a trash barrel. We have encouraged an expansion in consumption; but we were too lazy to think of, or incapable of deducing, the now obvious consequences.

Waste is responsible. Probably the Bible says little about waste because people in biblical times couldn't *afford* to waste much.

Jacques Ellul, in *The Meaning of the City* (Eerdmans, 1970), claims that the city, the ultimate in technology, has been an expression of men's rebellion against God. Man's attempt to shut himself off from creation and be sufficient unto himself began with Cain (Gen. 4:17), continued through Babel (Gen. 11:3–9), and reaches its ultimate expression in the Babylon of Revelation 17 and 18. God's perception of man's reliance on technology, rather than on the Heavenly Father, may be seen further in Abram's call from Ur to be a herdsman (Gen. 11–13), the curse placed on the rebuilder of Jericho (Josh. 6:26; 1 Kgs. 16:34), the children of Israel's general failure to build cities (Deut. 6:10; Josh. 24:13; 2 Sam. 5:6–9), and Jesus' refusal to sleep in Jerusalem (Matt. 21:17; Mark 11:11).

Ellul fends off two obvious rejoinders—the city of David and the city of God. His concept of the city of David is that, in the first place, it was not founded by God's people. Secondly, even in the building of the temple itself, Solomon's heart may have gone astray. First Kings 11:26–37 describes how in the midst of Solomon's building, God saw that Solomon was unfit to govern and caused the prophesying of Jeroboam's rebellion. Thirdly, and most important, the city of David is an illustration of man's search for a city not made with hands, whose builder and maker is God. Besides being an expression of rebellion, the city, as the ultimate in technology, reflects a God-given hunger, often perverted, for the heavenly Holy Place. Whether or not Ellul is completely correct, we must agree that our reliance on technology, though it provides us with many benefits, has greatly damaged our environment.

Christians who believe God's Word ought to be the leaders in protecting God's world, as Francis Schaeffer argues powerfully in *Pollution and the Death of Man*. Not only should we try to protect it because we believe it is God's world, but we should see the seemingly all-powerful Gross National Product as a symptom of idol worship, drawing men's hearts from eternal values to the selfish accumulation of treasures that moth and rust will surely corrupt. Unfortunately, we Christians have not been the leaders, and often not even followers, perceiving Communist plots (Earth Day is Lenin's birthday) or fearing upsets in the way of life that we, too, have come to love too much.

6. Certainty of punishment. After the fall, man's relation to his environment was changed for the worse (Gen. 3:17–19). After the Israelites did not allow their land to lie fallow as they had been commanded, the land was left fallow for them when they were placed in captivity (2 Chr. 36:21).

Finally, Revelation 6 and 8 mention disease, famine, fire, destruction of plants and fish, poisoned water, and the light darkened (by smog?). Perhaps these things will be the final result of the ecology crisis and man's other errors. Many scientists predict ultimate doom. So does God's Word. But it also predicts a new creation, a heavenly city (Rev. 21 and 22). Let us carefully tend the present creation, and at the same time look forward with a reverent mixture of fear and hope, mingled with shame, to the new one.

Chapter 7

GLOBAL HOUSEKEEPING: LORDS OR SERVANTS?

*We reflect the duality of the Incarnation
in our relationship to the earth.*

Loren Wilkinson | 1980

Today we find ourselves in a battle royal over how to act toward "the environment."

"Handyman for the earth" describes for Lewis Thomas the relationship each of us should cherish toward our planet. As he sees it, the earth has produced us. Now, because it has fallen on hard times, we owe it the devotion of tender care.

By contrast, many think "bulldozer of the earth" describes the modern Christian more aptly, and believe the Bible and the church have fueled the West's technological extravagance.

It may seem surprising, then, that among today's defenders of the earth the fine old biblical word "steward" has gained great currency. One conservation group, for instance, calls its donors "stewards." And a book about living on a wildlife preserve bears the title, *Planet Steward*.

In the Bible, a steward managed a household for the house-holder, his master. A steward was an *oikonómos*, one who gave order (*nomos*) to a house (*oikos*). *Oikos* is also used more broadly in the phrase, "house of Israel." And combined with the word for "dwell" it gives rise to *oikouménē*, which refers to the whole inhabited world.

We can see, then, why the new science studying this "house" we all live in, the world, was named "ecology" by nineteenth cen-tury German biologist Ernst Haeckel. Today when we use such terms as "eco-sphere" (which means about the same as the bib-lical *oikouménē*) and "ecofreak," we employ close cousins of the biblical word for "steward." It is the planet-wide dimension of the word that has made it (and its "eco" relatives) an appropri-ate way to express the new perspective on managing this house-hold planet.

What has stimulated this new interest? First, in taking a step outside our planet into deep space, we have been able to look back at ourselves and see that our *oikos* is limited—and thus requires an *oikonómos*, a steward.

Second, we have recognized that whatever else we are, we are organisms, enmeshed in a network of other life. The young sci-ence of ecology is teaching us that all living things affect our envi-ronment, and are affected by it. The main sources of the oxygen we breathe, for instance, are the phytoplankton in the seas and the vast rain forests of equatorial regions. Yet we are removing the tropical forests at a rate that will practically eliminate them by the end of the century. And we are treating the seas not as lungs for the planet, but as dumps for our waste. So by seeing that we too are organisms, depending on the organisms of the "ecosphere," we have gained a new concern for planetary management, "stewardship."

A third change producing this concern is a growing awareness—half-fearful, half-exultant—that we have a planet manager's powers. As our knowledge has increased, so has our ability to turn that knowledge into power. This is reflected in the title chosen by a leading technological optimist, Buckminster Fuller, for one of his books: *An Operating Manual for Spaceship Earth.*

These three changes in perspective—our recognition that the earth is limited, that we ourselves are organisms, and that we possess vast technological powers—underlie this broadening of the concept of stewardship to refer to management of this household planet.

Different from the Earth

Leaders in this movement, however, have accused the Christian world view of causing many of the problems that now make stewardship so urgently needed. They speak of irresponsibility, not to the planet's Creator, but to the planet itself. As this reasoning goes, the planet has produced us: now we owe it the wise and caring use of the powers it produced in us. Thus Lewis Thomas, a contemporary biologist with a strong sense of both man and planet as organisms, says each of us should be a "handyman for the planet." This is an appealing concept. Is there any biblical basis for the idea that humans have a responsibility to their *oikos* as well as to their Master? Critics of Christendom have said that the Bible has rather caused the trouble and its concept of "dominion."

The first two chapters of Genesis certainly reveal a strong doctrine of human dominion. It is clear, for example, that humans are different from anything else in creation: God made only them "in his image." Likewise the Garden of Eden was clearly created for them. This uniqueness in what humans *are* is borne out by a uniqueness in what they are told to *do*. Genesis 1:28 is explicit in its command: "And God said unto them, Be fruitful, and multiply, and replenish the earth, and subdue it; and have dominion over the fish of the sea, and over the fowl of the air, and over every living thing that moveth upon the earth."[1]

Two verbs forcefully express the intended human relationship to the earth: "subdue," and "have dominion," the Hebrew *kabash* and *radah*. The metaphor behind these words is instructive. *Kabash* comes from a Hebrew root meaning to tread down; it conveys the image of a heavy-footed man making a path by smashing everything in his way. The connotation of *radah* is no less harsh: it also conveys a picture of "treading" or "trampling" and suggests the image of a conqueror placing his foot on the neck of a slave.

These commands to men, who bear God's image, do not sound very stewardly. They seem more in line with those enormous powers over the earth that humans have recently developed. Nevertheless, it is clear from these two words that such power over the earth is appropriate. The idea of legitimate human dominion is restated clearly in Psalm 8: "Thou [God] hast put all things under his [man's] feet." (Interestingly, the passage continues the picture of trampling or treading begun in Genesis 1.) This view of the relation of humans to creation has dominated Christian thought, and perhaps explains why the ideal of "stewards of the earth" has not played a very significant part in Christian teaching.

---

[1] Unless otherwise noted, Scripture quotations in this article are from the King James Version.

Of the Earth

But it is important not to stop with this forceful picture of dominion and subduing. The Genesis account not only portrays man as different from the earth, and having legitimate power over it: it portrays him (as recent ecological studies have also confirmed) as enmeshed in the earth, and told to care for it. This other role of man's relationship to creation is reflected powerfully in the statement that God made man (Hebrew *adam*) out of the "dust of the earth" (Hebrew *adamah*). The words *adam* and *adamah* are obviously related. No translation catches the richness of the Hebrew pun here; it is as though the biblical writer declared that God made humans out of humus. Matching this intimate involvement with the earth, his *oikos*, man is given his task: "And the LORD God took the man, and put him into the garden of Eden to dress it and to keep it" (Gen. 2:15).

Again (as in Gen. 1:28) two verbs delineate human action. The word translated "dress" is elsewhere translated "till" or "work"; it is the Hebrew word *abad*, also the Hebrew word for servant. Though it is the most common Hebrew expression for agricultural labor it implies the labor is to be undertaken for the sake of the earth—not primarily for the sake of the laborer.

The other verb, *shamar*, here translated "keep," has the connotation of "being vigilant for the sake of another." When Adam and Eve were driven from the garden, the cherubim placed at the gate were told to "keep" or "guard" it, as man had been told to do; later, Cain used the same word when he asked, "Am I my brother's keeper?"

Dilemma

In these chapters—which provide the mandate for human stewardship of the planet—we thus find a striking polarity. On one hand, man is described as being, like God, transcendent over the earth, and told to dominate it; on the other, he is described as being immanent in the earth, and told to serve it.

These same two apparently contradictory perspectives underlie today's renewed interest in the concept of stewardship. Part of what prompts modern-day stewards is the recognition that humans are, in fact, humus: our life is enmeshed in the life of soil, air, water. But another source of stewardly concern is the fearful recognition that man has supreme manipulative power: we can transcend the earth; we can shape it; we can trample it.

Looking further afield in our culture we find the polarity everywhere. Man longs deeply to build cities, machines, power plants, and strip mines. Longshore-man-philosopher Eric Hoffer speaks for a large part of humanity when he declares: "Man should wipe out the jungles, turn deserts and swamps into arable land, terrace barren mountains, regulate rivers, eradicate all pests, control the weather, and make the whole land mass fit habitation for man. The globe should be ours and not nature's home."

But another part of us longs to flee the city—if not to the wilderness, at least to the suburbs. We seek the natural, the organic, the "wild." Sometimes the division is clear between one person and another; more often, however, we are individually torn within ourselves between these two views of human nature and the human task. We argue against the depredations of technology—then reinforce our antitechnological statement by traveling to the wilderness in our high-technology camping gear. On the other hand, we argue that the earth should be tamed—and breathe with pleasure the air wild nature produced, eat food bred from the wild earth's plants, and drink water stored for our reservoirs in the spongy humus of unlogged forest.

We cannot escape the dilemma: we are of the earth, and want to care for it; we are other than the earth, and want to dominate it. Remarkably, the dilemma of both our nature and our task is clearly set forth in Scripture.

Given such a dilemma, how are we to live? How are we to balance our legitimate urge to dominate the earth with our equally legitimate task to steward it, to look out for its welfare? Clearly, on biblical grounds, we owe a certain stewardship to the earth. God's command to tend the garden can only be deepened by our contemporary awareness of how thoroughly our human lives are entwined with the life of the planet. Yet Genesis also makes it clear that we are *God's* stewards of his creation. Thus we are stewards of the earth in a double sense: we owe the garden, which sustains us, care; and we owe its Creator our responsible management of it.

Resolution: Balance

The Christian's task of stewarding the earth might be easier if the Genesis account did not recognize so clearly the duality in our nature. But the duality is unmistakable: other than the earth, and of it; dominating the earth, and serving it. Presumably God intended man to achieve the balance between these two poles, and to learn to be both lord and servant.

But the tragedy of the human story is that we did not follow the way God established: we sinned, choosing to grasp at godhead on our own terms. Thus we began to set ourselves up as lords on the earth—only rarely exercising a lordship balanced by service. One way of understanding the Fall is to see it simply as the choice to have dominion, but not to serve; to lord, but not to husband. It is not that the towering achievements of human art, science, and technology are wrong. It is rather that man has usually undertaken them for himself alone, without an awareness of his rootedness in the earth, and his obligation to care for it.

Of course, man's relationship to the earth is only one of his relationships; his failure there is only one of his sins. We experience the same tension in our relationship with other people. We can use our separateness, our God-given individuality, to suck them up into ourselves, to increase our power at their expense. Or we can use our "transcendence" to be immanent in them—to "put ourselves in their place," to be touched with their infirmities. But whether we turn to the earth or to other persons, we are skewed and twisted: our "natural" proclivity is to expand our well-being at the expense of others.

We can understand biblical history as a long lesson teaching humans that they are to balance dominion with service; that the true Lord is a Servant. The lesson culminates in the death of Jesus. The disciples struggled with the lesson in their years with him, as we continue to struggle with it. They clearly expected lordship to mean dominion of the ordinary sort: the conqueror's foot on the neck of Rome, and themselves with a share in that power. Instead, Jesus began his kingdom by washing their feet.

The ultimate expression of God's dominion as service is the death of Jesus, "who, although He existed in the form of God, did not regard equality with God a thing to be grasped, but emptied Himself, taking the form of a bondservant, and being made in the likeness of men" (Phil. 2:6–8, NASB). This passage begins by calling for the impossible—"that each of you regard one another as more important than himself." Only the life-giving sacrifice of Christ provides the power for such an unnatural stewarding of others: "Have this mind in you which was also in Christ Jesus." If we are familiar with this passage, we think of it primarily with regard to interpersonal ethics. But the pattern established is the pattern for all stewardship. Just as God transcends his creation, so man transcends it: he is placed as lord over it. But just as God chose to become immanent in his creation "for the life of the world," so man must choose to bend his transcendence into immanence.

We are not saved out of the world; we are saved *for* it. This is the inescapable implication of Romans 8:19: "The creation waits in eager expectation for the sons of God to be revealed." Our "tending" of the garden earth is not a mere preservation, nor is it a man-centered destruction: rather, it is a transformation of the earth in light of God's purposes. This preserves the purpose and uniqueness of each thing, even as our own salvation presents us with true selfhood.

This view of the relationship between our salvation and the earth has not been common in Western Christianity, but it has long been an important doctrine of the Eastern church. One contemporary Eastern Orthodox thinker has written: "In his way to union with God, man in no way leaves creatures aside, but gathers together in his love the whole cosmos, disordered by sin, that it may at last be transfigured by Grace." Western Christianity might learn much from this aspect of Eastern tradition. But the basic principle—that man is redeemed back into his original stewardly role towards the earth—is inescapably biblical.

Implications of Balance

The secular concern for stewardship of the earth thus bears a certain harmony with biblical principles. Christians should be leaders, not followers, in such a movement, for God's stewarding of us in Christ provides us with not only an example, but the power to carry it out. What does it mean, specifically, for Christians to exercise stewardship of the earth? In general, it means we cannot act as though the maintenance of our own well-being is all important. That, of course, is basic Christian behavior. What a concern for Christian stewardship of the earth suggests, however, is that we extend our awareness of the impact of our actions beyond our family, friends, and neighbors, to all peoples of the earth, to future generations, and to the whole household: the *oikouménē*, or ecosphere—all the interrelated life of the planet.

Such a stewarding is enormously complex, for it must seek to match our understanding with the complexity of the ecosphere. This understanding of the earth's complexity is, after all, nothing more than carrying out in detail the command to know and name the earth's creatures. Nevertheless, within that complexity several principles, and some specific guidelines, can be pointed out.

1. No process of agriculture, mining, transportation, energy generation, waste disposal, recreation—in short, no resource-using human activity—should take place until its consequences for the household of life have been established with reasonable certainty. When we understand the breadth of our household, such concern becomes simply good "economy": stewardship.

2. As planet managers, we need to know how the planet works. Careful, loving, imaginative study of creation is thus not simply a secular necessity: it is a Christian duty. Too often we have acted out of ignorance of basic "ecological" or "household" principles the science of ecology now makes available to us.

3. The demands placed on stewards by both the human population and the whole ecosphere are complementary. The biblical picture of creation does not leave room for elimination of the nonhuman at the expense of the human; nor does it suggest that the demands of other creatures need diminish the true quality of human life. It is not a case, as one recent writer put it, of "people or penguins." There is room for the whole household—though it may take careful management to provide it.

4. Good stewardship does not mean abandoning technology. Man is indeed in dominion over the planet; it is legitimate for him to use his knowledge to increase his power. The more power he has, however, the more he must seek to use it for the whole world.

5. Good stewardship does not place on the future greater debts than it inherited from the past. This principle is particularly important in considering our use of nonrenewable resources like metals and fossil fuels. It suggests that if we use those things, part of their use should be diverted to establishing a substitute the future can use. For example, establishment of facilities for capturing and distributing renewable solar energy should be a major goal of the burning of nonrenewable oil or coal.

All these principles could entail serious costs, and might mean that we would have to live less luxuriously, eat differently, travel less. They certainly mean rejecting the assumption, implicit in our economic system, that growth is always good.

These are some of the implications of our stewardship—the legitimate human lordship of the earth, exercised after the mind and example of Christ, who gave himself "for the life of the world"—which bids us, in our lives, and for our great household, to do the same thing.

Chapter 8

A HANDFUL OF MUD

*Soil is life. Can we preserve it
for future generations?*

Paul Brand | 1985

I grew up in the mountains of South India. My parents were missionaries to the tribal people of the hills, and our lives were about as simple as they could be—and as happy.

There were no roads. (We never saw a wheeled vehicle except on our annual visit to the plains.) There were no stores, no electricity, no plumbing. My sister and I ran barefoot, and we made our own games from the trees, sticks, and stones around us. Our playmates were the Indian boys and girls, and our lives were much the same as theirs.

Rice was an important food for all of us. And since there was no level ground for wet cultivation, it was grown all along the streams that ran down the land's gentle slopes. These slopes had been patiently terraced hundreds of years before; and now every one was perfectly level, and bordered at its lower margin by an earthen dam covered by grass. Each narrow dam served as a foot-path across the line of terraces, with a level field of mud and water six inches below its upper edge and another level terrace two feet below. There were no steep or high drop-offs, so there was little danger of collapse.

Those rice paddies were a rich soup of life. When there was plenty of water there would be a lot of frogs and little fish. Egrets would stalk through the paddy fields on their long legs and enjoy the feast. Kingfishers would swoop down with a flash of color and carry off a fish from under the beak of a heron. And it was here I learned my first lesson on conservation.

I was playing in the mud of a rice field with a half-dozen other little boys. We were racing to see who would be the first to catch three frogs. It was a wonderful way to get dirty from head to foot in the shortest possible time. Suddenly, we were all scrambling to get out of the paddy. One of the boys had spotted an old man walking across the path toward us. We all knew him as "Tata," or "Grandpa." He was the keeper of the dams. He walked slowly, and was stooped over a bit as though he were always looking at the ground. Old age is very much respected in India, and we boys shuffled our feet and waited in silence for what we knew would be a rebuke.

He came over to us and asked us what we were doing. "Catching frogs," we answered. He stared down at the churned-up mud and flattened young rice plants in the corner where we had been playing. I was expecting him to talk about the rice seedlings we had just spoiled. Instead, the elder stooped down and scooped up a handful of mud. "What is this?" he asked. The biggest boy took the responsibility of answering for us all.

"It's mud, Tata," he replied.

"Whose mud is it?" the old man asked.

"It's your mud, Tata, this is your field."

Then the old man turned and looked at the nearest of the little channels across the dam. "What do you see there, in that channel?"

"That is water, running over into the lower field."

For the first time Tata looked angry. "Come with me and I will show you water." A few steps along the dam he pointed to the next channel, where clear water was running, "That is what water looks like," he said. Then we came back to our nearest channel, and he said again "Is that water?"

We hung our heads. "No, Tata, that is mud." The older boy had heard all this before and did not want to prolong the question-and-answer session, so he hurried on. "And the mud from your field is being carried away to the field below, and it will never come back, because mud always runs downhill, never up again. We are sorry, Tata, and we will never do this again."

Tata was not ready to stop his lesson as quickly as that, however. He went on to tell us that just one handful of mud would grow enough rice for one meal for one person, and it would do it twice every year for years and years into the future. "That mud flowing over the dam has given my family food since before I was born, and before my grandfather was born. It would have given my grandchildren and their grandchildren food forever. Now it will never feed us again. When you see mud in the channels of water, you know that life is flowing away from the mountains."

The old man walked slowly back across the path, pausing a moment to adjust with his foot the grass clod in our muddy channel so that no more water flowed through it. We were silent and uncomfortable as we went off to find some other place to play. I had experienced a dose of traditional Indian folk education that would remain with me as long as I lived. Soil is life, and every generation is responsible for all generations to come.

The Hand of Man

I have been back to my childhood home several times. There have been changes. A road now links the hill people with the plains folk, but traditional ways still go on. The terraced paddy fields still hold back the mud. Rice still grows. And the old man the boys call "Tata" is now one of the boys I used to play with 65 years ago. I am sure he lays down the law when he catches someone churning up the mud, and I hope the system holds for years to come. I have seen what happens when it doesn't.

The Nilgiri hills, or Blue Mountains, were a favorite resort in the hot season for missionaries from the plains. They were steep and thickly forested, with few areas level enough for cultivation, even with terraces. The forestry service allowed no clearing of the trees except where tea, coffee, or fruit trees were to be planted. These bushes and trees, in turn, held the soil—and all was well.

Thirty years after my encounter with "Tata" I was back in India, a doctor and a missionary myself, with a wife and growing family. We began going to the Nilgiris for every summer holiday, and our children reveled in the cool air and lush forests. But something was different, or soon became so.

A new breed of landowners had begun to take possession of the land. These new "farmers"—former political prisoners who, following India's independence, were given tracts of land—had not farmed before. They had never been exposed to a Tata teaching them the value of mud. They wanted to make money, and make it fast. They knew the climate was ideal for potatoes, and that there was a market for such a crop. Forests were thus cleared on sloping land, and potatoes planted. Two and even three crops could be harvested per year, and money flowed freely into their purse.

But harvesting potatoes involves turning over the soil, and monsoon rains often came before a new crop could hold that soil. Not surprisingly then, as my family and I returned to those mountains of boyhood memory, the water now looked like chocolate syrup. It oozed rather than flowed. We were seeing rivers of mud. I felt sick.

I went over to ask old Mr. Fritschi and his wife, a dear Swiss couple living in Coonoor on the Nilgiri hills, about the havoc that was being wrought and to find out if there was anything we could do. They had been missionaries of the Basel Mission but were long retired and now owned a nursery of young plants and trees. They loved to help and advise farmers and gardeners about ways to improve their crops. It seemed to me that these devoted people would know if there was some way to advise the landowners about ways to save their soil.

Mr. Fritschi's eyes were moist as he told me, "I have tried, but it is no use. They have no love of the land, only of money. They are making a lot of money, and they do not worry about the loss of soil, because they think it is away in the future, and they will have money to buy more." Besides, he continued, they can deduct the loss of land from their income tax as business depreciation.

Thirty more years have passed and we have left India. But every year I go back to visit Vellore Christian Medical College and take part in the leprosy work there. I do not, however, enjoy going back to the Nilgiri hills. I look up to those slopes and see large areas of bare rock of no use to anybody. Those deforested areas that still have some soil look like gravel. And the clear streams and springs that ran off from these areas 60 years earlier are dry today. When the rains come they rush in torrents and flood, then they go dry.

Oh Tata! Where have you gone? You have been replaced by businessmen and accountants who have degrees in commerce and who know how to manipulate tax laws. You have been replaced by farmers who know about pesticides and chemical fertilizers, but who care nothing about leaving soil for their great-grandchildren.

A Worldwide Drama

Outside of India I have seen another drama involving trees, soil, water, and human starvation working its tragic sequence. The place is Ethiopia.

I first came to Ethiopia in the early 1960s when I went to Addis Ababa on behalf of the International Society for the Rehabilitation of the Disabled. My task was to negotiate the establishment of an all-Africa training center for leprosy workers, with an emphasis on rehabilitation. I met Emperor Haile Selassie and his minister of health, as well the ministers of agriculture and commerce, the dean of the then-new University Medical College, and representatives of American AID and the Rockefeller foundation. Later I went to work in the new training center as a surgeon, teaching reconstruction of the hand and foot. But, as had happened so often in my life, it was the land that caught my attention. Most of our leprosy patients were farmers, and their future had to be in farming if they were not to be dislocated from their families and villages.

The emperor was very gracious as we talked about the problem. He gave us the use of tracts of the royal lands to farm. The Swedish churches had sent farmers into Ethiopia to teach the patients how to farm more efficiently; and it was a joy to see acres of tef, the local food grain, growing to harvest. Patients with leprosy were learning how to work without doing damage to their insensitive hands. We were grateful to the benevolent old emperor, and all seemed to be going well. Gradually, however, we began to see the real problems of that tragic country.

Camping out in the countryside, while visiting distant treatment centers, we were impressed with the way the countryside was fissured with deep canyons where streams had eroded the soil on their way to join the Blue Nile. Farms on the edges of these canyons were having to retreat year by year as their soil slipped away into the rivers. There had once been trees and forests on this land, but the trees had been felled for timber and firewood, and also to make way for grazing and cultivation.

What impressed me most, however, were the poor crops and stony fields that were cultivated by the peasant farmers. Every field seemed to be covered with great stones and boulders. Many of these stones were of a size that could have easily been levered up and rolled away to the edges of the fields where they would have made useful walls to hold the soil in and keep marauders out. As it was, it must have been a constant irritation to have to till and harvest between these rocks.

It did not take much inquiry to find out why such simple improvements had never been made. The peasants knew, and were frank to tell us, that if ever they made their fields look good they would lose them. The ruling race of Amharas, based in the capital city, contained all the lawyers and leaders of the country. Any good piece of land could be claimed by one of the city-dwelling Amharas simply by stating that it had belonged to his ancestors. Supporting documents were easy to obtain. In court the peasant had no chance. His only hope of being allowed to continue farming his land was to make it appear worthless.

Both the Ford foundation and the Rockefeller foundation had considered sending help to teach good farming methods and to halt erosion, but both insisted to the emperor that land reform had to come first. Only if the land were owned by the people who farmed it would it be taken care of in a way that would preserve it for generations to come. The peasants had to have confidence that their handful of mud would still be there for their children. If not, why not let it go down the river?

I believe the emperor wanted to introduce land reform; but if he tried, he failed. The Amharas were too strong for him. The established church, the old Ethiopian Orthodox church of which the emperor was head, had vested interest in the status quo, and was on the wrong side of real justice. This has happened so often in the past, when churches got comfortable and wealthy. We need to be watchful and aware today.

On a state visit to Egypt, Emperor Haile Selassie walked down to the river Nile and kneeled to scoop up two handfuls of the rich fertile mud on its bank. Raising his hands, he said, "My country." The Blue Nile had carried Ethiopia to Egypt, and the old emperor knew it. He could not send the mud upstream again and he did not have the courage to make the changes that would have arrested further loss.

Today the emperor is dead. Every cabinet minister with whom I negotiated for our training center is dead—they were killed by the firing squads of the revolution. There might not have been a famine today if the trees had not all been cut, if the land had not eroded away, if the absentee landlords of Ethiopia had not been so greedy, and if the church had insisted that justice should prevail.

I did not like the revolution or the foreign invaders who brought it about, but they would never have succeeded if the people had not been laboring under a sense of injustice. The new Marxist government has not suceeded in bringing back the trees or the land, and it has spent its energy in war. But the roots of Ethiopia's problems stem from generations ago—even before the leaders who have now died for their collective sins.

Kindred Sins

Today I live in Louisiana. I have no soil or water problems. In fact, my topsoil is so deep and so rich that I would not even try to plumb its depth. And the land is so flat that even when it floods my soil stays where it is.

But I cannot be at peace. My home is right beside the Mississippi River. I could probably throw a stone into the water from my roof. My house is an old one and built up on piles. At the time it was built, the occupants would expect to sit on their porch and watch the muddy waters of the Mississippi swirl under the house for a few days each year. If I were to analyze my garden soil, I would find that most of it came from Kansas and Ohio and Iowa and other states upriver. A farmer from Iowa could come to my garden, as the emperor of Ethiopia did in Egypt, scoop up a handful of mud, and say, "My farm!"

But no mud comes from Iowa to my garden now. The corps of engineers has built a dam, or levee, all along the bank of the river, so the mud runs straight out to sea. During the spring floods, I walk along the levee and look at that mud. They tell me that many whole farms flow past my house every hour. I know that Iowa has lost more than half its topsoil just in the hundred or so years since Americans started farming that land.

Because I am haunted by the mountains of India and by the erosion of Ethiopia, I have to ask why American farmers still lose soil. They tell me they know all about contour plowing, but say modern farming machinery is so big that it is impossible or uneconomic to plow around contours. So they just go straight up and down. They get it done faster—and lose the soil faster. This all gives better returns to the shareholders, and improves all the market indicators. Shareholders and members of the board are today's absentee landlords of the farm. They are not farmers. They tell me that only small family farms still do contour plowing, but they are going out of business. Big companies are buying them up, so they can use "efficient" methods.

They tell me that the American forests are replanted when they are cut, and I think that is probably true. But I also understand that wide clear-cutting is practiced even on steep slopes. It is a matter of pride that every part of every tree is used for timber or pulp or chipboard when it is cut. But then, nothing goes back into the land. There is no building of the soil, just depletion.

My Mississippi River is also the site now of scores of petro-chemical plants and herbicide factories. I have chemical plants to my right and industrial plants to my left. (The proximity of the river is convenient for getting water to cooling towers and receiving effluents.) All the trees downwind have turned white and died. They tell me it was fluorides, but it could have been any one of the effluents that have given parts of Louisiana the highest incidence of cancer in the country. Ten years ago all the cattle in this area were declared unfit to sell for beef because of unacceptable levels of tetrachlormethane in their fat. I wonder what the levels are in me and my family.

I look at the great Mississippi and think back to the days of Huckleberry Finn and his raft, when the river was largely water and fish. I look down now at the swirling mud and see it as no better than the Blue Nile, or the Cauvery River in India that carries mud from the Nilgiri Hills. Is there a common thread? It is not ignorance in all cases. Nor is it dire poverty (although that sometimes leads to the cutting of the trees for fuel). No, there would be enough for all if it were not for greed. More profit. Faster return on investment. A bigger share *for me* of what is available now, but may not be available tomorrow.

God has something to say to us about this. And he said it repeatedly by his prophets. Moses described in detail the care of the land in Leviticus 25. It was to be nurtured and given a regular sabbath year of rest. It was never to be sold on a permanent basis but regarded as a trust from the Lord. "The earth is [the LORD's], ... and you are sojourners ..." (25:23). Later, Isaiah pronounces God's judgment: "The earth dries up and withers, the whole earth grows sick; ... the earth itself is desecrated by the feet of those who live in it, because they have broken the laws ... and violated the eternal covenant (24:4–5 NEB). Hosea adds: "Because of this the land mourns, and all who live in it waste away; the beasts of the field and the birds of the air and the fish of the sea are dying" (4:3). God is concerned about his creation and looks to us whom he put in charge of it. We are to share in its redemption (Rom. 8:21), not be agents of its destruction.

My Legacy

I would gladly give up medicine tomorrow if by so doing I could have some influence on policy with regard to mud and soil. The world will die from lack of pure water and soil long before it will die from a lack of antibiotics or surgical skill and knowledge. But what can be done if the destroyers of our earth know what they are doing and do it still? What can be done if people really believe that free enterprise has to mean absolute lack of restraint on those who have no care for the future?

I cannot, however, conclude without a small balance of joy and an indication that God still has a church that produces people who care. In the final analysis it is not knowledge or lack of it that makes a difference, but concerned people. The sense of concern for the earth is still transmitted by person-to-person communication and by personal example better than by any other method. Old Tata still lives on. He lives in the boys who played in the mud, and they will pass on his concern for the soil and his sense of its importance to future generations.

Old Mr. Fritschi still lives on through his son. The love of trees he tried to promote in the Nilgiri hills is now being promoted by his son on the plains at Karigiri. A single dedicated person giving a good example is better than a lot of wringing of hands and prophecies of doom.

Ernest Fritschi was born in India and lived there long enough to love it, take Indian nationality, and marry a lovely Indian wife. He studied in Madras University, became a doctor, and then an orthopedic surgeon. Working with leprosy patients, he joined the Leprosy Mission and worked in many countries, including Ethiopia, and then became director of the Schieffelin Research and Training Center at Karigiri near Vellore.

The land for the center had been barren gravel with not a tree anywhere, and water had been hard to locate. I remember walking over the large acre-age before we started to build and thinking that it was no surprise the government had donated it so freely. It was good for nothing else.

Ernest, however, had faith in the land and was determined to prove that it could be productive of more than buildings and a hospital. Other directors had made a good start, but Ernest made a rule for himself that every year he would plant trees. He collected seeds and seedlings from everywhere and nourished them in his own garden until they were strong. Then he would plant them out just before the rains, and have them watered by staff and patients until they had root systems deep enough to survive. The hill that formed one border of the Karigiri land was bare and rocky, and the rains would send a rushing flood of water over the gravel of the hospital grounds. So Ernest built contour ridges of gravel and soil to hold the water long enough for it to soak in.

I remember the hospital and its surrounding staff houses and chapel as they grew. They were grey and white and stood out on the skyline. They could be seen for miles as the only structures breaking the monotony of the gravel slopes. Today, as I approach that hospital, it is hidden in a forest with trees higher than the tallest buildings. The place has been declared a sanctuary by the environmental department of the state government in recognition of what already exists. The whole area is full of birds; we counted and identified over forty species in one afternoon. The water table, falling in most places, was rising last year under the gravel at Karigiri. Soil is building, not being lost.

What is a few acres among the millions where the reverse is true? It is important to me because it sounds a message. One man can make a difference. Dedication is what is needed. And faith. It is important, too, because the man who made this little revolution is not a professional farmer or a government official. He is a doctor who loves trees, soil, and water. He was sometimes criticized by his board of governors who said his goals and objectives should be to treat and rehabilitate leprosy patients. Money, they argued, should not be diverted to other goals, like farming and reforestation. But he proved that concern for soil and trees benefits patients too. Buildings do not need air conditioning when they are shaded by trees. Patients who see and participate in good practices on the land learn to reproduce the same when they go home.

Not far from there is the Christian Medical College, founded by the beloved American doctor Ida Scudder. She insisted on building the college on an extensive piece of land where there would be room for gardens and trees. She was followed by others who had the same view, including the first Indian director, Dr. Hilda Lazarus, who doubtless had claims to fame in her own medical specialty but whom I remember for her love of trees.

Dr. Lazarus is long gone, but her trees and philosophy remain. In my day we used to get excited and concerned about new drugs and new diagnostic equipment, but today when I visit the Christian Medical College, I find the director more likely to be excited about preserving the water table, and growing the right kind of crops and preserving the soil. This is health, and this is hope for the future. There is still life in the land, and God still blesses those who recognize "the earth is the LORD's."

I am a grandfather now. My grandchildren do not call me Tata, but I rather wish they would. It would not mean much to them, but it would remind me that, in addition to the immortality of our spirit, we all have a sort of immortality of our flesh. If the kids called me Tata, it would remind me that, down the centuries, there may be many generations of people who will bear my humanity, who will enjoy life, or who will suffer in proportion to the care that I now take to preserve the good gifts that God has given us. Part of that care is in teaching and in example.

My grandson is called Daniel, and the next time he comes to visit me I shall take him out into my garden and scoop up a handful of mud. I shall ask him, "Daniel, what is this?"

Chapter 9

IS THERE ROOM
FOR PROLIFE
ENVIRONMENTALISTS?

Kim A. Lawton | 1990

laire Brown of Norristown, Pennsylvania, has a deep concern about the environment and wildlife. For many years,
she has been a steady contributor to the National Wildlife
Federation and a frequent supporter of the Audubon Society
and the Sierra Club.

She is also prolife. So when she discovered this summer that
these groups are lobbying in Congress against prolife legislation
she supports, she was shocked and dismayed. "I felt personally
betrayed," she told *Christianity Today*. "I'd like to help [these
groups] out, but I can't understand an organization that supports
animal life and yet has, from what I can gather, little regard for
human life. I think this is outside their charter," she said.

A growing number of persons who are prolife shares Brown's concerns. "Several major environmental organizations have become increasingly active in promoting proabortion policies on the federal level," said National Right to Life Committee (NRLC) Legislative Director Douglas Johnson. "Many Americans who support the Bush administration's prolife policies are unknowingly contributing to environmental organizations that lobby to nullify those policies," he added. While some environmental groups acknowledge their support of abortion—support based mainly on concerns of overpopulation—other groups say the NRLC is "inaccurate" in its claims.

The controversy is likely to come to a head this month as Congress debates the Foreign Aid Appropriations Bill. At issue will be two measures that the NRLC says make up "the most important antiabortion policy of the Reagan years": the Mexico City Policy and the Kemp/Kasten Amendment.

The Mexico City Policy, announced by Ronald Reagan in 1984, prohibits the US government's family-planning program from funding organizations that campaign for legalized abortion internationally or promote abortion "as a method of family planning" in foreign countries.

The Kemp/Kasten Amendment, enacted in 1985, prohibits US family-planning dollars to any group that "supports or participates in the management of a program of coercive abortion or involuntary sterilization." The primary loser under the amendment has been the United Nations Population Fund (UNFPA), which supported China's population program that includes compulsory abortion. Neither of these measures cuts any money from the total US family-planning budget; both merely redirect funds to programs that can comply with the regulations.

Environmental Arguments

The Sierra Club has been candid about its stand. Last year, the 450,000-member group filed a brief using environmental arguments to urge the US Supreme Court to uphold its 1973 decision legalizing abortion. "If abortion were not an option, the strains on the environment would be even greater," the brief said. The group's official position is that abortion is "an acceptable means of controlling population growth."

Other groups deny they are supporting abortion. The National Wildlife Federation (NWF), which claims 5.6 million members, has not taken a position on abortion in any of its resolutions. However, the group has endorsed a bill that, in effect, would overturn the Mexico City Policy.

"We want to safeguard the right of consultation between a woman and her doctor about her condition, especially in life-threatening cases," said NWF's chief executive officer, Jay D. Hair, in a written statement to *CT*. "The International Family Planning Act seeks to correct these deficiencies currently present in the Mexico City Policy." Hair further said that NWF supports modification of the policy to ensure that "any funding restrictions applied abroad are consistent with those imposed in the US reflecting fundamental rights of privacy and federal law governing family planning services provided in this country."

Hair denied their "right to privacy" provision is a covert prochoice plank. "It deals with the right to freedom of speech between a woman and her physician ... in cases where the woman's life is in danger," he said. The NRLC's Johnson says this is a "duplicitous" response. "The Mexico City Policy in no way interferes with any 'medical service' other than abortion," he said. "Moreover, the Mexico City Policy has always included an explicit exception which permits organizations to provide abortion counseling, referrals, or even actual abortions in cases of life endangerment, rape, or incest," he said.

The NWF also supports resumption of funds to UNFPA because, Hair said, "cutting off the funds for effective family-planning organizations like UNFPA denies desperately needed birth control services to women in developing countries." Hair added that his group would like to see restrictions retained on the funds going to "involuntary sterilizations or to coerce any person to accept family planning." He said their involvement in family-planning issues stems from the organization's concern about population growth and the "additional pressures on natural resources and the environment."

The National Audubon Society, while also asserting it "does not take a position for or against abortion," has been involved in lobbying campaigns against the Mexico City Policy and the Kemp/Kasten Amendment. The organization was unable to provide a spokesperson to comment on its stand for *CT*, but in a letter to a member, the group supported overturning the antiabortion language because it "adds nothing" to previous family-planning laws.

Johnson reiterated that the NRLC has "no position" on family planning. "We have no problem with organizations that are supporting family planning, but we do have a problem with those that are calling for the removal of the antiabortion conditions that currently govern funding," he said. The NRLC has released a list of environmental groups that are not involved in "proabortion lobbying." Included on the NRLC list are the Conservation Foundation, Environmental Defense Fund, Greenpeace, National Parks and Conservation Association, Trout Unlimited, and the World Wildlife Fund.

Caught in a Touchy Spot

Many Christian environmentalists feel caught in a touchy situation with the debate. Dave Mahan, associate director of the AuSable Institute, said that although he is opposed to abortion, he is also uncomfortable with the issue being brought up in the environmental context. "Overpopulation is a significant concern in many parts of the world, and it is having serious environmental effects," he said. "Christians need to face that."

Mahan said he fears tying in abortion and family planning may cause Christians to walk away from all international family-planning efforts. "As Christians, we have a responsibility in helping support people who want to practice family planning, but in methods that we would agree with," he said. "And we must promote those [methods] within the environmental organizations that we support." Mahan opposes wholesale pullouts from environmental groups because of the abortion issue, and points to the American Bar Association's reversal of a prochoice stance as an example of the effectiveness of working for change from within. "To me, nobody has a higher calling than Christians to protect all forms of life," he said.

The issue is expected to be a politically contentious one again this fall. Last year, President Bush vetoed a foreign-assistance bill that contained resumed funding for the UNFPA. He is likely to do the same this year if either the Kemp/Kasten Amendment or the Mexico City Policy is overturned by Congress.

Chapter 10

—

ARE WE OUR PLANET'S
KEEPER?

*Our problems with the environment are
not merely technical, they are spiritual.*

William A. Dyrness | 1991

C hristians have had a mixed record when it comes to concern
for the environment. Some have felt the deterioration of
planet Earth is a sign of the last days, while a growing number—
citing the biblical principle of stewardship—are working hard
to care for their created context. The real question is this: How
serious is the "crisis" the media speak about? And more crucial,
what is an appropriate biblical concern?

We might conclude from news reports that, since the first
"Earth Day" in 1970, things have continued to grow worse. Rain
forests in Brazil, according to UN estimates, are disappearing at
the rate of fifty thousand acres a day; tons of topsoil are lost each
year in the American Midwest; the movement of the Sahara down
into Africa is measured in miles per year.

This last devastation struck me in a personal way recently while living in Kenya. There I often watched Kikuyu women bent under great loads of firewood weighing as much as fifty pounds. My wife, an anthropologist, discovered these women would walk for hours each day to find firewood in order to cook for their families. Looking down from the air, we saw giant, barren circles surrounding villages where women had scraped the ground clean in their frantic effort to eke out a living. There we saw clearly a struggle between human life and care for the Earth. Were we to work to preserve the landscape or to help the people in their struggle for survival?

Since coming back to America we have been struck by the ease with which we can bemoan the population or environmental problems of people in the Third World. Meanwhile, our 8 percent of the world's population continues to use 40 percent of Earth's resources, glibly assuming that our technical prowess will somehow solve these global inequities.

Hopeful Signs

More and more, however, these problems are seen as not merely technical, but religious in character. We will not find the answers in our laboratories (though more time should be spent on these issues there), but in the depths of our national soul.

On this score there are hopeful signs. Primary among them is the growing recognition of the seriousness of these issues and the necessity of addressing them on several levels. A 1990 *New York Times* poll indicated that 84 percent of Americans see these concerns as a serious national problem; 71 percent are willing to increase their taxes to solve them; 56 percent are even willing to see jobs lost (presumably not their own) to address the problem.

And progress has been made. Since the early 1970s: we have reduced the emission of carbon dioxide (the pollutant mainly at fault for the so-called greenhouse effect) from our cars by 85 percent; we have cleaned up many lakes and rivers as well as many other areas polluted with toxic waste. But what progress have we made in addressing the religious dimension?

Here I find the most cause for encouragement. More and more, ecological concerns are being addressed in the context of values and religious commitments. Unfortunately, many are proposing "new age" types of answers. But at least people are beginning to acknowledge that the underlying problem is a religious one. Christians are more frequently being invited to address these questions. Twice last year, around Earth Day, I was invited to address meetings sponsored by religious coalitions who wanted to find out what the Bible and what evangelicals have to say about ecology.

This is encouraging because Christians have not always been welcome at ecology conferences. In 1967 ecologist Lynn White published a now-famous article blaming the environmental crisis on the Christian view of Creation. Since then, Christians have been on the defensive, hiding out on the fringes of the ecology movement. But with the recent revival of interest in religion, Christian perspectives on these things are being given a new hearing. In what follows, I would like to lay out four biblical principles of Christian concern for the Earth that may win a new hearing in our postsecular era.

God's Good Creation

The first principle is that the Earth is God's good creation.

One of the most basic questions the environmental movement faces is why we should care for the Earth. Most discussions assume that care for the Earth is necessary for human and global survival. But the Christian has a far more comprehensive answer: We care for the Earth because its value reflects the goodness of

God himself. Its beauty and value are not accidental, but built in by its Creator. In a sense, then, any attack or injury to this goodness reflects on God—it has an overtone of blasphemy to it.

We human beings are put here to "work" and "take care of" this goodness (Gen. 2:15). Notice that we do not create its fertility, but we can encourage and protect it; and, sadly, we can injure it. So there is a good order, in which humans play a key role, but it is an order that serves a higher purpose: to glorify God.

Ecologists talk a great deal about this "good order," but they come at it another way. Holmes Ralston, for example, in his important book *Philosophy Gone Wild* (1989), argues that we have a duty to the Earth to "stabilize the ecosystem through mutually imposed self-limited growth." This imperative is based on the assumption that we ought mutually to preserve life. Pioneer conservationist Aldo Leopold put it this way: "A thing is right when it tends to preserve the integrity, stability and the beauty of the biotic community. It is wrong when it tends otherwise."

Now this is all good as far as it goes, but it does not go far enough in two directions. On the one hand, *sustainability*, while a worthy goal, is ultimately unachievable. In his book *Entropy: Into the Greenhouse World* (1989), Jeremy Rifkin points out that current conservation measures should be seen as a "transitional adaptation" along the road to a far more radical transformation of values. The quest for "stability" or "homeostasis" (and the recycling that supports it) is important, but in the end it is not nearly radical enough.

But there is an even more serious limitation of the "sustainability" thesis. Behind our Western discussion of ecology and natural order lies a massive assumption: Life as it is on the Earth is good and so must be preserved. But what if life is not good, but brutish and mean? Balance is easy for us to endorse after a good dinner in a heated building, but what does it mean to the woman hauling fifty pounds of wood several hours a day?

The problem with our search for stability of the ecosystem is that something has gone dreadfully wrong with the system. It is sick unto death, a sickness that is narrated in the early chapters of Genesis. Adam and Eve's disobedience had immediate and long-term ecological effects: "Cursed is the ground because of you," Adam is told (Gen. 3:17). Moreover, the problem, the Bible makes clear, is not only—or even mainly—in the environment, it is in us, all of us. As Isaiah put it: "We all, like sheep, have gone astray, each of us has turned to his own way" (53:6).

Liberation

It appears we are stuck in a deteriorating situation, desperately in need of the second biblical principle: *liberation*.

There is a sober realism to the biblical account of human life on the planet. After the Earth is cursed, Adam and Eve are put out of the garden, and soon after, Cain kills his brother Abel. What is wrong with the Earth issues in a loss of paradise and great human disorder.

To address this disorder God did not use half-measures. When Israel became enslaved to Egypt, he did not merely give them the law with provision for weekly recycling. He smashed the powers that held them in bondage, delivered them from Egypt, and planted them in the fertile Land of Canaan.

In the New Testament, God intervened in a final way in Christ's life to bind the powers that hold the world in slavery and to deliver the prisoner. "In Christ God was reconciling the world to himself" (2 Cor. 5:19).[1] And Paul elsewhere tells us that

---

[1] Unless otherwise noted, scripture quotations in this article are from the Revised Standard Version.

"creation waits in eager expectation for the sons of God to be revealed ... in hope that the creation itself will be *liberated* from its bondage to decay" (Rom. 8:19, 21).

If the cosmic disorder is caused by sin, the most important ecological principle is liberation from bondage to sin. What might this mean for the environment? I think it will mean different things for different parts of the world.

For us in the West, it will mean liberation from what Robert Bellah calls our "advanced poverty." We are in bondage to a way of life that is destructive not only to our environment, but to our families, our friends, our health, even our souls. We need to be set free. And no talk of the environment will make much progress apart from this fundamental recognition.

For the rest of the world, the cry is for liberation from the crushing weight of economic poverty. The World Bank reports that eight hundred million people live in what it calls "absolute poverty"—that is, having per-capita incomes of less than two hundred dollars per year. In our generosity, we are anxious to help them stop their slash-and-burn farming, their having large families, their scouring the land for firewood. What they need is liberation from the poverty that drives them to scrape clean the Earth to survive.

The fundamental liberation for all of us is from our sin, that rebellion against God that keeps us in bondage. But this rescue will lead to transformed lives and communities. Moreover, I believe the transformation called for in the West and in the Third World are profoundly related. Notice that it is precisely that from which we both need liberation—we from our wasteful lifestyles, they from their grinding poverty—that is most destructive to the environment. Could it be that apart from our deliverance from our bondage to affluence they will not be freed from their poverty?

It is significant that Jesus struck this note of liberation in his first sermon at Capernaum: "The Spirit of the Lord is upon me, because he has anointed me to preach good news to the poor. He has sent me to proclaim release to the captives and recovering of sight to the blind, to set at liberty those who are oppressed, to proclaim the acceptable year of the Lord" (Luke 4:18–19).

Jubilee

In fact, Jesus is quoting from a passage in Isaiah that many believe relates to the third principle of Christian ecology: *jubilee*.

All the realities we have considered come together in the biblical principle of jubilee. The jubilee is an extension of the sabbath principle, that one in every seven days or years should be set apart for rest and refreshment. Interestingly, the principle applies not only to people but to animals and even the land itself.

Every fifty years Israel was called to celebrate a supersabbath called the jubilee: "You shall hallow the fiftieth year, and proclaim liberty throughout the land to all its inhabitants; it shall be a jubilee for you, when each of you shall return to his property and each of you shall return to his family.... [In this year] you shall neither sow, nor reap what grows of itself. ... For it is a jubilee; it shall be holy to you" (Lev. 25:10–12).

As this is explained in Leviticus, there are three components to this event. First, to relieve poverty the land is redistributed and all debt is released. Second, the land is meant to lie fallow so that its fertility can be restored. Finally, the human family and community is celebrated and strengthened.

Jesus announces the presence of this jubilee reality in Luke 4 and when he urges: "Come to me, all who labor and are heavy laden, and I will give you rest" (Matt. 11:28). His Earth-shaking work is meant to include the devastation of the environment as part of the ravages of sin in its purview. But the question immediately arises as to what this means for us.

At first blush, such reordering seems either wildly impractical or dangerously revolutionary. Even if we might understand what this means in an agrarian economy—everyone understands something of the benefits of land reform in Central America and the Philippines—what could this mean in a modern industrialized nation?

In the March 1990 issue of *Tikkun*, Jewish scholar Arthur Waskow proposed that the jubilee model be used to develop strategies for dealing with economic inequality and environmental issues. First, he proposed that through taxation, capital be made available for financing Third World projects. Second, he urged periodic sabbaticals on research and development to assess the impact of projects on economic inequality and the environment. Third, he suggested we make regular and inclusive celebrations of community and family empowerment a high priority of our political life.

While we may have questions about some of these proposals, they do suggest there may be some industrial equivalent to the biblical "land reform" policies. Land reforms have proven possible and helpful in some places, but other reforms are also necessary. Obviously, much thought and planning must still be done. But if we are to preserve our Earth, this work must be given a high priority.

Repentance

These momentous changes can only come about if we take our fourth and final principle with sufficient seriousness: *repentance*.

If the problem is not in creation alone but in us as well, in our abuse of the land and of our neighbors, then things will not change apart from a radical spiritual change in our hearts and our communities. The Bible describes the radical response that is appropriate in a single word: *repentance.*

We must turn our lives around and inside out. The death and resurrection of Christ put before the world the only chance for real deliverance. To follow Christ, then, is at the same time to respond to the Earth's ecological crisis.

In the end, it is not only encouraging that Christians have become more concerned about the future of the Earth, it is essential that they continue in this path. For it is finally only the gospel that frees people from their sins and will one day free the Earth.

Chapter 11

EARTH SUMMIT: SEARCHING FOR A SPIRITUAL FOUNDATION

Loren Wilkinson | 1992

T he Earth Summit in Rio de Janeiro may or may not go down in history as a turning point in humankind's treatment of planet Earth. But it quite likely will stand as the first celebration of a new synthesis of world religions.

An article published in the conference newspaper on how to find one's way around Rio suggested using the giant statue of Christ that stands on a mountain peak above the city as a reference point: "Just remember where you are staying or going in relationship to Christ and you should never get lost." With the international conference drawn to a close, one of the many questions remaining was, where was the Earth Summit going in relationship to Christ?

Apart from a reference to the Christ statue in the opening remarks by Brazilian President Fernando Collor de Mello and a quotation from Leviticus by the Israeli representative, most religious input came via the conference's Global Forum, the non-governmental meeting held on nearby Flamengo Beach. The majority of the talk there, however, sounded more like vague pantheism than Christianity.

An all-night vigil held there on June 4 opened with "invocations of the sacred" by some 30 religions, and concluded with an address by the Dalai Lama and a Hare Krishna mantra. On another occasion, a large contingent from the United Church of Christ joined with members of several other religions in a demonstration, which opened with the singing of the hymn "Were You There When They Crucified My Lord?"—substituting the word *Earth* for *Lord.*

Saving Earth's Souls

Some Christian observers said the forum's religious smorgasbord illustrated a search for a spiritual center for a "new ethic" of Earth care. In fact, Maurice Strong, the Canadian businessman who organized the summit, said that "any workable decisions made at UNCED [the United Nations Conference on Environment and Development] will have to have deep moral, spiritual, and ethical roots if they are to be successfully implemented."

Some evangelicals presented a Christian view of environmental issues at meetings during the forum. But many found themselves on the summit's outskirts, preferring to focus on saving souls rather than caring for creation.

One downtown demonstration by evangelicals startled even its organizers by drawing between five hundred thousand and a million people, who heard Brazilian evangelist Caio Fábio assert that rejecting God's truth always leads to disastrous consequences in nature, society, and religion.

But unlike Fábio, many Brazilian evangelicals did not connect saving the environment with the gospel. For instance, the

Brazilian Evangelical Fellowship drew crowds to their dance and mime group inside the forum. Dozens professed new faith in Christ, but little was said connecting personal salvation and the environment. Another group representing the rapidly growing Brazilian charismatic community held an all-night prayer vigil at a church outside the forum grounds.

A few church leaders openly opposed the Earth Summit. One Brazilian pastor told his congregation the Sunday following the meeting that the forum had experienced financial problems. Drawing applause, he added, "I hope they have more problems."

Some Christian groups, however, did go beyond the message of personal salvation to address the environment. Albert Gore, head of the US Senate delegation, spoke to an enthusiastic and well-attended forum gathering, disclaiming any interest in "proselytizing" but asserting that the basis for his own thinking was that the Earth is God's creation, entrusted to humankind's care.

Other Christian groups set up display booths or small gatherings at the forum. They included Food for the Hungry, the Christian Environmental Alliance, World Vision of Brazil, the Summer Institute of Linguistics, and the Consortium on Religion and Ecology.

The delegation of the World Council of Churches (WCC), which met during the summit's first week in a slum community in Rio, issued a letter on Pentecost Sunday. "The Spirit teaches us to go first to those places where community and creation are most obviously languishing. ... Here we meet Jesus, who goes before, in solidarity and suffering."

A New Paradigm

Despite such efforts, the Christian presence at the forum was swamped by a plethora of feminist, universalist, and monist groups, who argued that a new religious paradigm must replace the old one, which was shaped by patriarchy, capitalism, theism, and Christianity. Many blamed the "old paradigm" for the environment's destruction.

Among those seeking converts were the Baha'is; Ananda Marga, a Hindu sect with mainly Western members; Global Heart, a New Age organization; and Findhorn, a Scottish New Age group.

Chapter 12

REDEEMING THE ENVIRONMENTALISTS

*Humanity will find some spirit
to guide its environmental
concerns. Will it be Christian?*

Ronald J. Sider | 1993

I n March 1990, in Seoul, South Korea, I attended an international conference on Justice, Peace, and the Integrity of Creation sponsored by the World Council of Churches. I heard many persuasive claims about the way Christians had distorted humanity's mandate to have dominion over the Earth—the consequence of these distortions being a ravaged creation. I became concerned, however, when I noticed that no one had mentioned the fact that human beings have an exalted status within creation, in that they alone are created in the image of God.

So I proposed a one-sentence addition to the document we were debating. From the floor, I asked that we add a sentence affirming that, as we confess these misunderstandings, we none-theless "accept the biblical teaching that people alone have been created in the image of God."

The drafting committee promptly accepted the addition but dropped the word *alone.* I pointed out that this undercut the basic point. Are trees and toads also created in God's image? When the drafting committee remained adamant, I called for a vote. And the motion lost! At that moment, a majority of attendees at this important convocation were unwilling to say what historical, biblical theology has always affirmed: that human beings alone are created in the image of God.

As my experience illustrates, in today's environmental movement there is a lot of theological confusion. Actress Shirley MacLaine says we must declare that we are all gods. Disciplined but unchastened Catholic theologian Matthew Fox says we should turn from a theology centered on sin and redemption and develop a creation spirituality, with nature as our primary revelation and sin a distant memory. Australian scientist Peter Singer says any claim that persons have a status different from monkeys and moles is "speciesism." Several decades ago historian Lynn White argued that it is precisely the Christian view of persons and nature that created the whole ecological mess. Meanwhile, many evangelicals come close to celebrating the demise of the Earth, enthusiastically citing the decay as proof that the return of Christ is very near.

These and other factors will tempt evangelicals to ignore or denounce environmental concerns. But that would be a tragic mistake—for at least three reasons. First, because the danger is massive and urgent. Second, because there are evangelistic opportunities that arise out of environmental concern. And third, because if we do not offer biblical foundations for environmental action, we will have only ourselves to blame if environmental activists turn to other, finally inadequate, worldviews and religions. With wisdom and a renewed appreciation of the wholeness of God's plan for redemption, we can lead the way forward in the healing of our Earth.

Why Be Involved

An urgent problem. That we are in trouble is increasingly clear. Gaping holes in the ozone layer, polluted rivers, expanding deserts, denuded mountainsides, air-poisoned cities, and spiraling carbon emissions producing global warming—all sound the warning. In the last forty years, we have lost one-fifth of our topsoil and one-third of our rain forests. Leading scientists are so frightened that even prominent secularists like Carl Sagan have issued an urgent plea to the religious community to help find solutions to impending ecological disaster.

Evangelistic opportunities. The very urgency of the problem has created tremendous evangelistic opportunities. As one reads the environmental literature, the deep yearning for religious meaning becomes clear. Many environmentalists have rejected the materialistic "scientism" that drives our technoculture. They are right in thinking that secular naturalism, which has been so influential in the last two hundred years, cannot solve environmental problems. The tragedy is that when these folks yearn for religious solutions, they assume that historic Christianity has nothing to offer. So they turn to goddess worship, nature spirituality, Eastern monism, and New Age nonsense.

What an opportunity—if we have the courage, intellectual vigor, and faith. Instead of rejecting environmentalism lest our theology become contaminated, we must stride boldly into the mainstream of the green movement, showing how biblical faith offers a better foundation for environmental engagement. We need to imitate Paul's bold strategy in the face of the Athenians' religious confusion and spiritual groping. Paul praised their religious yearning and told them about the God for whom they did not have a name (Acts 17). If we do the same, naming God in the midst of the massive contemporary longing for religious foundations, we may be surprised at the evangelistic results.

Christian leadership. Third, evangelicals must become environmentalists to make sure that a biblical rather than a monist worldview shapes what will undoubtedly be one of the most central global problems of our lifetime. Make no mistake: Modern folk will find some spiritual foundations to guide and shape their environmental concerns. If it is not biblical faith, then it will be something far less adequate.

There is a spiritual battle going on. Satan would dearly love to persuade modern folk that the best way to solve our environmental crisis is to jettison historic Christianity. The truth, of course, is exactly the reverse. The best foundation for saving the creation is by worshiping and obeying the Creator revealed in Jesus Christ.

Called to Garden

The only way to make sure that the biblical worldview plays a central role in shaping key environmental decisions is for large numbers of biblical Christians to join enthusiastically in the environmental movement. As we pray, teach, and act, five biblical principles will be especially important.

First, whereas a one-sided view of either God's transcendence or immanence compounds our problems, a biblical combination of both points the way through our dilemmas. If we focus only on God's immanence (his presence in the world), we land in pantheism where everything is divine and good as it is. If we talk only about God's transcendence (his radical separateness from creation), we may end up seeing nature as a mere tool to be used at human whim.

The biblical God is both immanent and transcendent. He is not a cosmic watchmaker who wound up the global clock and then let it run on its own. God continues to work in the creation. In Job we read that God gives orders to the morning (38:12), that the eagle soars at God's command (39:27), and that God provides food for the ravens when their young cry out in hunger (38:41). The Creator, however, is also radically distinct from the creation. Creation is finite, limited, dependent; the Creator is infinite, unlimited, self-sufficient.

Second, we should gratefully learn all we can from the book of nature without in any way abandoning biblical revelation. When Matthew Fox tells us that we can get most or all the revelation we need from creation, we will firmly reply that the biblical revelation of redemption from sin through Jesus Christ is as true and essential as ever in our environmental age.

Third, human beings are both interdependent with the rest of creation and unique within it, because we alone have been created in the divine image and given stewardship over the Earth. Christians have at times forgotten our interdependence with the rest of creation. Our daily existence depends on water, sun, and air. Everything is interrelated in the global ecosystem. The emissions from our cars contribute to the destruction of trees—trees that convert the carbon dioxide we exhale into the oxygen we need to survive. Christians today must recover an appreciation of our dependence on the trees and flowers, the streams and forests. Unless we do, we shall surely perish.

But the Bible insists on two other things about humanity: Human beings alone are created in the image of God, and we alone have been given a special "dominion" or stewardship.

It is a biblical truth, not speciesism, to say that only human beings—and not trees and animals—are created in the image of God (Gen. 1:27). This truth is the foundation of our God-given mandate to have dominion over the nonhuman creation (Gen. 1:28; Ps. 8).

Tragically—and arrogantly—we have distorted dominion into domination. Lynn White was correct in placing some blame for environmental decay on Christianity. But it is a misunderstanding of the Bible, not God's Word itself, that is at fault here.

Genesis 2:15 says the Lord put us in the garden "to work it and take care of it." The word *abad*, translated "work," means "to serve." The related noun actually means "slave" or "servant." The word *shamar*, translated "take care of," suggests watchful care and preservation of the Earth. We are to serve and watch lovingly over God's good garden, not rape it.

The Old Testament offers explicit commands designed to prevent exploitation of the Earth. Every seventh year, for instance, the Israelites' land was to lie fallow because "the land is to have a year of rest" (Lev. 25:5). Failure to provide this sabbatical for the land was one reason for the Babylonian captivity (Lev. 26:34, 42–43). "I will remember the land," Yahweh declared.

If we have no different status from that of mammals and plants, we cannot eat them for food or use them to build civilizations. We do not need to apologize to brother carrot when we have lunch. We are free to use the resources of the Earth for our own purposes. Created in the divine image, we alone have been placed in charge of the Earth. At the same time, our dominion must be the gentle care of a loving gardener, not the callous exploitation of a self-centered lord. So we should not wipe out species or waste the nonhuman creation. Only a careful, stewardly use of plants and animals by human beings is legitimate.

Clothing the Lilies

Fourth, a God-centered, rather than a human-centered, world-view respects the independent worth of the nonhuman creation. Christians have too easily and too often fallen into the trap of supposing that the nonhuman creation has worth only as it serves human purposes. This, however, is not a biblical perspective.

Genesis 1 makes clear that all creation is good—good, according to the story, even before our first ancestors arrived on the scene. Colossians 1:16 reveals that all things are created *for* Christ. And according to Job 39:1–2, God watches over the doe in the mountains, counting the months of her pregnancy and watching over her when she gives birth! The first purpose of the nonhuman creation, then, is to glorify God, not to serve us.

"The heavens are telling the glory of God; and the firmament proclaims his handiwork. Day to day pours forth speech, and night to night declares knowledge. There is no speech, nor are there words; their voice is not heard; yet their voice goes out through all the earth, and their words to the end of the world" (Ps. 19:1–4 RSV).

It is important to note that God has a covenant, not only with persons but also with the nonhuman creation. After the flood, God made a covenant with the animals as well as with Noah: "Behold, I establish my covenant with you and your descendants after you, and with every living creature that is with you, the birds, the cattle, and every beast of the earth with you, as many as came out of the ark" (Gen. 9:9–10 ESV).

Jesus recognized God's covenant with the whole of creation when he noted how God feeds the birds and clothes the lilies (Matt. 6:26–30). The nonhuman creation has its own worth and dignity apart from its service to humanity.

Insisting on the independent dignity of the nonhuman creation does not mean that we ignore the biblical teaching that it has been given to us human beings for our stewardship and use (Gen. 1:28–30; Ps. 8:6–8). Always, however, our use of the non-human creation must be a thoughtful stewardship that honors the creation's dignity and worth in the eyes of the Creator.

The Earth's Hope

Finally, God's cosmic plan of redemption includes the non-human creation. This fact provides a crucial foundation for building a Christian theology for an environmental age. The biblical hope that the whole created order, including the material world of bodies and rivers and trees, will be part of the heavenly kingdom confirms that the created order is good and important.

The Bible's affirmation of the material world can be seen most clearly in Christ himself: Not only did the Creator enter his creation by becoming flesh and blood to redeem us from our sin, but the God-man was resurrected *bodily* from the tomb. The goodness of the created order is also revealed in how the Bible describes the coming kingdom: the marriage supper of the Lamb, where we will feast on bread, wine, and all the glorious fruit of the earth.

Unlike Hindu monists who think the created order is an illusion to escape, biblical people know that the creation is in itself so good that God is going to purge it of the evil introduced by the Fall and restore it to wholeness. Romans 8:19–23 tells us that at Christ's return, when we experience the resurrection of the body, then the groaning creation will be transformed: "The creation itself will be liberated from its bondage to decay and brought into the glorious freedom of the children of God." In Colossians 1:15–20 we read that God intends to reconcile all things, "whether things on earth or things in heaven," through Jesus Christ. That does not mean that everyone will be saved; rather, it means that Christ's salvation will finally extend to all of creation. The Fall's corruption of every part of creation will be corrected.

The prophets often spoke of the impact of human sin on nature (Gen. 3:17–18; Isa. 24:4–6; Hos. 4:3). But they also foresaw that in the messianic time nature would share in salvation: "In that day I will make a covenant for them with the beasts of the field and the birds of the air" (Hos. 2:16–23; see also Isa. 55:12–13). In the coming kingdom, I hope to go sailing on an unpolluted Delaware River.

The Christian hope for Christ's return must be joined with our doctrine of creation. Knowing that we are summoned by the Creator to be wise gardeners caring for God's good Earth, knowing the hope that someday the Earth will be restored, Christians should be vigorous participants in the environmental movement. Our motives are many. We must preempt worldviews that would undermine both Christian faith and a lasting environmental solution. We will discover, perhaps to our surprise, that environmental engagement grounded in biblical truth will attract many spiritually lost contemporaries to our Lord. Also, we may be able to save our grandchildren (should the world still exist 40 years from now) from ecological disaster. Most important, we will honor the Creator of this gorgeous and astonishingly intricate cosmos.

Chapter 13

—

HOW CHRISTIAN IS
THE GREEN AGENDA?

Loren Wilkinson | 1993

T he environmental movement divides and confuses
Christians, keeping us at arm's length from a crucial arena
of societal engagement. Many withdraw from environmentalism as an infectious carrier of New Age ideas. At last year's Earth
Summit in Rio, this was the response of the rapidly growing
Brazilian evangelical church. In North America, similar tendencies are apparent in books and articles that dismiss population
pressure, global warming, and ozone depletion as pseudoprob-
lems, and belittle specific actions such as recycling or wilderness
preservation.

Sometimes these Christian "anti-environmentalists" use-
fully remind us of the jungle of agendas and ideologies in which
environmental concern moves. But to deny the reality of an environmental crisis is an enormous mistake for those who worship
the Creator. Such a denial neglects a major human responsibility

and withholds the gospel from one of the places where it most needs to be heard.

At the same time, Christian participation in some aspects of environmentalism embraces uncritically an emerging religious philosophy founded on the oneness of all things. In Rio, religious leaders attending a preconference "Sacred Earth" meeting issued a declaration of faith that "the universe is sacred because all is one." It announced the need "to evolve earth ethics with a deeply spiritual orientation" and suggested that the ecological crisis is a spiritual crisis resulting not from sin, but from ignorance.

Many Christians find it difficult, in the religious pluralism of the environmental movement, to stand against such syncretism. The problem is made worse by the appearance, as Christian works, of books like Matthew Fox's *The Coming of the Cosmic Christ*. That work dismisses as an Augustinian perversion any idea of original sin, welcomes the Earth itself as a kind of Christ, and dismisses as "Christofascism" any theology that speaks of the unique revelation of God in Jesus.

Yet apart from the posturing and contentiousness that marked the Rio conference, there are indications that Christians are beginning to assess environmental issues with more theological rigor and biblical accuracy. It is an area we can no longer avoid: the issues are forced on us today by fears that the tragic proportions of Hurricane Andrew and the African drought, for example, may be linked to human activity. And the philosophical underpinnings of environmentalism demand an answer to calls for a new "earth spirituality" in which we are told to recognize that we are part of a sacred Earth. (See "Is the Earth Alive?" on page 109).

The Origins of Environmentalism

The "environmental movement" is less than thirty years old. It emerged in the early 1960s, prompted by Rachel Carson's book

Silent Spring, by growing concern over nuclear war and testing, and by widespread awareness of the damage brought about by postwar growth and technology. Christian (though not necessarily evangelical) concern over these issues dates back to this time as well. In 1961 in the World Council of Churches' New Delhi Assembly, Lutheran theologian Joseph Sittler pointed out the declining health of the world's environment and called for the churches to reaffirm that Christ was Lord of all creation. At that time, however, even in the socially aware World Council (as pastor H. Paul Santmire writes), "response to Sittler's address at New Delhi was mainly one of polite indifference." There was little serious discussion of the environmental implications of Christian faith (evangelical or otherwise) until the late 1960s.

Ironically, it was an attack on the church (rather than any threat to creation itself) that galvanized Christian theological response.

In 1967, *Science* magazine published an address given by medieval historian Lynn White to the American Association for the Advancement of Science. That paper ("The Historic Roots of Our Ecologic Crisis") called Christianity "the most anthropocentric religion the world has ever seen" and claimed that through such ideas as human dominion, the desacralizing of nature, and belief that ultimate human destiny is with God (and not the Earth) Christendom has encouraged a destructive use of creation.

Lynn White's case against Christendom (valid or not) has become conventional wisdom in the environmental movement, and Christians continue to discover—and try to refute—its argument. One of the first extended evangelical responses was Francis Schaeffer's *Pollution and the Death of Man*, published in 1970. Schaeffer acknowledged the extent of the problem, and the inadequacy of both pantheism, on the one hand, and a world-rejecting Christianity, on the other, to deal with it. He founded his Christian response on a Reformed theology that recognized both our shared creatureliness (he was not ashamed to speak of the Earth as "our fair sister") and the unique role of human beings as creatures responsible to God. He called on churches to become "pilot plants" demonstrating the possibility of a "substantial healing" of the damage brought about by human greed.

An even more substantial work that appeared in 1970 was H. Paul Santmire's *Brother Earth*. A Lutheran pastor, Santmire critiqued American Romanticism, which sentimentalized nature, and European theology, which mechanized it. In its place, with remarkable biblical and theological thoroughness, Santmire sketched an ethic of "The Created Realm of God" and an "Ethic of Responsibility."

In 1977, Calvin College assembled a team of evangelical scholars to address "Christian Stewardship of Natural Resources." The result, *Earthkeeping: Christian Stewardship of Natural Resources*, was an important resource throughout much of the 1980s for Christians interested in the subject. But for a variety of reasons, including the US political climate of the past decade, environmental concern receded. Neither the culture at large nor evangelical Christians took much notice of environmental issues until quite recently.

Early evangelical thinking on the subject tended to suggest that the chief value of creation is to fuel human industry. That kind of anthropocentrism is inadequate. Yet in response, environmentalists have gone to the other extreme. Their explanations have often diminished the human to nothing more than one node in a cosmic web. The early "conservation" movement has grown into a philosophically more radical "deep ecology." In response, evangelical thinking has been prompted into a more biblical understanding of God's concern for the whole creation.

Healthy Planet, Healthy Humans

Evangelicals also have been compelled to defend the crucial biblical teaching on the distinctive role of human beings in creation—unpopular as that doctrine is in much of the environmental movement. In fact, many thoughtful Christians harbor suspicions of the environmental movement because it has seemed to be more concerned about nonhuman creation than human needs. Even socially concerned evangelical groups like Evangelicals for Social Action and the Sojourners community have, until recently, tended to regard the environmental movement as a luxury of the comfortably developed northern nations and an excuse to ignore the deep human needs of the poor.

That perception is changing, however, among Christians and non-Christians alike. In 1987, a UN report of the Commission on Environment and Development titled *Our Common Future*, explains that a healthy planet and a healthy human population together make up one goal, not two: Humans will not prosper if the Earth languishes, an insight that is certainly consistent with what the Bible calls "*shalom*," or true peace. Increasingly, Christian missions and relief organizations have come to recognize that environmental and developmental needs are not only compatible, but inseparable. Paul Thompson, an executive with World Vision, speaks of a kind of "Damascus Road" experience when he realized a few years ago that meeting human needs without a larger caring for the Earth was unbiblical and ultimately impossible.

Another recent recognition by evangelicals of this essential harmony was the Oxford Declaration on Christian Faith and Economics, hammered out among Christians of widely differing economic persuasions in January 1990. Theologians and economists were able to sign a statement asserting, "God the Creator and Redeemer is the ultimate owner." The declaration went on,

"When we abuse and pollute creation, as we are doing in many instances, we are poor stewards and invite disaster.... Economic systems must be shaped so that a healthy ecological system is maintained over time."

An Evangelical Response

Evangelical Christians can and should do more than just talk and theorize about the environment. We could begin by becoming aware of our creatureliness and delighting in it as a gift from God. That worshipful awareness should lead to changes in our use of creation. Christian individuals and churches could provide models of a different, less wasteful, more thankful way of life. For Christians in the wealthy world, this is one of our greatest challenges.

Caring for creation also can mean doing the best work we can in our chosen vocation. Hidden from public view in the Earth Summit, for example, was the work of Susan Drake, a State Department negotiator. She played a major role in crafting many of the US positions on environment, often against considerable opposition and spiritual struggle. Throughout the process, she said she was helped immeasurably by the prayer support of Christians in her church. At a key point in organizing the Earth Summit several years ago, the mere suggestion of holding such a meeting had died because of disagreements among the many UN nations organizing it. Susan persuaded the differing nations to agree on a formula by which the summit could go forward. Thus without the courageous and prayerful work of an unpraised Christian, there would not have *been* an Earth Summit in Rio.

Similar examples abound as Christians translate their concern for creation into their work in influential ways. In Washington State, Ruth Scott acts as wilderness manager for

Olympic National Park, bringing her concern for care of creation into the management decisions affecting the mountain and rain forest vastness of one of the nation's treasures. In England, Ghillean Prance, a Christian who heads up the Royal Kew Gardens, has become a world authority on rainforest botany (see profile in *CT*, July 22, 1991, p. 26).

Among institutions, certainly one of God's gifts to the church in the US has been the AuSable Institute for Environmental Studies. This well-equipped laboratory, library, and study center in the woods of Michigan used to be a Christian camp, but in the early 1970s it became the site of one of Michigan's more productive oil wells. Under the guidance of a far-sighted board, the income from the oil has funded an endowment that supports environmental education among Christian College Coalition schools. Headed by Cal DeWitt, professor of environmental studies at the University of Wisconsin, the AuSable Institute has hosted productive meetings of evangelical scientists and theologians from all over the world, resulting in the publication of a number of books and a chance for environmentally concerned Christian leaders to think together on the issues. If there is an evangelical center for care of creation, it is probably here.

Last summer, at a meeting sponsored by the Oxford Center for Mission Studies, the AuSable Institute, and supported by the World Evangelical Fellowship, Christian scholars from five continents examined the same issues addressed by the Earth Summit, such as balancing human needs and the needs of the Earth. In an environment of worship and prayer, the results were considerably different: a World Evangelical Network was formed to encourage evangelicals worldwide to think about their care of creation in the light of biblical and theological reflection, and to generate the resources to do so.

Toward a Doctrine of Creation

Important theological issues are at stake in the environmental movement; evangelical clear-headedness on the issues requires a more thorough doctrine of creation. After all, it is God's good creation that is at risk—not "nature" or "resources" or even "the environment."

Yet the creation-evolution debate has reduced the high biblical concept of creation to a spate of arguments about its how and when. The tragic result has been that whole generations of Americans (Christian or not) think that a belief in "creation" commits one to the notion that God's creative acts took place only at the beginning of time. Missing is the robust biblical picture of a triune Creator, transcendent and immanent, by whose Spirit each living thing is quickened and renewed (Ps. 104:30), and in whose Word "all things hold together" (Col. 1:17).

Christians today are underrepresented in the biological sciences. Yet these disciplines reveal that creation is an unfolding process, not just a one-time act. As we develop a richer understanding of God's ongoing activity of creating, perhaps the study of creation will be seen as an act of praise for the Creator, as well as a way to refute reductionist evolutionary theories. It is shortsighted and self-contradictory to regard life on Earth as an accident; it is just as shortsighted to ignore what creation tells us about itself.

A second theological issue involves the "curse" on the Earth. This doctrine looks back to the Fall to explain the apparent harshness of the present created order in which all living things must devour something—soil, plants, animals—to live. But do we let it explain too much? Ecology has been described as the study of who is eating whom, a definition that makes plain that some forms of death are integral to the created order that God called good. Perhaps our repugnance at a biosphere in which creatures eat each other may be a bit like Uzzah's steadying the ark of the covenant. The ark of creation is a rough place, and God's idea of goodness is apparently much wilder than our own.

In addition, many have located the consequences of the curse in the creation itself. But our present woes are due rather to our sinful use of and relationship to the Earth than to any malfunction of the created order as much. Hosea's words make the situation clear: After a blunt, familiar catalogue of human sinfulness, he concludes, "Because of this the land mourns, and all who live in it waste away; the beasts of the field and the birds of the air and the fish of the sea are dying" (4:3, NIV84). Our goal should be to restore our proper relationship with the Earth, to make it one of mutual blessing.

A third theological issue raised by the environmental movement is eschatological: What is the fate of the Earth in God's ultimate plan? Premillennial thought (especially in America) sometimes emphasizes the idea of an imminent, literal destruction of the Earth through divine wrath. The new heaven and the new earth, in such a view, replace the old, from which humans alone are saved. Using this framework, some Christians interpret environmental problems, such as population pressure, global warming, and species extinction, as pointers to the end time: not exactly to be welcomed, but neither to be resisted through futile efforts to save a world dismissed as "the late, great planet Earth."

Other Christians, convinced that God has not made a throwaway world, are rediscovering a deep biblical theme that sees the gospel as good news for all of creation, not just humans. They are rediscovering the truth that redemption is not human salvation *out of* a doomed creation, but rather the *restoration* of all God's purposes in creation. Theological support for this view comes from theologians as diverse as Irenaeus in the second century and John Calvin in the sixteenth.

Closely connected to eschatology is a fourth biblical theme: the place of humanity in creation. This is of crucial importance in an ideological atmosphere that suggests that the best things humans can do is to reduce the self-valuation that has led them to create the problems in the first place. Here the all-important principle is stated by Paul in Romans 8: Creation *waits* "in eager expectation" for the children of God to be revealed. In ways we hardly understand, it will be the human privilege to *complete* creation and be its voice of praise to the Creator.

A final theological idea in need of further evangelical reflection is a *biblical* cosmic Christology. The New Testament teaching that our Redeemer Jesus Christ is also our Creator and Sustainer has not been sufficiently stressed in Protestant thought. And the doctrine is confused now by the theological laxity of Matthew Fox, whose "cosmic Christ" is little more than a principle of interconnectedness available to all through the Earth itself.

The full biblical doctrine is more adequately stated by Irenaeus, who in the second century declared: "For the Creator of the world is truly the Word of God: and this is our Lord, who in the last times was made man, existing in this world, and who in an invisible manner contains all things created, and is inherent in the entire creation, since the word of God governs and arranges all things. ... He came to His own in a visible manner, and was made flesh, and hung upon the tree, that he might sum up all things in himself."

On this foundation, a Trinitarian understanding of the Creating and Redeeming God, evangelicals can build a more spacious understanding of the gospel. The gospel is good news indeed, announcing a renewal of creation that begins in the hearts of men and women—God's image bearers and stewards—who have been reconciled with him. That is the true foundation on which our care for creation should be based.

Chapter 14

———

IS THE EARTH ALIVE?

How Gaia has become earth goddess,
scientific theory, and a New Age icon.

Tod Connor | 1993

I s it science or is it religion? Not even the promoters of Gaia agree completely. Gaia is the New Age darling of spiritual feminists, neo-pagans, political environmentalists, and animal-rights activists. Yet in the past three years, more than one hundred *scientific* and *technical* articles have been written on Gaia theory. Gaia, the Greek earth goddess, has scientists hotly debating the reality of her existence.

The Gaia hypothesis is the scientific expression of the pre-Christian belief that the Earth is a living creature. As *Environment* magazine describes it, the idea is "that the earth's lower atmosphere is an internal, regulated, and necessary part of life itself, and that, for hundreds of millions of years, life has controlled the temperature, chemical composition, oxidizing ability, and acidity of the earth's atmosphere."

The basic concept of Gaia theory was advanced more than twenty years ago by James Lovelock, an atmospheric scientist and inventor. No charlatan, he is a respected member of Britain's elite Royal Society. Lovelock initially thought of calling the scientific concept of a living Earth the Biocybernetic Universal System Tendency/Homeostasis. During a quiet walk in the English countryside, his neighbor, William Golding (author of *Lord of the Flies*), suggested "Gaia" instead. Science will never be the same.

Lovelock's US collaborator is Lynn Margulis. They began working and writing together more than fifteen years ago. She is an internationally known professor of microbiology at the University of Massachusetts at Amherst. Her most recent published work is *Microcosmos*, cowritten with her son, Dorion Sagan (from her first marriage to Carl Sagan). The book traces the evolution of life from its original bacterial ooze. She is the kind of scientific heavyweight that gives the Gaia hypothesis much of its respectability.

From Theory to Theology

Gaia had her scientific "coming out" party at the American Geophysical Union's 1988 Chapman Conference in San Diego. The uneasy marriage of science and religious philosophy dominated much of the discussion. James Kirchner, a physicist/philosopher, offered the most challenging critique: he argued that the attempt by scientists to figure out "whether the earth *really is* alive" accomplishes little and diminishes the reputation of the scientific community.

Kirchner contends that Gaia is an awkward, amorphous grouping of ideas with dubious provability. While he is willing to accept that "biota [plants and animals] affect the physical environment" and that "physical environment shapes biotic evolution" (both of which most scientists have accepted for one hundred years), he does not accept the notion that the biota are part of a "global cybernetic [computerlike] control system, the purpose of which is to create biologically optimal conditions." From the beginning, this tenet has been basic to Lovelock's hypothesis.

The religious aspects of Gaia theory, meanwhile, encompass a wide array of interpretations and responses. The Lindisfarne Association is an international gathering dedicated to the development of planetary culture. One of its cofounders, William Irwin Thompson, is a former history professor at MIT. The aim of Gaian politics for the nineties, according to Thompson, is to realize that we are all "organelles within a planetary cell."

Lindisfarne's other cofounder, James Morton, is dean of the Cathedral of Saint John the Divine in New York City. Eschewing the idea of Gaia worship or praying to the goddess, he nevertheless believes that modern theology must reincorporate the Earth. He contrasts his contemporary creation theology with fundamentalist creationists who explicitly oppose the notion of evolution. To this purpose Morton created the Gaia Institute; he commissioned Paul Winter to compose a full-blown choral mass entitled *Missa Gaia*; and he even had Lovelock, an avowed agnostic, preach at a Sunday service.

Lovelock and Margulis chafe at the continual allusion to religion. Lovelock received twice as many "religious" letters as "scientific" ones when he published *Gaia: A New Look at Life on Earth*. Always the optimist, he says Gaia may be the first religion with a "testable scientific theory embedded in it." Margulis, on the other hand, takes greater offense: "The religious overtones make me sick," she said in a 1986 interview. But more recently she has mellowed. "Gaia is less harmful than standard religion. It can be very environmentally aware. At least it is not human centered."

Gaia has a magical allure. It undermines biblical creation by imputing a kind of divine power to the Earth, while offering a science that resonates with ancient mysticism. Lovelock compares Gaia's appeal to that of the Virgin Mary: "What if Mary is another name for Gaia? Then her capacity for virgin birth is no miracle or parthenogenetic aberration, it is the role of Gaia since life began."

G. K. Chesterton once said that "it is exactly where biology leaves off that religion begins." Gaia, in its broadest application, has the potential of eradicating any distinction between the two.

Gaia's religious appeal is reflected in goddess festivals held in New York, San Francisco, Toronto, Boulder, and Amherst. Leaders of spiritual feminism, such as Merlin Stone who wrote *When God Was a Woman*, are attracting thousands of enthusiastic followers. To these spiritual feminists, the scientific theory is icing on Gaia's cake. "What contemporary feminism wants to give birth to," says Rabbi Leah Novick, "is the Goddess." The spiritual feminists are minimally concerned about physical reality and quantitative data.

This approach is anathema to the geophysicists who are grappling with Gaia as a scientific hypothesis. One of the foremost spokespersons in this area is Rowena Pattee Kryder of the California Institute of Integral Studies in San Francisco. She has developed an elaborate "scientific" theory based on the "language" of Gaia—how Gaia "talks to herself" and to us, her children. If we are "addicted, confused, and express disempowering tendencies, Gaia reacts with earthquakes, tornadoes, floods, and extreme weather changes that force us to reassess our values, work together, and create a way of life anew," Kryder asserts. And whenever "some conscious living entity" becomes enlightened about its true nature and its relationship to other living things, "Gaia is happy and experiences intrinsic joy herself."

Gaia theory may not be at the forefront of the ecology movement, but its ideas influence many environmental issues. For instance, supporters of Gaia often argue against any special status for humanity among living creatures. Such a position is what has led PETA (People for the Ethical Treatment of Animals) to destroy research laboratories and Earth First! to put metal spikes in trees (to thwart the chain saws of lumberjacks). One noted activist, Ralph Metzner, compares human beings to a cancer spreading across the globe. Humanity has a "reckless disregard for the delicately balanced interrelationships of the whole system," he states. The notion that human beings are intrinsically more valuable than a tree or a bug is now construed as a form of bigotry. Instead, all organisms are seen as vitally interrelated, and *all* plants and animals are said to have a *right* to survive.

Finding Good in Gaia

As Christians, where do we fit into the debate over Gaia?

First, we can acknowledge the seriousness of the environmental crisis. This concern provides much of the motivating force for those interested in Gaia. Wasting precious resources and being insensitive to the science of the Earth (geophysiology) *is* a kind of sin. God warned the Israelites: "If you defile the land, it will vomit you out as it vomited out the nations that were before you" (Lev. 18:28).

Second, we need to avoid a knee-jerk rejection of the entire Gaia theory. Gaia is the current consensus builder within the New Age. But the ideas underlying Gaia theory are not intrinsically evil because they carry the name of a pagan goddess. Our Puritan forebears refused to use the names of the days of the week because of their pagan origins. The Gaia hypothesis, viewed as a scientific tool, can be constructive and stimulating. According to Genesis, God created the plants and the fish and the birds on the fifth day, before he created humanity. His creation was alive. *Life* is not easy to define, and this is where the scientific character of Gaia is most intriguing and technical. This does not challenge Christian belief nor does it threaten Christian faith.

The real problem with Gaia theory is not the scientific aspect but the religious tinkering to which it is being subjected. *We know* that the spiritual nature of humankind, our unique place in creation, is resolved by the Cross, not by microbiology. Christianity finds strength in being "human centered," in sharp contrast to the views of Lovelock, Margulis, and the goddess worshipers. "Human centered" does not mean centered on human nature, rife with greed and insensitivity; instead, it refers to that which was made in the image and likeness of God. The destruction of the world around us is a reflection of not being "God centered" as human beings. Christ, as both God and man, is our center, our truth, and our life. The pollution and defilement we encounter exists through ignorance or rejection of God.

In 1988, Mother Teresa and James Lovelock got into an argument at Oxford University's Global Forum for Survival. Mother Teresa said that if we take care of the people on the planet, the Earth will survive. Lovelock countered that if we take care of the Earth, humanity's problems will be solved. In 2 Chronicles, God hints that both of these views are true. If God's people will "turn from their wicked ways; then will I hear from heaven, and will forgive their sin, and will heal their land" (7:14 KJV).

The beauty and complexity of the Earth are God's gifts to us. Christians should be at the forefront of the ecology movement so that the glory of God is not pre-empted by a narrow humanistic agenda or an "antihuman" value system. We are not to conclude that the Earth is good and humanity merely evil, but we are to treat God's gifts with gratitude and sensitivity because that is his will. Christians should not abandon environmental concerns because of the taint of Gaia-inspired pseudoscience. Rather, the emergence of the spiritual side of environmentalism provides us with the opportunity to offer life-giving truth to an increasingly fearful humanity.

Chapter 15

——

ECO-MYTHS

Don't believe everything you hear about the church and the environmental crisis.

David N. Livingstone, Calvin B. DeWitt, Loren Wilkinson | 1994

You are at a neighborhood block party. Conversation is lagging—until somebody mentions "the environment." Suddenly your problem is not keeping talk going, but keeping tempers under control.

Fueled by misconceptions, misinformation, and even showmanship, the environmental debate rages in the popular media. One side likes to quote Rush Limbaugh, who paints Vice President Al Gore and friends as "tree huggers"; the other charges "rape of the Earth."

It is not very different in evangelical churches. When it comes to God's creation, evangelicals want to have ardent convictions, though misunderstandings and myths get in the way. Is concern for the earth *biblical*? Should our theology shoulder the blame for the crisis? Is there nothing we can do to make a difference?

CT decided to take such questions to key evangelical thinkers and leaders. When the Evangelical Environmental Network offered to cosponsor a symposium, *CT* signed on. A dozen people representing an array of disciplines spent the better part of two days late last year hitting the issues head-on. Many of the symposium participants stayed on to help shape "An Evangelical Declaration on the Care of Creation." As expected, there was plenty of vigorous and interesting discussion.

The question arose, for example, concerning whether there really *is* a problem. Nobel laureate Henry Kendall, professor of physics at MIT (one of the few nonevangelicals present), set the stage by reviewing quantifiable evidence. Citing studies on water resources, oceans, soil, and atmosphere, he noted that the scientific community generally agrees that all is not well.

A public-policy shaper also joined the group, putting to rest the notion that all who work for environmental causes are neopagan New Agers. Susan Drake, a former UN representative for the Environmental Protection Agency and now senior conservation adviser for the US State Department, told how Christian faith guided her work in high-level, international environmental forums.

Bunyan Bryant, from the School of Natural Resources and Environment at the University of Michigan, showed that African-Americans are particularly vulnerable to the effects of pollution. Studies show a disproportionate number of Blacks living close to hazardous waste-disposal sites.

Contributing editor Thomas Oden, concerned that "evangelicals not allow themselves to be co-opted by an agenda that is essentially politically motivated," urged symposium participants to think through a uniquely Christian approach to the issues.

The writers included in this *CT* Institute do just that. Their presentations at the symposium were particularly helpful in tackling "eco-myths." They offer insights that are sure to keep the church's discussion going.

Myth 1: The Church Is to Blame

David N. Livingstone

In 1967, historian Lynn White, Jr., provoked a furious controversy by suggesting Christianity was largely to blame for the world's environmental problems. His article in *Science* magazine, "The Historical Roots of Our Ecologic Crisis," argued that Christianity had to shoulder such responsibility because its theology was hostile toward the natural order. White's article has been quoted and vigorously debated ever since. Some found in White's analysis a justification for seeing the church as the planet's enemy.

But White's article must first be read in the light of his self-professed Christian faith. His father was a Presbyterian professor of Christian ethics, and White himself remained a lifelong Presbyterian and a frequent contributor to church publications.

Because his article is more often referenced than read, many have missed the subtleties of his argument. White argued that ecological problems grew directly out of the Western world's marriage between science and technology, a marriage that gave birth to power machinery, labor-saving devices, and automation. That is the first point. However, the intellectual origins of this transformation, he said, actually predate both the Industrial Revolution of the late eighteenth century and the scientific revolution of the seventeenth.

It was the Middle Ages, he argued—and, specifically, the medieval view of "man and nature"—that brought a decisive shift in attitude: people no longer thought of themselves as *part of* nature but as having dominion *over* nature. According to White, this ruthless attitude toward nature later joined forces with a new technology to wreak environmental havoc.

White ultimately traced this exploitative attitude to the triumph of Christianity over paganism—what he called "the greatest psychic revolution in the history of our culture." Christianity, he insisted, told people that humans had a *right* to dominate nature, and it was therefore "the most anthropocentric religion in the world." All this contrasted with earlier religious traditions in which every tree, spring, and stream had its own guardian spirit. By eliminating animism, he wrote, "Christianity made it possible to exploit nature in a mood of indifference."

White's assessment was more complex than this résumé might suggest. He recognized that Western Christianity encompassed a variety of distinctive theological traditions, some of which—notably that of Saint Francis of Assisi—were quite reverential toward the created order. Nevertheless, he explicitly insisted that, insofar as Christianity undergirded both science and technology in the West, it bore "a huge burden of guilt" for a natural world now seeing increasing degradation.

Since the appearance of White's article, the idea of blaming Christians for the environmental crisis has attracted a wide range of committed defenders. Max Nicholson, for fourteen years director-general of the Nature Conservancy in Great Britain, for instance, insisted that organized religion in general and Christianity in particular were ecologically culpable because they taught "man's unqualified right of dominance over nature."

Historian Arnold Toynbee found in biblical monotheism the mainsprings of "Man's improvidence" toward the natural order. To him, the only solution was to revert to pantheism. Similarly, educator and regional planner Ian McHarg claimed that Judeo-Christian theology produced "the tacit Western posture of man versus nature" by asserting "outrageously the separateness and dominance of man over nature."

The Prosecution Falters

The arguments of White and his defenders have also been widely criticized, of course. There is much about their position that is questionable. In 1970, historian Lewis Moncrief expressed misgivings about looking for single causes for the environmental crisis. Instead of pinning blame for environmental recklessness on Judeo-Christian dogma, he argued for the significance of a range of cultural factors. Two were especially prominent: democratization in the wake of the French Revolution and, in the American context, the frontier experience. On the one hand, such developments led to affluence, changed production and consumption patterns, and problems of waste disposal. On the other hand, the absence of a public and private environmental morality, the inability of social institutions to adjust to the ecological crisis, and an abiding—if misplaced—faith in technology were the ultimate fruits of America's frontier experience.

The work of Chinese-American geographer Yi-Fu Tuan throws doubts on White's thesis in a different way. Tuan scrutinized the environmental situation in Asia and discovered that, despite its different religious traditions, *practices* there were every bit as destructive of the environment as in the West. Tuan clearly showed how the "official" pro-nature line in Chinese religions, for example, was actually vitiated by behavior. Deforestation and erosion, rice terracing and urbanization have all exacted an immense toll on the environment and effected a gigantic transformation of the Chinese landscape. Nor is Tuan's an isolated judgment. Erich Isaac speaks of the destruction wrought by Arab imperial expansionists on vast tracts of the Old World and of the devastation of central Burma by Buddhists. Such are ignored, if not suppressed, among critics of the Judeo-Christian West.

From a different perspective, the Oxford historian Keith Thomas insists that the coming of private property and a money economy led to environmental exploitation and the demise of what he termed the "deification of nature." The "disenchantment" of the world, as he put it, was less a theological achievement than an economic necessity. Alongside the Judeo-Christian emphasis on the human right to exploit nature's bounty, he pointed out, was a distinctive doctrine of human stewardship and responsibility toward creation. This is also the thrust of philosopher Robin Attfield. The idea that everything exists to serve humanity, he emphatically insists, is *not* the biblical position. This led Attfield to assert that there is "much more evidence than is usually acknowledged for ... beneficent Christian attitudes to the environment and to nonhuman nature."

God, the Wise Conservationist

As the rise of science and technology brought about profound environmental changes, Christian clergy and scientists alike outlined strategies to moderate damage to the natural habitat.

Concerned over wasteful land practices, John Evelyn (1620–1706), a founding member of the Royal Society and a Latitudinarian churchman, published in 1662 his famous *Silva, A Discourse of Forest Trees and the Propagation of Timber in His Majesty's Dominions.* Here Evelyn appealed for the institution of sound conservation practices, drew attention to agricultural encroachment on forest land, highlighted the ecological problems of unrestrained grazing, and warned of dangers from charcoal mining. His was a *managerial* approach to the environment, adapted to the rationalizing tendencies of the new mechanical world order. *Efficiency, production, management* were the watchwords of this pioneer conservationist. Precisely such arguments could also receive explicitly theological support.

Thus, John Graunt presented his *Natural and Political Observations upon the Bills of Mortality of* 1662—a demographic analysis—within the context of natural theology. Graunt, using comparative population ratios, directed his readers' attention to the high incidence of pulmonary disorders from pollution in the metropolis.

The orderliness of the world machine, he argued, attested to the sovereignty and beneficence of its Grand Architect. Humans must exercise stewardship over the natural world to ensure that they did not efface or erase the marks of its Designer. Moreover, God was seen as a wise conservationist, and people, made in his image, were to act as caretakers of his world.

The stewardship principle had already been firmly established in John Calvin's injunction: "Let him who possesses a field, so partake of its yearly fruits, that he may not suffer the ground to be injured by his negligence; but let him endeavor to hand it down to posterity as he received it. ... Let everyone regard himself as the steward of God in all things which he possesses."

Now, in the mid-seventeenth and early eighteenth centuries, a form of beneficent dominion surfaced in the writings of Matthew Hale and William Derham. Hale, England's lord chief justice, wrote in 1677 that the human race was created to be God's viceroy, and that its dominion and stewardship roles were intended to curb the fiercer animals, protect the other species, and preserve plant life. It was the task of humankind "to preserve the face of the Earth in beauty, usefulness and fruitfulness."

Derham, a clergyman and author, believed that the Creator's "Infinite Wisdom and Care condescends, even to the Service, and Wellbeing of the meanest, most weak, and helpless insensitive Parts of the Creation."

The Beetle's "Precious" Life before God

Cultural changes during the eighteenth and early nineteenth centuries drove people to think about their relationship to the environment even more. In response to worldwide geographical discovery, revelations about the size of the universe, and geological reports of an immensely old Earth, thinkers began more seriously to question the idea that the world existed solely for human benefit. Some argued that the human species was one more link in the chain of nature. The seeming secularism of such realizations should not blind us to the fact that it became increasingly acceptable *within* the Christian church to believe that all creatures were entitled to respect and civility.

Some theologians began to see that, in the Old Testament, animals were regarded as good in and of themselves—not just for their potential service to humanity. John Flavell, a late-seventeenth-century Presbyterian divine, described the horse as his "fellow creature"; Christopher Smart, the eighteenth-century religious poet, insisted that the beetle's life was "precious in the sight of God"; the Calvinist minister and hymnwriter Augustus Montague Toplady abhorred the digging up of anthills; and John Wesley instructed parents not to let their children cause needless harm to living things—snakes, worms, toads, even flies. So powerful, indeed, was this Christian impulse toward a new sensibility that Keith Thomas comments,

> [T]he intellectual origins of the campaign against unnecessary cruelty to animals ... grew out of the (minority) Christian tradition that man should take care of God's creation. ... Clerics were often ahead of lay opinion and an essential role was played by Puritans, Dissenters, Quakers, and Evangelicals.

One of the consequences of this changing sensibility was a growing sense of ecological interconnectedness. Consider the "arca-
dian" vision of English minister Gilbert White, whose famous
Natural History of Selborne, published in 1789, recorded the natural order of the village from its bird life to seasonal change. White
saw remarkable ways in which his region's ecological diversity
actually constituted a complex unity. He conceived of all this in
providential terms. God had so contrived and constituted this
coherent natural order that everything fitted together "economically." Why? Because like its Creator, White insisted, "Nature is a
great economist." He found a doxological aspect to this economy:
the humble earthworm's indispensable activity in the soil bore
witness to the "wisdom of God in the creation."

Similarly providentialist, though decidedly more rationalist,
was the contribution of the Swedish botanist Linnaeus (1707–78),
arguably the greatest natural historian of the Enlightenment. To
Linnaeus, the classification of life was nothing less than a tool
for uncovering the very order of God's creation. Linnaeus even
saw himself as a second Adam, the namer extraordinaire. Divine
design lay at the heart of the Linnaean project. And nowhere is
this more clearly evident than in an essay he penned in 1749
on "The Oeconomy of Nature" in which he readily detected the
hand of God in nature's order. Because God was the Supreme
Economist and Divine Housekeeper, the study of nature's economy could, at once, confute atheism, justify the social order, and
help humans see their creaturely position as continuous with, yet
separate from, nature.

Where Blame Is Due

To the extent that the church has failed to take concern for the
environment seriously, it must accept its share of the blame. We
must not substitute irritation at Christianity's critics for serious

self-criticism. But that need not keep us from reappropriating insights from Christian tradition that have been lost or suppressed. We need to cull our heritage for intellectual and spiritual resources to meet today's environmental problems.

I have concentrated on voices within the modern Western Christian tradition. There are many earlier voices as well, such as Francis of Assisi. Committed to a life of poverty and a gospel of repentance, Francis treated all living and inanimate objects as brothers and sisters and thereby insisted on the importance of communion with nature. Some believe Francis came close to heresy in his tendency to humanize the nonhuman world and have turned to other sources.

Sixth-century monastic leader Benedict is one of those. He emphasized stewardship, insisting on integrating scholarly work with manual labor. In this he represents an early wise-use approach to the natural order. Benedict drew on ethical resources embedded even earlier in the patristic period. The commentary on the six days of Creation in the hexaemeron of Basil the Great (c. 329–79), for instance, displays a profound interest in nature. His intent, like that of his contemporary Ambrose (c. 339–79), was to illustrate the wisdom of the Creator from the balance and harmony of nature, and to insist on the partnership between God and humankind in improving the earth. Similarly, in the fourth century, Chrysostom believed that animals should be shown "great kindness and gentleness for many reasons, but, above all, because they are of the same origin as ourselves."

One researcher scrutinized Asia and discovered that, despite its different religious traditions, environmental practices there were every bit as destructive as in the West.

All these need to be heard. It is the conceptual and practical testimony of figures like these that prompted Attfield to conclude, "Belief in man's stewardship is far more ancient and has been far more constant among Christians" than the assaults of critics would suggest.

Attending to these hidden riches within the Christian heritage can do more than clear our name. They might well provide the impetus for changing worldwide environmental behavior. The scholar and theologian can and should take a vital role in addressing the current situation—and leading the church forward.

Myth 2: It's Not Biblical to Be Green
Calvin B. DeWitt

I am amazed to hear Christians sometimes say that biblical faith has little in common with the environmental cause. Even worse, some evangelicals fear that teaching people to enjoy and respect creation will turn them into pantheists.

My experience has been very different. For over fifty years I have been inspired and awed by God's creation. From keeping a painted turtle in a tank at age three to caring for a backyard zoo during my youth, I gained deep appreciation for God's creatures. Because I attended a Christian school, heard two sermons every Sunday, and had parents who not only tolerated the creatures under my care but brought me up in the way I should go, there was never any question where the natural abundance around me came from. All creatures were God's—his masterpieces. They were the ones about which we sang each Sunday, "Praise God, all creatures here below!"

As a youth I savored Article II of the Reformed tradition's Belgic Confession. In answering "By What Means Is God Made Known to Us?" the first part affirms, "by the creation, preservation, and government of the universe; which is before our eyes as a most elegant book, wherein all creatures, great and small, are as so many characters leading us to see clearly the invisible things of God."

This theme of how creation tells of God's glory and love is echoed throughout Scripture: God lovingly provides the rains and cyclings of water, provides food for creatures, fills people's hearts with joy, and satisfies the earth (Ps. 104:10–18; Acts 14:17). It is through this manifest love and wisdom that creation declares God's glory and proclaims the work of the Creator's hands (Ps. 19:1). Creation gives clear evidence of God's eternal power and divinity, leaving everyone without excuse before God (Rom. 1:20).

But today we often acknowledge God as Creator without grasping what it means to be part of creation. We have alienated ourselves from the natural processes. We abuse God's creation without realizing that we thereby grieve God.

Of God's magnificent provisions in creation, I want to identify seven. These provisions, many of which are celebrated in Psalm 104, point to the beauty and integrity of what God has made. Through the ages they have led to wonder and respect for the Creator and creation. They also magnify the seriousness of our era's sometimes reckless disregard of our Father's world.

Seven Provisions of Creation

1. *Earth's energy exchange with the Sun.* Our star, the Sun, pours out immense energy in all directions, heating anything in the path of its rays. A tiny part of the Sun's energy is intercepted by our planet. This energizes everything on Earth—all life, ocean currents, the winds, and storms.

The thin layer of gases that envelops this planet has a very important function here. This layer contains water vapor and carbon dioxide and other "greenhouse gases" that trap energy and delay some of its return to space. Earth becomes warm—but not too warm.

The provision of these greenhouse gases—in just the right amounts—makes Earth warm enough to support the wondrous fabric of life we call the biosphere. It works very much like the glass of a greenhouse that lets sunlight in, but makes it difficult for the heat to get out. We experience this "greenhouse effect" on the sunny side of our houses and in our cars when parked in sunlight.

The Sun's energy also contains lethal ultraviolet radiation. This can break up chemical bonds that hold together molecules and thus disrupt and destroy living tissues. Of special concern is the breaking up of DNA, the genetic blueprint of living things. Doing so can kill microscopic creatures and induce cancer in larger ones.

But here we find another remarkable provision of the Creator. For in the gaseous envelope of Earth—high in the atmosphere— we find a gas that absorbs ultraviolet light: ozone. This forms the "ozone layer" or "ozone shield." Not much ozone is present; although it spans a layer several miles deep, if you collected it at thirty-two degrees Fahrenheit at sea level around the Earth, it would measure only about one-eighth inch thick. Yet that is enough to prevent most of the Sun's ultraviolet radiation from penetrating our atmosphere.

If the biblical psalmist had known of this provision by the Creator, perhaps we would have had this verse in one of the Psalms:

> The creatures that dwell in the shelter of God's providence
>   rest in the shadow of the Almighty.
> God covers his earth with a protective shield;
>   God guards the life he has made to inhabit Earth.

2. *Soil and land building.* Many of us know from gardening that soil can be made more productive through tilling and composting. This process also takes place unaided by human cultivation. Climate, rainfall, and soil organisms work together to make soils richer and more supportive of life. This entails a remarkable variety of cycles: the carbon cycle, water cycle, nitrogen cycle, and so on. This symphony of processes enables even bare rock eventually

to support a rich fabric of living things. What a remarkable provision! It nurtures the fruitfulness of creation.

But this soil building teaches patience. It may take a century to produce an eighth inch of topsoil. In this way the land is nurtured, refreshed, and renewed.

3. *Cycling, recycling, and ecosystems*. Recycling is not a recent invention. The whole creation uses and reuses substances contained in soil, water, and air. Carbon dioxide breathed out by us—and raccoons, lizards, and gnats—enters the atmosphere later to be taken up as the carbon-based raw material from which to make the carbon-based stuff of life. This is in turn transferred to the animals and microscopic life that depend upon it for food. And soon these consuming creatures return the carbon back to the atmosphere through breathing, or by their own death and decay.

Water, too, is recycled. Taken up by animals, it is released through breathing, sweating, and ridding of wastes—finding its way into the atmosphere, or through sewage-treatment plants back to rivers and streams. Taken up by the roots of plants, some is pumped up through the bundles of tubing in the roots, stems, and leaves of plants and back to the atmosphere. That moisture joins water evaporated from lakes, streams, and other surfaces and forms rain and snow that again water the face of Earth.

Thinking of such provision, the psalmist wrote,

He makes springs pour water into the ravines;
    it flows between the mountains.
They give water to all the beasts of the field;
    the wild donkeys quench their thirst. ...
He waters the mountains from his upper chambers;
    the earth is satisfied by the fruit of his work.
    (Ps. 104:10–13)

4. *Water purification.* Some water percolates through the soil to the ground water below and supplies the springs that feed wetlands, lakes, and ravines; we call this *percolation.* In many water-treatment plants in our cities, water is purified by having it percolate through beds of sand. In similar fashion, water that percolates through soil or rock is filtered, but usually over much greater distances. The result: by the time we pull up water to our homes by our wells, it usually is fit to drink.

This is more remarkable than it may at first seem. Water is often called "the universal solvent," meaning that it dissolves practically anything. How then could water ever be purified? Should it not always be contaminated with dissolved materials from everything through which it passes? Because of creation's natural distillers, filters, and extractors, the answer is no. There is remarkable provision in creation for the production of pure water.

5. *Fruitfulness and abundant life.* Of the known flowering plants alone, there are two hundred fifty thousand species—orchids, grasses, daisies, maples, sedges. And each of these inter-relates with water, soil, air, and other organisms, forming the interwoven threads of the household of life we call the biosphere. When I was in ninth grade, I recall learning that there were one million different species of living creatures. In graduate school, I learned that it was five million, and today we believe it is some-where between five million and forty million. This biodiversity is so great that we have just begun to name the creatures. This is just the kind of provision you would expect from a remark-ably creative Genius. "The earth is full of your creatures," said the psalmist. "There is the sea, vast and spacious, teeming with creatures beyond number" (Ps. 104:24–25).

6. *Global circulations of water and air.* Because of its 23.5-degree tilt, our Earth gets unequally heated from season to season. Both

seasonal and daily differences cause differentials in Earth's temperatures. This, in turn, produces temperature gradients that drive the flow of water and air from place to place.

Atmospheric and oceanic circulations are vital provisions for maintaining life. Carbon dioxide produced by animal and plant respiration and oxygen produced by photosynthesis are released to air and water. Carbon dioxide is moved around so that it comes into contact with plants that reincorporate it. And oxygen, produced by photosynthesis of plants, is similarly circulated by air and water currents. Global circulations provide the "breath" of life on a planetary scale.

7. *Human ability to learn from creation.* Human beings are endowed by God with minds that integrate what creation teaches us. Through observation and experiment, we are able to revise our models of the world to represent reality better. Our mental models are further nurtured and refined by the cultures we grow up in. This capability is essential for meaningful human life.

Seven Degradations

Human beings can mute and diminish God's testimony in creation. We have the ability, in the words of Revelation 11:18, to "destroy the earth." Nearly every day now, we learn about new destructions of land and creatures. While some reports are dramatized and overstated, professional technical literature again and again describes new and increasing instances of environmental degradation. What I present here as "seven degradations" draws upon scholarly literature accepted by the scientific community. That means I have not gotten my information from government or university reports, newspapers, opinion polls, television, talk shows, or popular articles. Practically every one of these degradations is a destruction of one of God's provisions for creation.

1. *Land conversion and habitat destruction.* Since 1850, people have converted 2.2 billion acres of natural lands to human use. This compares with Earth's total of 16 billion acres that have some kind of vegetation and current world crop land of 3.6 billion acres. This conversion of land goes by different names: deforestation (forests), drainage or "reclamation" (wetlands), irrigation (arid and semiarid ecosystems), and opening (grasslands and prairies). The greatest conversion under way is tropical deforestation, which removes about 25 million acres of primary forest each year—an area the size of Indiana. The immensity of this destruction illustrates our new power to alter the face of Earth. In the tropics, we do it to make cheap plywood, bathroom tissue, hamburger meat, and orange juice, among other things, but it destroys the long-term sustainability of soils, forest creatures, and resident people.

2. *Species extinction.* More than three species of plants and animals are extinguished daily. If there are indeed forty million species, then the rate may be several times higher.

3. *Land degradation.* What once was tall-grass prairie we now call the Corn Belt; here we grow the corn that feeds hogs, cattle, and us. In much of this prairie, two bushels of topsoil are lost for every bushel of corn produced. Pesticides and herbicides made it possible to plant corn, or any crop, year after year on the same land. Crop rotation—from corn to soybeans to alfalfa hay to pastures—has been abandoned.

4. *Resource conversion and wastes and hazards production.* Some seventy thousand chemicals have been created by our ingenuity. Unlike chemicals made by organisms and the earth, some cannot be absorbed back into the environment. Among them are many specifically designed to destroy life: biocides, pesticides, herbicides, avicides, and fungicides.

5. *Global toxification.* Of the thousands of chemical substances we have created, hundreds have been discharged or have leaked into the atmosphere, rivers, and ground water. This happens through "disposal" and from vehicles, chemical agriculture, homes, and industry. Some join global circulations; DDT has shown up in Antarctic penguins, and biocides appear in a remote lake on Lake Superior's Isle Royale. Cancer has become pervasive in some herring gull populations.

6. *Alteration of planetary exchange.* Earth's exchange of energy with the Sun and outer space is fundamental to the planet's circulations of air and water. But burning and exposing carbon-containing materials to oxygen brings rising concentrations of atmospheric carbon dioxide, allowing less heat to escape to outer space, thereby enhancing the greenhouse effect. This creates global warming.

Adding to the effects of increasing carbon dioxide are other greenhouse gases, such as chlorofluorocarbon (CFC) refrigerants in our air conditioners and refrigerators. Melting snow caps, receding glaciers, and a slowly rising sea level demonstrate that Earth's temperature has been rising very slowly over the centuries. There has been some debate on the degree to which this is happening, but that it is happening seems clear. And this rise likely will accelerate, with consequences not only for Earth's temperature but also for the *distribution* of temperature across the planet, with consequent changes in patterns of rainfall and drought, and even—ironically—lower temperatures in some places in the world. CFCs operate not only as greenhouse gases. They also destroy ozone in Earth's protective ozone layer.

7. *Human and cultural degradation.* One of the most severe reductions of creation's richness concerns cultures that have lived peaceably on the land for centuries. In the tropics, cultures

living cooperatively with the forest are being wiped off the land by coercion, killing, and legal procedures that deprive them of traditional lands. Their rich heritage of unwritten knowledge is being lost. Names of otherwise undescribed forest creatures are forgotten; so are uses of the wide array of tropical species for human food, fiber, and medicine.

A Place for Evangelicals?

Six centuries before Christ, Jeremiah described the undoing of creation: "I looked at the earth, and it was formless and empty; and at the heavens, and their light was gone. ... I looked, and the fruitful land was a desert; all its towns lay in ruins before the LORD, before his fierce anger" (Jer. 4:23–26). Neglecting to do God's will in the world is not new, and its environmental consequences have been known for more than two thousand years (Jer. 5:22–23, 31; 8:7).

The evangelical community has been slow to get involved in environmental issues. But it is not too late. In the early 1970s there were few evangelicals involved in world hunger. Today some of the best relief operations are done by these deliberative evangelicals. They did not just start handing out food. They got the best minds together, collected the scriptural material, and carefully planned.

That needs to happen again. Our environmental situation presents a significant opportunity. To be *evangelical* means to proclaim the good news. Part of our proclamation is that the environment is God's *creation*. If we do not make God the Creator part of the good news, we are crippling our faith and witness. We will lose sight of what the Belgic Confession called "a most elegant book" wherein all creatures help us—and others—to see the invisible God.

Myth 3: There Is Nothing
Christians Can Do
Loren Wilkinson

Headlines trumpet news of environmental crises, with some experts claiming apocalyptic scenarios where we will either burn or freeze within a generation. Another vociferous group claims just the opposite: there is no real ecological problem, only hysterical environmentalists. Despite their divergent messages, both groups offer Christians the same temptation: to think there is nothing we can do to help the situation.

But this is simply not true. There are many strategies Christians can and should pursue to help care for creation.

One of the earliest evangelical books on the environment—Francis Schaeffer's *Pollution and the Death of Man*—made one of the wisest observations: Christian households and churches need to be "pilot plants" of the new creation. There the world can see, acted out in individual lives and in communities, the healing of creation that only comes from being in fellowship with God in Christ. Eugene Peterson's rendering of Philippians 2:15 suggests the difference we can make: "Go into the world uncorrupted, a breath of fresh air in this squalid and polluted society. Provide people with a glimpse of good living and of the living God" (Message).

What does "good living and the living God" mean when it comes to creation? What can we *do?* Here are some suggestions, organized in ever-widening spheres of influence:

Individual Action

First, we become *aware.* We learn how God cares and provides for us through creation. That means, for example, knowing where our food, water, and energy come from and where our waste products go. (There is no "away" in God's creation.) What farms produced the food in our last meal? How were the plants grown? How far was it transported to get to our table? To what former wetland is our garbage hauled? Into what bay or river are our toilets flushed (and after what degree of processing)? What forests were pulped to produce our paper? These questions are not intended to reduce us to guilty inaction, but to make us know that it is through God's creation that we live.

We also need to practice the principles of "reduce, reuse, recycle"—not out of environmentalist legalism but in conscious delight of being God's free, redeemed, and responsible stewards:

We *reduce*, for example, because, though creation is for our use, it has worth far beyond the use we make of it. The more we learn the impact of our choices on creation, the more likely we are to learn to be content with less.

We *reuse* because God did not make a throwaway world. So repair the shoes or toaster to give them new or longer life. If we must bring things home in packaging, we ought to consider the second life the packages might have. And we ought to be willing to pay more for things that have a longer life.

And we *recycle* because God does. "To the place the streams come from, there they return again," says Ecclesiastes 1:7.[1] Increasingly, however, we have built a civilization whose residues—plastics, tires, Styrofoam™—do not fit into the created cycles. So when we must discard what we have used, we need to recycle.

To these three R's, Christians have good reason to add two more:

We *resist*. Our culture often defines our value in terms of how much we consume. We need to resist this consumerism that is fed

---

[1] All Scripture quotations in this article are from the New International Version.

by advertising and television. Perhaps a television set is one thing we should *not* repair when it breaks. In few other areas can we better demonstrate "good living" and our allegiance to "the living God" than by refusing to be shaped by our consumerist culture.

But that negative choice opens up a glorious, positive one: We *rejoice.* The more we learn about God's provisions for the earth, the more wonderful it seems. Isaiah's words should describe our experience of creation: "You will go out in joy and be led forth in peace; the mountains and the hills will burst into song before you, and all the trees of the field will clap their hands" (Isa. 55:12).

Community Efforts

We should get in the habit of using the theological term *creation* instead of the more secular *environment* or *nature.* The bedrock of our action is that we are *creatures*, responsible to God our Creator for our use of his gifts in creation. A congregation that speaks only of "the environment" may well come to feel that its wastebaskets full of plastic-foam cups on Sunday morning offend only some politically correct fad.

We also need to broaden our understanding of the word *stewardship.* Inside the church, the term is restricted almost entirely to matters of money. But increasingly, it is being used outside the church to speak of our care of creation. The word opens a door to witness, for it invites the question, *"To whom is the steward responsible?"*

If the church is to be a model of "good living and the living God," we also need to be aware of what our buildings and practices convey about God and the genuinely good life. All the principles of caring for creation that we practice as individuals—reducing, reusing, recycling, resisting, and rejoicing—should be evident in our corporate life as well. To recycle (or avoid) the Sunday flood of paper, to make our church buildings and parking lots available to wider use—these make for good stewardship. Ultimately, to a pagan world beginning to glimpse something of God through creation, these acts function as pre-evangelism.

Church members should also consider reducing their impact on creation through sharing. Many things that we own—from lawn mowers to vacation homes—could well be shared.

Finally, churches should resist an increasing tendency to leave God's creative acts out of worship. Much new worship music exalts God in his majesty, but speaks very little of *what* he has done and made. New music in the church would be enriched if it were to follow the pattern of an old carol: "Joy to the world! the Lord is come; / let earth receive her King; / Let every heart prepare him room, / And heaven and nature sing." That's good theology, and good worship.

Public Witness

Christians have recently begun to be more aware of their need to be politically active. We need to extend that activity to policies that influence our care of creation. It is important to shape the way our governments and economies work. We need to bring the full meaning of words like *creation* and *stewardship* into the public arena. Here are four principles for wider involvement.

- Many of the most important political decisions related to the care of creation are influenced greatly by opinions of local people. Zoning hearings to increase the density of an area, or to allow roads, industry, or power plants, invite public participation. It is important to use such forums in order to save our communities, and to do so publicly in the name of God the Creator.

- Just as we have (rightly) evaluated candidates for office on their records on such issues as abortion and attitude toward the family, we need to evaluate also their attitudes toward creation.

- A major problem in our civilization is the barrier between cities and the agriculture that supports them. (The average food item in North America is transported more than 800 miles.) This leads to ever-larger farms and ever-fewer opportunities for stewardship and contact with the creation that supports us. To remind people of their vital connection to the land, we therefore need to encourage urban gardens, farmers' markets, and local, small-scale agriculture—and to point out (as Paul did to the pagans in Acts 14:17) that it is God who "has shown kindness by giving you rain from heavens, and crops in their seasons, and provides you with plenty of food, and fills your hearts with joy."

- Some of the most eloquent and effective voices for the care of creation come from environmental groups in which there is no Christian presence (and often an implicitly anti-Christian bias). Christians should consider participating in such groups, both because their agenda—caring for creation—should be a Christian's agenda, and because these organizations desperately need a Christian witness. The environmental movement is an ethic looking for a religion, and it is no surprise that many people in it have turned to native and pagan religions when no Christian voice speaks with and to them.

Chapter 16

CHRISTMAS UNPLUGGED

*Why spending less and turning
off TV should be part of the
church's mission to the world.*

Bill McKibben | 1996

I'm looking forward to Christmas—no dread of the busyness, no fear of drowning in the commercialism. I know what Christmas Eve will be like: we'll cut the tree in the afternoon and bring it in and decorate it. We'll go to church, where I will sweat with my Sunday-school class as they try to remember their lines for the pageant, and then I'll relax in the knowledge that it is the small mistakes (the drooping halo, the three-year-old shepherd using his crook as a hockey stick) that really stick most fondly in people's minds. We'll come home, read the Christmas story once more, put up our stockings, and go to bed. In the morning, we'll open the stockings and find the candies and pencils and tiny jokes inside; we'll exchange one or two homemade presents—photo albums, raspberry jam made in the summer's heat—and then we'll go outside to play in the snow, or into the kitchen, cooking for the great dinner ahead. In other words, a completely normal Christmas minus the mounds of presents.

The story of how my family arrived at this quiet and beloved Christmas (which means, of course, a much quieter December than most of our friends experience, without a single trip to the mall, and a January without a credit-card debt) has to do with many things: with carbon dioxide levels in the atmosphere, with our worries about what a consumer culture meant for our daughter—and with the conviction, nurtured by our church, that there was more real joy to be had from Christmas if only we could unplug it: more real connections with that glad day in the past, and more real hope for a troubled future.

To understand what I mean, you need to begin by looking hard at what we've done to this planet. We all know that you can guess with some accuracy a human being's behavior by looking at his physical and social surroundings. If a parent is self-absorbed, lazy, or forced by economic pressure to be absent, then a family often falls apart. On a slightly larger scale, when a community's institutions—schools, parks, churches—begin to wither, you know its people have succumbed to a kind of privatized selfishness.

And if you look at the largest measures of environmental health, you can make similar judgments. The ever-increasing levels of carbon dioxide, the steadily rising rates of ultraviolet radiation, the fast-growing list of extinctions: these testify not so much to technological failure as to human failure. We need to confront that failure in the hopes of building something new and joyful in its place.

We need to begin with a few basics. I find as I travel that there is a tendency, even among those who care about such issues, to underestimate the pressures on the natural world. We tend to list "the environment" as one issue alongside a hundred others—drugs, the deficit, and so on. But it is much more than that; it is less an issue than a context, the basic context in which we all must live our lives. And it is coming unraveled.

In the next fifty years we will probably see Earth's population hit its maximum. Toxic pollution, fossil fuel use, ozone depletion, soil erosion, and a dozen other phenomena that environmentalists have been warning us about will put enormous pressure on this planet.

In the area I study most closely, global climate change, the world's scientists are now in agreement that we have begun to warm the planet. This warming is in its very early stages—1995 was the warmest year to date, but it only reflects about a fifth of the warming the scientists say we will see by midcentury—and already you can begin to see what happens. Over seven hundred dead in a short Chicago heat wave. Highest grain prices in twenty years on the Chicago Board of Trade as the farmers of the world's farm belts struggle to feed an expanding population while simultaneously coping with yield-destroying high temperatures.

We do not quite realize our danger yet; the most recent presidential campaign, with its call from both sides for cutting gas taxes, is proof of that. One reason we don't is because of the casual way we have of discussing environmental problems. By grouping together everything from global warming to river pollution, we obscure crucial differences and delude ourselves as to the progress we've made.

What Goes In ...

Although we have made major strides in addressing some ecological problems—urban air pollution, lake contamination, lead poisoning, and so on—it does not follow that this means *anything* about our capacity to solve other environmental problems, because those other problems are fundamentally different.

Consider what comes out of the tailpipe of a car. One byproduct of burning gas is carbon monoxide, the chief ingredient in smog—brown, dirty, dangerous to breathe, and now largely eliminated by the installation of catalytic converters; that's why Los Angeles is noticeably cleaner than it used to be.

But carbon *dioxide* comes pouring out that exhaust pipe, too. When you burn a gallon of gasoline, which weighs about eight pounds, you release five and a half pounds of carbon dioxide. The average car releases its own weight in CO_2 annually. It is invisible, and it does nothing to us directly. But it is the chief heat-trapping gas now altering the most basic terrestrial forces on the planet— its molecular structure traps heat that would otherwise radiate back out to space. And here is the real catch: there is no catalytic converter, no technology, that can do anything about it. All you can do is drive smaller cars, and drive them less—and we, of course, are doing neither, and so the CO_2 continues to build up in the atmosphere.

The difference between these two types of environmental problems—between things like smog, rivers that catch on fire, and radiation leaks from atomic plants on the one hand, and global warming, habitat destruction, and overfishing on the other—is simply this: the first is caused by some mistake, something going wrong. It can therefore be fixed with relative ease. The second is caused by things going pretty much as they should go, simply at much too high a level.

And it is those more serious and deeper problems that concern me most. We are in the fast-moving water above the rapids, and there is no way to paddle backwards. It will take all the skill and cohesion we can muster to get through intact.

Think of it in this way: we have vastly speeded up the changes in our societies and economies in the twentieth century, and seen people and communities strain, and in some cases crack, as they try to keep up. Now, as the twenty-first century dawns, we are taking the always-before-stable physical systems and forcing them to speed up just as quickly. And there is no good reason to suppose they will adapt.

Job Talks Back

For people of faith, however, the problem is even deeper than the practical one I have described. People have always polluted—always needed to alter and manipulate the land around the places they lived or farmed. But that did not raise the deepest theological questions. Now, in the short period of ten or twenty years, we have so quantitatively increased the scope of our alterations that they have become *qualitatively* different. We are altering the most basic forces of the planet's surface—the content of the sunlight, the temperature and aridity—and that brings out the most powerful questions about who is in charge.

If you wanted to give a name to this theological problem, I think you could say that we are engaged in *decreation*. God, before getting around to humans, created birds and sea creatures and beasts and creeping things, and he pronounced them all good; he saved a breeding pair of each aboard the ark. Now we toss them off the ark.

In the book of Job, God speaks from the whirlwind, taunting Job's powerlessness—where were you, he asks, when I set the boundary of the oceans? Can you summon forth the rain clouds and crack them open? Job had to sit down and shut up, but increasingly we can talk right back to God. We can spit in his face, the old geezer: our habits and behaviors, by raising the temperature, now threaten to determine how high the seas rise, and where it will rain, and where it won't.

As I said at the beginning, it is our behaviors, our *desires*, that are really at the bottom of this mess, not our technologies.

Let's look again at global warming. Carbon dioxide is an inevitable byproduct of fossil fuel burning. If you buy an electric car and hook it up to a fossil-fuel-fired power plant, then all you've done is move the problem upstream; now the carbon dioxide pours out of the power plant's smokestack. Let's say you double the efficiency of the car's engine so it burns only half the gasoline. That's possible—in fact, we have done it over the last decade. But we have simultaneously doubled the total number of miles driven in this country, which wipes out the whole gain. A massive, much-heralded EPA project to reduce energy use by half at the American Express Corporation was wiped out by only 700 people switching from cars to Jeep Cherokees or Suburbans or those big 4×4 pickups. With the constant pushing by the electric utilities, the average American household added one of those compact fluorescent bulbs during the 1980s—and on average added seven incandescent bulbs as well, one reason that per capita electric consumption went up 11 percent on average. If you double fuel efficiency and simultaneously double the size of the economy, you get precisely nowhere.

We need technical change, but more than that we need behavioral change. Much more than we need electric cars we need buses and bicycles and the shifts in our ideas of what is desirable that would cause us to use them. The American way of life, insofar as it revolves around consumption, drives our physical problems.

Consumption is an issue uniquely suited for faith communities. Among the institutions of our society, only the church and the synagogue and the mosque can still posit some reason for human existence *other* than the constant accumulation of stuff. Our businesses thrive on constant growth; our politicians avoid hard choices by flogging the economy to grow more quickly (in the immortal words of William Jefferson Clinton, "It's the economy, stupid."); even our educational institutions have designed themselves to fit easily into this happy picture. We have made most important decisions—as individuals and as a nation—in recent decades by answering the question: Is it good for the economy?

Religious institutions, which grew up before this emphasis, inherited a different set of concerns—in many ways, a contradictory set of concerns—and those contradictions, among other things, have weakened the power of religion in the economic era. We profess to believe that we cannot worship both God and mammon; we profess to worship someone who told us to give away, not accumulate; we profess to follow a tradition that in its earliest and purest forms demanded communal sharing of goods and money. But we have by and large bracketed off those central portions of the message. And we are not alone in this. Virtually every religious and philosophic tradition has similar figures and similar teachings, in a line that runs from Buddha through Jesus and Francis, to Thoreau and Gandhi. Martin Luther King, Jr., said at the end of his life that it was not racism or imperialism or militarism that represented our root problem, it was materialism. But for all our pious lip service, we have regarded those people as unrealistic cranks.

This is a powerful moment for rehabilitating Christ the crank. What are the atmospheric chemists telling us? What are the climatologists saying? In many ways, the same things we have heard from Christ and his disciples: Simplicity, they say. Community. Not because it is good for our souls, or for our right relation with God, but because without simpler lives, the chances of stabilizing the planet's basic workings are slim. Because without community, the chances for buses and trains and other necessary efficiencies are nil. This confluence of the hardheaded and the softhearted may make for a powerful moment, an unpredictable time when the world could turn quickly in new directions.

The $100 Christmas

If we in religious communities are going to do anything about it, we have to recognize just how strong the consumerist ethos is. It has taken root in all of us, basically unchallenged. Fertilized by a million commercials, it has grown into what we call a wolf tree where I live, a tree whose canopy spreads so wide that it blots out the sun, that it blots out the quiet word of God. Churches, obviously, do not have the power to compete head-on, and few of us junkies are ready to go cold turkey. But increasingly there are signs that people are asking deep questions: "Isn't there something more than this?" And the churches can help build this momentum in important ways, beginning with those things it has the most psychological control over.

Chief on this list is the celebration of Christmas, not only the most beloved of church holidays, but also the most powerful celebration of consumerism. Just how powerful can be judged from the fact that it has become a major gift-giving holiday in Japan, despite the conspicuous lack of Christians there. And it is not entirely well-understood. A few years ago, in Kyoto, one department store filled its center window with an enormous effigy of a crucified Santa Claus.

Christmas is a school for consumerism—in it we learn to equate delight with materialism. We celebrate the birth of One who told us to give everything to the poor by giving each other motorized tie racks.

A few years ago, with a couple of friends, I launched a campaign in our Methodist conference in the Northeast for "Hundred Dollar Holidays," recommending that families try to spend no more than a hundred dollars on Christmas.

When we began, we were very long faced, talking a lot about the environmental damage that Christmas caused (all those batteries!), and the money that could instead go to social justice work, and so on. But what we found was that this did not do the trick, either for us or for our fellow congregants.

What did the trick, we discovered, was focusing on *happier* holidays. Though we continued to stress the one-hundred-dollar figure as an anchor for families pushed and pulled by the tidal forces of advertising and social expectation, we talked about making Christmas more fun. The poster we used suggests many alternatives to a store-bought Christmas, things that involve people doing things for each other and for creation.

We were amazed at how well this worked, even on the limited scale on which we were trying it out—many people thanked us for "giving them permission" to celebrate Christmas "the way I always wanted to celebrate it." It taught me a useful lesson: that the effect of consumerism on the planet is mirrored precisely in its effect on the soul; that finding true joy means passing up momentary pleasure; and that joy, that deep bubbling joy, is the only really subversive force left in our society. The only way to make people doubt, even for a minute, the inevitability of their course in life is to show them they are being cheated of the truest happiness. And Christmas is a good school for this education, because it can be such a wonderfully giddy party for the birth of a baby.

It also turns out to be a pretty radical idea. The retail economy is massively geared toward "the fourth quarter," banking annually on the fact that people will rush into stores to buy things they don't need. So to question the wisdom, and the pleasure, of that consumption is to question an awful lot about our consumer society. We had several newspaper columnists attack us on the grounds that, while we might be right, we would also undermine the sacred economy. And it gave us a good opportunity to write back and say, Surely American consumer capitalism, defended always as the most rational of all systems, doesn't demand the corrupted celebration of Christ's birth in order to make ends meet.

Great American TV Turnoff

Another practical idea involves a feature of our lives even more entrenched than Christmas, and that is television. It has become the essential anchor of the growth culture, our endless moral tutor. Children spend more time staring at it than they spend in school; when asked if they wanted to spend more time with the tube or with their father, more than half chose TV. New research indicates it makes us fatter and less physically healthy all the time—but it also, and more profoundly, changes the shape of our minds. Are you worried about a decline in family values, in community spirit? Then you are worried about television.

The debates over things like violence on TV miss the point, I think. I wrote a book once that involved watching everything that came across the largest cable network then in existence on a single day. I had 2,400 hours of videotape by day's end, and I spent a year looking at it, asking myself: What would the world look like if this was your main source of information? If you distilled all those thousands of game shows and talk shows and sitcoms and commercials down into a single notion, it would be this: You are the most important thing on the face of the earth. Your immediate desires are all that count. Do It Your Way. This Bud's for You. We are led daily, hourly, into temptation.

And there is something else: television and its attendant technologies create a constant buzz around us, an unrelenting torrent of image and sound that make it difficult for us to think for ourselves anymore—to rise to occasions. That's one reason I am a board member of a group called TV Free America, which every year sponsors a turnoff week in schools around the nation. Last year three million kids took part. And increasingly the idea is spreading to churches. Not only are the turnoffs endorsed by the American Medical Association, the Children's Defense Fund, and the Natural Resources Defense Council, but also by the Congress of National Black Churches, the National Religious Partnership for the Environment, and the Family Research Council. Last winter the pope called for TV-free Lent, a campaign we are just beginning here.

Again, the emphasis will not be on renunciation; it will be on the great pleasure that comes when you turn off the television and rejoin the living world. And on the opportunity to reflect—to think—in the stillness of the unplugged world. Solitude and silence and darkness have always been key parts of the religious life, but they have been banished by TV. We need to reclaim them, and in so doing break the materialist enchantment that now holds us in its thrall, shrug off some of the witchcraft that makes us long constantly for things that will not satisfy us.

The center of Our Lives

These questions about consumption, like the questions about the new environmental damage, get near the deepest theological questions. If we were built, then what were we built for? We know what hawks were built for—it's announced in every fiber of their bodies. But what about us? Why do we have this amazing collection of sinews, senses, and sensibilities? Were we really designed to recline on the couch, extending our wrists perpendicular to the floor so we can flick through the television's offerings? Were we really designed in order to shop some more so the economy can grow some more? Or were we designed to experience the great epiphanies that come from contact with each other and with the natural world? Were we designed to witness the goodness all around us, and to protect and nourish it? Just as "the environ-ment" is a context, not an issue, so is "consumption." It defines at the moment who we are—and who we aren't.

This is a profound moment for religious people. On the one hand, our species asserts itself as never before. We have grown large enough to alter creation—whether by the single great explo-sion of a nuclear weapon, or the billion muffled explosions of pis-tons inside engines spewing out carbon dioxide. As Oppenheimer said on that New Mexico afternoon testing of the A-bomb, we have become as gods. And not just the nuclear engineers—anyone with a car, anyone with a credit card.

Yet, at the same moment, we have acquired the intelligence to see what we are doing—not just the scientific understanding of things like the greenhouse effect, but the dawning ecological understanding of the way that everything is linked to everything else, that creation is a fabric far richer than any of our predeces-sors could have understood (though, of course, they may have sensed it more deeply than we do). The age-old struggle between God and mammon, always before a personal and never-ending battle, now has a time limit and a bottom line.

It is really an issue of who or what we put at the center of our lives. In the environmental debates, there has been a lot of discussion about anthropocentrism versus biocentrism versus theocentrism. Most of this debate seems empty to me, assuming as it does that most of us put any of these things at the center. If we followed any of them in a sincere fashion, we would be well on the way to solving our environmental and social problems. Anthropocentrism, if we really placed humans at the center of our concern, would lead inevitably to the kind of sharing necessary to heal the environmentally destructive gaps between rich and poor; were we truly anthropocentric, we would feel grave shame at our own overconsumption. But, of course, we are not. We are me-centric. We are I-dolatrous. That is what consumer society has schooled us to be.

The question now is, how can we break out of it? Some have criticized secular environmentalists as "pagans" because they profess a biocentrism, a view of the world that puts all living things at its center. But they are far closer to orthodoxy than most of the rest of us who still put ourselves at the sweet center. We need to put God there. And then we need to realize that this involves more than the smug announcement that we have done so.

Having God at the center imposes certain limits on our behavior. If we are not to wreck God's creation, then there are certain things we simply must not do; we simply must not continue consuming as we now are. And there are certain things we must do; we must share our bounty with those of the rest of the world, finding somewhere a middle ground so they don't follow our path to consumer development. These things are in one way extraordinarily difficult. But we know the deep and certain joy they can bring, and so we can say with some confidence that at least they are possible. At least they are worth a try.

And we will know if we are succeeding by the evidence all around us. Creation will let us know if we are rebuilding our house, restoring its foundations. Are species continuing to the out? Is the temperature continuing to climb? Our communities will show us if we are really changing. Are the numbers of absurdly rich and absurdly poor beginning to decline? Are we rebuilding institutions other than the mall, places like schools and parks and churches? The environmental crisis is so deep and so fundamental that our response will reveal who we most truly are.

———

In the meantime, I'm looking forward to Christmas. There's one more tradition we always observe, one begun many centuries ago by Saint Francis. We take some bird seed out into the woods near our homes, and spread it far and wide. The minute we leave I have no doubt that jays and squirrels and chickadees and shrews descend, happy to have their day's food without a day's work. This is such a joyful morning that all creation deserves to share in the celebration!

Chapter 17

GREENING OF
THE GOSPEL?

*Evangelical environmentalists press to
add creation care to the church's mission.*

Randy Frame | 1996

C al DeWitt in 1977 sat alone in his office at Calvin College reading the Gospel of John. He had read John 3:16 countless times in his Christian life, but this time he noticed something different in the well-known passage, "God so loved the world."

"That day, it bowled me over," DeWitt recalls. Noticing the Greek word *cosmos (world* in English), DeWitt was deeply moved by the idea that Christ's death had eternal implications not only for the rebellious human race, but for the *cosmos,* all of creation, as well. That day was a turning point in DeWitt's understanding of biblical mandates for care of God's creation and stewardship of the earth.

DeWitt has gone on to become a leading light in the contemporary movement among evangelicals toward environmental awareness and activism. In recent years, that movement has blossomed in size and influence. It also has drawn its share of criticism from within evangelical ranks.

Birth of a Movement

For nearly two decades, DeWitt has been pressing church leaders to affirm the church's role in caring for the environment.

In 1979, he became director of the Mancelona, Michigan–based Au Sable Institute, which had been reorganized around the goal of environmental stewardship. Au Sable sponsored yearly forums, where a few dozen evangelical leaders gathered to focus on the Bible and creation. "Nobody was raising any green flags," DeWitt recalls. "We were just rediscovering the Creator. Many of us knew that the Scriptures had a lot to say about the Creation, but we began to realize that some of the key things were central texts of evangelical Christianity."

The words of some hymns DeWitt had sung all his life began to sound odd, he says, citing, "This world is not my home, I'm just a-passin' through" as an example. "I can't sing that anymore," says DeWitt, "because I believe that God sees this earth as a valuable home for us, a home that he graciously provides and waters."

When those leaders who had gathered at Au Sable returned to their churches, Christian colleges, and parachurch groups, they continued the reflection and started new discussions, thereby planting some of the seeds of the contemporary evangelical environmental movement. "The Au Sable Institute has probably been the single most powerful force in bringing Christians together on these issues," says Fred Van Dyke, a biology professor at Northwestern College in Orange City, Iowa.

For his part, DeWitt is hesitant to call it a movement. "It's deeper than that. I see it more as a revival, because people are finding new life in their faith as they encounter God in all his fullness."

Whether a movement or a revival, something is definitely happening. "There's a major groundswell being felt within the evangelical church," says Joseph Sheldon, professor of environmental science at Messiah College in Grantham, Pennsylvania, where forty-four students are majoring in the subject. "More and more people are realizing that their theology is not entirely limited to humanity, but that God is concerned about the creation."

This groundswell can be documented in many ways, including by the increase in evangelical organizations dedicated to creation care. The Evangelical Environmental Network (EEN), Christians for Environmental Stewardship, the Christian Environment Project, and the Christian Society of the Green Cross are among the Christian organizations that have formed within the past three years. "For many years, we felt very lonely," says Scott Sabin, executive director of the San Diego–based Floresta, founded in 1984. "But that's all changed."

Even organizations not known primarily for an emphasis on creation stewardship, such as InterVarsity Christian Fellowship (IVCF), are taking a look at environmental issues. Staff workers are being trained and encouraged to engage chapter members in projects to protect and preserve the environment. Terry Morrison, IVCF's director of faculty ministries, says, "We're trying to get our people to think in terms of creation care at all levels of our ministry."

Evangelical relief-and-development organizations have in recent years become more intentionally environmentally aware. Last year's annual gathering of the Association of Evangelical Relief and Development Organizations (AERDO) included a major emphasis on environmental stewardship. "I became an environmentalist while I was working with World Vision trying to alleviate poverty," says AERDO board member Paul Thompson.

"You can't alleviate poverty without addressing issues of environmental degradation." Thompson cites, for example, the relationship throughout much of the Third World between deforestation and the resulting inability of the land to retain ground water and to produce food people need to survive.

Higher Education

One of the strongest indicators of a grassroots movement among evangelicals toward an environmental focus can be found at Christian colleges.

At least two dozen Coalition for Christian Colleges and Universities (CCCU) schools now offer environmental science majors, and most of those programs are less than five years old. At one of the forerunners—Taylor University in Upland, Indiana—students may choose from among six subspecialties under the environmental science category, including biology, chemistry, economics, and environmental management.

At Au Sable, environmental science majors from one hundred colleges and universities take highly specialized courses. "We view it as an extension of Messiah College," Sheldon says. "It gives us—and other coalition schools—a program that approaches the strength of what you'd find at a major university."

According to DeWitt, the creation-care revival on Christian college campuses goes beyond course offerings and majors. "It's penetrating the entire curriculum, and it's influencing everything from the way cafeterias are run to the way the grounds are kept."

Twenty CCCU member institutions are participating in the two-year Global Stewardship Initiative, financed by a Pew Charitable Trusts grant. The program focuses on the interrelated areas of environmental degradation, resource consumption, and population growth.

Not only has it increased the number of environmental courses being offered at Christian schools, it has also facilitated networking among like-minded Christian scholars, many of whom have embarked on joint publishing efforts.

Sleeping with the Enemy?

The movement's popularity, however, has not shielded it from the concerns of some Christian leaders. Critics claim the movement has failed to maintain enough distance from a secular environmental movement laden with humanistic and pantheistic views.

"Caring for Creation" kits distributed to churches by EEN, however, address such commonly asked questions such as "Isn't concern for the environment a part of New Age Religion?" and "Why should we be anxious about environmental problems when God is in control?" Among the respondents are World Vision President Robert Seiple and Regent College theologian J. I. Packer.

The key to remaining distinct from secular environmentalists, according to EEN Director Stan LeQuire, is to focus on Scripture. Such a commitment has led evangelicals to part paths with secular counterparts at some points. Extreme advocacy for animal rights, for example, is not common among evangelicals. LeQuire stresses that human beings are the "crowning achievement" of God's creation.

Also, although evangelical environmentalists in general consider world population growth an important concern, they have consistently held to a pro-life stance.

"Sometimes we hear of people who have found relevance in their Christian faith as a result of what the Bible says about creation care," LeQuire says. "We find that very rewarding."

Some of the divisions between evangelical environmentalists and their critics can be traced to different scriptural interpretations. E. Calvin Beisner, associate professor of interdisciplinary studies at Covenant College in Lookout Mountain, Georgia, claims that Christian environmentalists have "almost completely neglected" the biblical doctrine of the Curse, resulting from the fall of humankind in Genesis 3.

Beisner says that because of the Curse, "We cannot expect to find nature untouched by human hands as in and of itself good or even neutral. We ought instead to find it under the Curse and in need of redemptive transformation."

Northwestern College's Van Dyke, however, says, "The earth is under a curse because of human disobedience toward God. We find nowhere in the Bible where God tells us that matter is inherently sinful."

Divided over Methodology

The differences between these two perspectives goes beyond Scripture to public policy and scientific analysis.

For instance, EEN participated in a major campaign that included radio spots in 18 states supporting the 23-year-old Endangered Species Act (ESA), which had come under attack earlier this year in Congress.

Peter Illyn, executive director of Christians for Environmental Stewardship, defended ESA during the Republican National Convention at the invitation of Republicans for Environmental Protection. "God created the different species and called them good," Illyn says. "When species go extinct, we're bouncing checks in the trust fund that God called us to manage."

Wheaton (Ill.) College environmental economist P. J. Hill in principle supports protection of endangered species, but he maintains that ESA discriminates against humans who own property where such species are located. "The cost of saving endangered species should fall on all of us, not just on those on whose land the endangered species dwell," Hill says.

Richard Land, president of the Southern Baptist Christian Life Commission, considers the ESA "an unmitigated disaster," adding that the act "has done much to ruin individual human lives and to trample upon basic property rights."

Hill applauds evangelical environmentalists for spurring more thought about environmental issues. But he believes many in the movement are too quick to reach questionable conclusions. "Implicit in a lot of the writings is that modern capitalism will necessarily cause the earth to run out of resources. I dispute that presumption."

He maintains that environmental concerns must be weighed against other important principles. "In my work in institutional design, I try to figure out how to construct environmental programs that get results, but in the least expensive and fairest ways, Hill says. "A lot of people in the Christian environmental movement fail to recognize the complexity of these issues."

Crisis or Not?

Environmental activists, both Christian and secular, have been labeled as reactionaries who overstate environmental problems.

Geochemist Edwin Olson, retired professor at Whitworth College in Spokane, Washington, comments, "People figure if they can tick off a dozen problems, you've got a crisis. But when you begin to look at each one separately, you find that some aren't as big as we thought, and some may not be problems at all."

Beisner, too, maintains that environmentalists have a crisis mentality. "The potential risks involved in increasing atmospheric carbon dioxide get major play," he says. "The potential benefits get no mention at all." Beisner cites research establishing that increased carbon dioxide levels result in increased crop yields. In theory, "it may produce global warming, but it has also contributed to efforts to feed more people at lower prices."

Northwestern College's Van Dyke acknowledges a relationship between carbon dioxide and increased photosynthesis. But he adds, "The effects that go with it will have long-term negative consequences, including an overall warming effect and the shifting of agricultural zones."

Messiah College's Sheldon observes that the environmental movement's critics often are not experts in a natural science. Sheldon says that most natural scientists, including Christians, strongly agree that the earth's global environmental problems are real and must be addressed.

Ray Grizzle, associate professor of environmental science at Taylor University, maintains that Christians' criticism of the environmental movement is based at least partly on a disdain for science, a disdain he says could have disastrous consequences.

"There has been some hype by environmentalists," Grizzle notes, saying that some scientists have a vested interest in inflating dangers in order to get a paper published or to obtain funding for a research project.

Nevertheless, he believes that the scientific community's warnings of possible environmental disaster are too serious to ignore.

"A lot of people are looking for conclusive proof," Grizzle says. "But this is not like going into a laboratory and manipulating data. The experiment is with the earth, and it's a one-time experiment. I'm concerned that when the ozone is depleted and we're all dying of skin cancer, people will say, 'Well, I guess you proved it. We were wrong.' "

Sheldon's prescription for change starts with a new way of thinking, beginning with the assertion that the earth's resources are limited. "We must realize that we can't have ever-increasing growth in a finite system," Sheldon says.

Sheldon calls for intensive efforts to find alternative fuels for automobiles, greater energy-efficiency requirements for appliances and new homes, and more recycling.

"We don't need to give up all our comforts," he says. "The standard of living in the United States is not that much different from Canada and Europe, and yet the negative impact on the environment in the US is much higher."

According to EEN's LeQuire, the ultimate issue is not science or economics. "Our emphasis is biblical," he says. "The Bible has a lot to say about how we should be living with regard to the creation. All the warnings from scientists could be proven wrong tomorrow, and we would go right on doing what we're doing."

Chapter 18

——

GOD'S GREEN ACRES

*How Calvin DeWitt is helping
Dunn, Wisconsin, reflect the
glory of God's good creation.*

Tim Stafford | 1998

I met Cal DeWitt, the environmentalist, some years ago at a conference on world population. He was expounding eloquently on the need for living in harmony with God's creation when I asked him, in an offhand way, whether he had seen any place that would serve as a model.

My question was not, I admit, entirely innocent. In my experience, environmentalists can be very clear on what aspects of modern life they are against, but when asked what kind of society they admire, they may refer to the way Native Americans once lived on the land, or to some remote tribe in Central Africa. I am looking for an environmental vision that applies to modern America, suburbs and cities and all.

So DeWitt's answer surprised me. "Yes," he said cheerfully, "Dunn, Wisconsin."

"Dunn? Where's that?" I asked, suspecting a commune in the northern woods that raised organic vegetables for the farmer's market.

"Just south of Madison," he told me. "It's my town."

Dunn, the Un-Town

I visited Dunn in late spring last year. Leaving the freeway behind me, I took a meandering road through Wisconsin farm country, cornfields covering easygoing hills patched with black and brown oak woods. I was looking for a town to appear, but it never did. The first thing I learned about the town of Dunn, Wisconsin, is that it's not a town. In Wisconsin, the place where you find stores and schools and inevitable taverns—what I call a town—is a village. A town in Wisconsin is a subset of the county, a square of open country six miles on a side.

That doesn't imply, however, that there is no "there" to Dunn. At one time few residents thought much about the locale. They lived in the country "just south of Madison." That has changed quite dramatically over the twenty-five years since DeWitt came to live there. Now the four thousand citizens say proudly what town they live in. They note the difference (perhaps not so visible to others) when they cross over the town line into other towns. DeWitt says that one of the most notable developments of recent years is the expansion of the town cemetery, previously overgrown and almost forgotten. People in Dunn feel they belong to the place and plan to plant their bones there.

Eyes to See

Calvin DeWitt is a wetlands ecologist who teaches in the University of Wisconsin's interdisciplinary Institute for

Environmental Studies. He's also director for the Au Sable
Institute, a Christian study center in the Michigan woods that
offers summer field courses for Christian college students. He is
a formidable scholar, recognized by the university as one of its
best teachers. Ron Sider says he is "Mr. Evangelical" regarding
the environment—the person with the scholarly credentials, the
outspoken faith, the long track record.

What he is best at, though, is field trips. He has a way of taking
students into the most ordinary landscapes and showing them
a creation they hadn't seen. He is good at explaining complex
features of the terrain and its living creatures, and he conveys a
sense of wondering joy as he does it. DeWitt sees the world as a
scientist and as a Christian, and he puts remarkably little space
between those two. He is committed to preserving nature, but
it isn't humanity against nature for him. Rather, he sees nature
serving humanity by offering testimony to the glory of God.

It is one thing to proclaim God's glory on field trips. It is quite
another in the vexed and politicized subject of land-use planning.
Dunn's north boundary runs a mere stone's throw from Madison,
a city that is spreading fast into the dairy, corn, and soybean farmland all around. When the DeWitts bought their home in 1972, the
familiar process of turning farmland to suburb was well under
way. Small subdivisions and five-acre "farmettes" were spreading
across the landscape. Farmers whose children showed no interest
in farming could foresee selling out to home builders for a bundle.

DeWitt was studying rural land-use decisions and, as part of
his research, went to observe a meeting of the Dunn town board,
an elected council of three. The discussion was over a new hot-
mix and rock-crushing plant that the town council had approved.
Some of the neighbors were upset at the prospect of the plant polluting their environment, but the supervisors were in no mood
to listen. One of them rudely told the dozen attendees that they

were wasting time trying to argue the issue; if they didn't like the decision they should elect somebody else, but in the meantime, just go home.

DeWitt had come to observe, but these comments drove him to his feet. He spoke passionately to the small gathering on the nature of democracy. He spoke of an active, involved citizenry, not a passive electorate that votes every few years on who should make decisions for them.

The talk made an impression, and shortly thereafter he was invited to a meeting in a local farmer's living room. The purpose was to recruit a slate to run for the town board, to throw out the old, unresponsive supervisors. DeWitt was new to Dunn, but he was asked to stand for election.

DeWitt the Politician

It is not easy to imagine Cal DeWitt running for elected office. He seems too idealistic for the grit of governance. "I often use Rembrandt for an illustration," he says. "Is it conceivable that we could give acclaim to the artist but not to his masterpieces? Is there anyone who honors Picasso without any reference to his paintings?" Our proper relation to God's creation is awe and wonder, DeWitt says. This does not sound like a land-use stump speech.

Once, he told me, he stopped his car on the Interstate freeway near Gary, Indiana, and tried to read Psalm 19 aloud. "I looked up into the night sky and couldn't see any stars because of all the lights and pollution. The noise of traffic was deafening. Semitrailers slammed by, literally sucking at my car. The psalm made no sense at all there. I thought, 'Here is a community that has been deprived, and has deprived itself, of nature's testimony.'"

DeWitt worries when human creation entirely supplants God's, when the natural world is so blotted out by city as to be unknown. He worries, too, about mental deprivation. "For some of my students, *Star Trek* is more real than the biosphere. They can tell you more about the star-ship *Enterprise* but don't know the boundaries of the town they live in. We even abstract nature in science, so it doesn't provide for awe and wonder."

In the world of politics, the Dunn town board sat very near the bottom of the food chain. Most planning decisions rested with the county. The town government was responsible for plowing snow and repairing local roads, and little else. Furthermore, many Dunn residents were vague on whether they lived within Dunn's boundaries, as their mail was addressed through one of the local villages. There was no cafe or post office where the people of Dunn gathered. Few paid attention to town elections.

Nevertheless, DeWitt approached his campaign with all the verve of a military assault. He helped mobilize a large pool of volunteers and dedicated himself to visiting every home in the town personally. He is an affable, easygoing conversationalist who treats even his enemies like old friends. His style of campaigning is perhaps best captured by his conversation with pike fishermen.

Some of Dunn's constituents, DeWitt explains, have settled in the area strictly for the pike. So, as DeWitt tells the story, he greets one such fisherman outside his home and asks cheerily, "How are things going with the pike nursery?"

The man looks confused, so DeWitt repeats the question.

"What's a pike nursery?" the fisherman asks.

"You like to catch pike?" DeWitt says. "I understand they get pretty big in this lake."

"Yeah, they do. Real big."

"Well," says DeWitt easily, "they don't start out that big. They start out as little ones. The place the little pike come from is what you call the pike nursery. I figured if you were a pike fisherman you would be able to tell me how things are going in the pike nursery."

The guy summons his neighbor, also a fisherman, and asks if he knows where pike come from. His neighbor doesn't know. DeWitt suggests they ask some more of their buddies. By now they're curious. Eventually there are eight pike fishermen standing around in the yard, none of whom knows where pike come from. So DeWitt explains that mature pike go into the marshes to spawn, and the little pike live in the shallow safety of the marshlands until they're big enough to venture out into the lake. That's one of the reasons DeWitt is running for town council, because the marshes are getting spoiled. If there isn't a marsh, there isn't a pike nursery; and without a pike nursery, there soon won't be any pike.

Needless to say, DeWitt won the pike-fisherman vote. He believes firmly that "when people really know their world, they will take care of it." A lot of his neighbors love the country—that's why they live in it—but they didn't really understand it. For DeWitt, loving the country and understanding its ecology go naturally together. His goal was not merely to win an election but to build a broad understanding of and involvement in town decisions.

The Moratorium on Development

DeWitt won his election and was able to scuttle the hot-mix plant. ("He did it with a filibuster," says supervisor Eleanor White. "Cal kept talking and talking. ... He wore them down.")

Two years later, DeWitt was elected town chairman, and an ally, Ed Minihan, became a supervisor with him. Their two votes controlled the board, but it took some clever work for them to figure out how to use their power effectively. They learned that every new construction site needed town permission for access off the town roads. They used that as the choke point to control development.

There was a certain "last-one-in-close-the-door" quality to these restraints, as most of DeWitt's allies were recent arrivals from the city who wanted the countryside preserved as they had found it. Rosalind Gausman, who married into an old farm family, told me that DeWitt and his group were seen as "new people coming in and taking over our town. I had [Cal] pegged as an outsider and a troublemaker." Old-time farmers felt their property rights slipping away.

Their alarm grew when the town board slapped a two-year moratorium on all property subdivisions. Dunn had never had a land-use plan, and the continuing surge of applications for land divisions meant the council couldn't get its head above water. The debate was often framed in terms of development: Are you for or against it? But DeWitt noted that when people said "development," they only meant housing tracts. "We said, 'We're for development. We want to develop farms.' "They wanted Dunn to grow in a way that would make sense to its citizens and preserve the qualities that they loved. A moratorium would give them time to think through a plan.

Housing developers sued the town, which managed to survive through some good legal counsel and a one hundred thousand dollar surplus built up by not building any roads for a year. Gausman says, "Cal is so amazing—how he could have a room full of hostile people, and he could calm the crowd. He would let them talk, would really try to understand them. Then he would start explaining his side. He would just calm things down. He always listens to people."

Prairie Fire

DeWitt also likes to talk, and when he talks, his love for nature and his awe toward its splendors always comes through. When I first arrived in Dunn, Cal and Ruth DeWitt welcomed me to their home, set on a drumlin nearly surrounded by marsh. Cal was busy at his computer, manipulating images from a digital camera he had just acquired. He enthusiastically showed me how the software could be used to extract environmental data from a photograph of daffodils blooming on his lawn. Then, while Ruth prepared dinner, he walked me around the drumlin.

A drumlin, as DeWitt explained to me, is a cigar-shaped pile of rock and soil left by an ancient glacier. DeWitt pointed out the glacier's path, from Lake Waubesa just out of sight to the north, down the silver marsh at his front door, and on to Lake Kegonsa south and east. A mile away, on the other side of the marsh, ran a thin strip of black. 'That's prairie," Cal said. "It's just been burned a few days ago." Fires are set in the marshlands at regular intervals, he explained, one section at a time, for both prairie and marsh depend on wildfire to sustain their balance.

Over dinner, we talked more about fire. "People ask me why I have a lawn around the house instead of prairie," Cal said. "I used to want to bring the prairie in a lot closer, but I learned that's not the most practical thing to do." He told how, lighting backfires to burn the grasslands on his property, he underestimated the power of wildfire. The fire department arrived just in time to save the house.

Suddenly Cal got up out of his seat, a look of excitement on his square, Dutch features. By his porch light, he pointed out the characteristic features of a burr oak tree growing near the door. A burr oak has thick, fire-resistant cork bark, which expresses itself in knife-edged ridges running up and down the trunk and along all but the thinnest branches. DeWitt took some time explaining this to me, telling me the relation of this oak tree to the cork trees of Spain, making me punch my fingers into the firm resiliency of the bark. I was not sure why he was excited until he began to talk about fire again.

"An oak savanna like this one is an island in the fire," he said, his voice full of awe. "When the marsh and prairie burn, the fire will usually peter out in the oak savanna, because the tall grasses don't grow in the shade of the trees. Occasionally, though, a fire will get into the crowns of the trees. The oak savanna would be destroyed except for the burr oak, which won't burn through. These cork ridges will light, and glow, but the heat won't penetrate to the life of the tree. If you see a burr oak after a wildfire you see every branch outlined in red, glowing with fire."

The Budding Naturalist

DeWitt grew up in Grand Rapids, Michigan, the child of devout Christian Reformed parents. His father was a house painter who encouraged his son to pursue whatever he loved. What Calvin loved was studying God's creatures. He had a pond in his back yard where he kept all nine species of Michigan turtles. He maintained a zoo with other wild creatures, including an extensive aquarium in the basement. Their home was on an ordinary forty-foot-wide city lot, but DeWitt used his bicycle to explore nearby fields and forests.

Educated in Christian Reformed schools, including nearby Calvin College, DeWitt never conceived of science as opposed to God. The book of nature was God's other book, a revelation of his nature.

When DeWitt went for doctoral studies at the University of Michigan, he expected a rigorous challenge to his faith, but he found that if his professors were materialists, they weren't dogmatically so. He was surprised to find a secular university such a congenial place for a Christian.

That's characteristic. Where others see sharp divisions, he finds it easy to unite his faith and his science. When it was popular in his field of ecology to blame Christianity for the degradation of the natural world, he established the Au Sable Institute with its explicitly Christian basis. He enthusiastically speaks of the Christian faculty and graduate students that he works with at the University of Wisconsin, a place hardly known as a bastion of faith.

DeWitt is reticent when asked his thoughts on evolution. He finds the whole discussion of origins very bookish, quite removed from the actual observation of God's handiwork. "Whatever God did is what God did. Whatever means he is using to create is okay with me," he says. Evolution has never been a cutting issue for him, he says. "Sometimes [it is] for two or three days, when I'm with people who think it is very important. Then I'm out in the field, singing psalms, enjoying God's marvelous work, and the discussion doesn't seem so significant."

Land-Use

The plan for Dunn, Wisconsin, began with taking inventory. That's a natural approach for DeWitt. He hoped that when people got a firm understanding of their land, they would find that they mostly agreed on how to treat it. Taking inventory gave time to defuse the winners-and-losers mentality that land-use decisions often create.

A newly formed plan commission compiled a detailed description of their town's geology, water resources (including lakes, rivers, and streams), woodlands, wetlands, wildlife, fisheries, historic and cultural resources. They mapped bird flight patterns and assessed pollution in all surface water. They studied how locations for homes and businesses affect their surroundings. The University of Wisconsin and governmental authorities provided all kinds of expert testimony. Eventually, the town published their study so that every citizen could become familiar with the town's natural resources.

"Coming to know their place, they liked what they found and decided to care for it and keep it." That is DeWitt's published summary. The land-use plan the town wrote into law essentially tried to keep Dunn the way it is by severely limiting new subdivisions and businesses. It enabled property taxes for farms to be set on a basis that assumed agricultural use (rather than on a higher basis assuming the land's use for housing). Plans for parks and trails were made. Roadsides were replanted to prairie. Preserves were plotted out. And every detail of the plan assumed the active involvement of its citizens.

For example, community parks are planned and developed by the neighborhood they are in, not by a town parks department. Someone building a new home can live in a trailer on the property while he builds—to encourage families on a limited budget—but only if they personally get the okay from all their neighbors.

The plan, in fact, was adopted by a referendum, even though the town board had legal authority in itself. The idea was to involve as many citizens as possible in discussions about the plan.

You can certainly argue over the plan. By limiting building, the planners have made Dunn a kind of park land for Madison. Housing in Dunn is bound to grow expensive, simply by the law of supply and demand. Other locales will have to carry the burden of providing housing and jobs for a growing population. (Nearby villages will continue to expand, and Madison itself will push in other directions.) Dunn isn't everybody's solution.

Clearly, though, it's the favored plan of the people of Dunn. In the early days there were lawsuits and meetings where people shouted, and one election where the reformers were voted out of office. (Two years later they were voted back in.) In recent elections, there hasn't even been opposition. Most of the old-time farmers have come to see that, as town clerk Rosalind Gausman says, "these guys are not out for their own good." In fact, one of the clearest objectives of the Dunn plan is to create conditions where farming can be a viable way of life forever.

In a 1996 referendum, Dunn voted to raise its taxes, the money to be used to purchase development rights for crucial parcels of land. The idea is to lock in the land-use plan permanently. It helped that a frugal approach to town government had kept their taxes lower than anywhere else in the area.

User-Friendly Environment

I concluded a day-long tour of Dunn standing with DeWitt in a small oak grove overlooking the northwest corner of the town. Looking north, we could just make out a ribbon of cars and trucks moving on the Madison beltway. Otherwise, the scene was an American pastoral, now preserved permanently as farmland and park. Through complicated negotiations, Dunn officials had succeeded in using their new tax dollars to buy a large tract of the land there, then reselling it, stripped of its development rights, to a local farmer. DeWitt told me about the pig farmer who had increased his farm's economic viability, about the heirs of a large tract who had agreed to sell to the town for a reduced price, and about others involved in delicate financial negotiations. Just a few days before, the town had celebrated with a picnic on the grounds where we stood.

I noticed a stand of small conifers, aliens in the landscape, growing on the northern edge of the oak grove. I asked DeWitt whether they would be removed.

"No," he said. "If we were the Nature Conservancy [an environmental preservation group, which has bought land for preservation in nearby marshes] the conifers would go, because they aren't indigenous. But they make a good wind screen for picnickers, so we'll leave them."

In a small way, that captures DeWitt's philosophy. He's not such a purist that human concerns have to get out of nature's way. Rather, he seeks ways for the natural world and the human world to live as neighbors. That's good for the natural creation, because when humans live with it and get to know it, they love it and want to take care of it. And it's good for humans, because through the natural world they get a dose of the reality of God's reign. Community is a natural result. Picnics—an expression of community—are a result. DeWitt takes a serious interest in picnics.

Lessons Learned

DeWitt really thinks we can find common ground between environmental concerns and humanity's needs when we *experience* the creation (as distinct from arguing about it). That's why, in his university classroom, his chief objectives are "awe and wonder" and "developing community." He takes his students on field trips to develop both. He believes, in fact, that the natural world offers the best resource for saving the university from its factionalism, its rigidity, its inhumanity.

It's the same with Dunn. People scattered in a country setting, commuting elsewhere, often live isolated lives. Dunn has no gathering place where they bump into neighbors—not even a school. (Dunn's children go to school in nearby villages.) Yet Dunn's environment brought its citizens together. Through the long, ongoing process of figuring out how to care for Dunn and to keep it, they came to know and value each other.

Does Dunn offer anything to the rest of America, cities and suburbs and all? Two things, I believe. First, it reminds us that God's beautiful creation can exist harmoniously on the very border of a large city. Madison will have Wisconsin marsh and farm a bike ride away, perpetually.

Second, it suggests that the beauty around us really can help us find common ground. Not, of course, that decisions about the land are easy to make. Differing political and economic ideas, applied to the environment, can make for heated combat. Yet when people take a break from arguing and actually look at the world God has made, they generally want to keep it and care for it. It's a rare person who doesn't value parks, whether they are as grand as Yellowstone or as ordinary as a prairie path reclaimed from an old railroad. It's a rare person who feels no sense of loss in seeing condos line the Gulf Coast, or hearing of the extinction of any species. Dunn, Wisconsin, is one small example of how people can come together around such deep, instinctive responses. It is an example not just of preserving nature. It is also people and community who are being preserved.

Chapter 19

———

HEAT STROKE

*The climate for addressing global
warming is improving.*

Editorial | 2005

I n May, Richard Cizik, governmental affairs vice president
for the National Association of Evangelicals, talked to *The
Wall Street Journal* about human-induced climate change (often
referred to as "global warming"). Cizik pointed to polls of the
NAE membership that revealed "even George Bush supporters
believe you have to offer something more ... than simply voluntary
measures" to address the problem.

Cizik identified himself as "one of those Bush Republicans,"
but added, "I disagree with the President on this one."

Soon Cizik and Bush may be able to agree. In August, the
administration finally acknowledged that the climate change
since 1970 cannot be accounted for in purely natural terms, and
that "smokestacks and tailpipes are the likely cause." According
to *The New York Times*, that judgment was delivered "in a report

to Congress accompanied by a letter signed by the secretaries of energy and commerce and the President's science adviser."

The administration has previously brushed off such reports or even suppressed them. Now it is time for whoever leads the United States to address its contribution to the problem. Attitudes are changing across the board. In August, *Business Week* carried the cover line, "Global Warming: Why Business Is Taking It So Seriously." The article shows that major energy companies realize that it is to their advantage to make voluntary changes that preempt government actions and save them money.

Not everyone is persuaded about the link between human activity and climate change. But the scientific data have grown increasingly solid as the Intergovernmental Panel on Climate Change's reports moved from 1994 to 1997 to 2004. The real danger is to wait until the data are undeniable. While ExxonMobil, the world's largest publicly traded oil company, has been dragging its feet, the second largest has been a pioneer of change. BP chief executive John Browne has called on governments and industry to undertake a drastic shift to boost the use of technologies that could help slow down the buildup of greenhouse gases. "It would be too great a risk to stand by, do nothing, and to wait so long that when the impact on the climate really does begin to be felt, you have to take action which is so disruptive as to cause serious damage to the world's economy," Browne told the Council on Foreign Relations in June.

Who or What Is to Blame?

Global climate change is not on every citizen's list of hot issues. The small shifts in temperature documented by scientists are hard to feel in your own backyard. And when you read that the average global temperature will change by somewhere between 2.5 and 10.4 degrees from 1990 to 2100, it sounds trivial.

It isn't. While the numbers sound small, the effects are likely to be great. Because climate systems are complicated, the changes will ripple out to result in more frequent heat waves, drought, torrential rains and floods, increased tropical diseases in now-temperate regions, and increased peak wind and precipitation in tropical cyclones.

While warming will no doubt benefit some frigid regions, these sorts of disasters will disproportionately impact the poor. American Christians give generously to relief and development organizations when people are devastated by droughts or floods or hurricanes. Clearly, we care about the victims of such "natural disasters." To borrow from Bob Pierce, founder of World Vision and Samaritan's Purse, our hearts are broken by the things that break the heart of God. This month, representatives of Christian relief and development organizations are meeting for a briefing on climate change and an opportunity to discuss how they can face these challenges.

But what if our actions are contributing to these "natural disasters" even as we contribute our dollars to relieve their victims? What if the likelihood of extreme weather is increased by the amount of fossil fuels we burn to light and heat our homes and to run our cars? Right now, we don't have many individual choices for change. But collectively, we do.

Reachable Goals

When it comes to climate change, collective activity is a touchy subject. Many have objected to the Kyoto Protocol to reduce greenhouse gases. And truly, as a writer in the *Harvard International Review* said this summer, "International coordination is likely to slow and divert truly effective action."

The *Harvard International Review* writer stressed the importance of national plans that can be tailored to individual economies. The United Kingdom has stepped out in front and set ambitious, but reachable, goals. The European Union is working on its own plan. As individual nations see the importance of taking action, the problems can be addressed without serious economic repercussions and without creating nightmarish international bureaucracies.

In the United States, Senators John McCain and Joseph Lieberman have introduced legislation that would set targets and create a trading system that would allow companies to reduce emissions in a way that is responsive to the market economy. This bill is an excellent starting point for whatever plan the Congress and the administration will eventually develop. Individually, Americans should weigh the advantages of low-emissions technologies such as hybrid vehicles. Business will more quickly respond to consumers than to government regulation. And consumer demand has the power to lower prices.

But time is important. With each passing year, we lose the ability to slow and minimize the effects of global warming. This is our Father's world, and it is filled with our brothers and sisters. Christians should make it clear to governments and businesses that we are willing to adapt our lifestyles and support steps toward changes that protect our environment.

Chapter 20

———

ENVIRONMENTAL WAGER

*Why evangelicals are—but shouldn't
be—cool toward global warming.*

Andy Crouch | 2005

T he theory is taken for granted by nearly every scientist
working in the field. But because it is difficult to confirm
experimentally, a few vocal skeptics continue to raise pointed
questions. The skeptics find a ready audience among evangelical Christians, with groups like Focus on the Family saying that
"significant disagreement exists within the scientific community
regarding the validity of this theory."

I'm not talking about evolution. Or maybe I am. The issue in
question is not our distant past but our near future. The theory
is the all-but-unanimous scientific consensus that human beings
are changing the climate by emitting gigatons of carbon into the
atmosphere, and that if we do nothing to change our behavior,
the warming trend that has taken hold for the past century may
well become a runaway gallop.

Prompt action could not only avert the worst consequences—extreme drought and ocean levels rising as much as three feet by 2100—but could actually open up a new era of prosperity through the development of new, more efficient technologies. Some evangelical leaders—including the editors of this magazine—have called for action to address climate change. But the Bush administration, which generally listens carefully to conservative Christians, apparently hasn't heard enough to reconsider its indifference. For many churchgoers, the issue seems murky, its complexity amplified by claims of "significant disagreement."

There is in fact no serious disagreement among scientists that human beings are playing a major role in global warming. The Intergovernmental Panel on Climate Change, whose scientific working group was chaired for many years by the evangelical Christian Sir John Houghton, concluded in 2001 that "most of the warming observed over the last fifty years is attributable to human activities." These conclusions, Houghton points out, were vetted by more than one hundred governments including the United States: "No assessments on any other scientific topic have been so thoroughly researched and reviewed."

Unfortunately, there is another politically loaded issue where scientific agreement has failed to convince the public. If evangelicals mistrust scientists when they make pronouncements about the future, it may be because of the history of antagonism between biblical faith and evolution. As pro-evolution philosopher Michael Ruse points out in a recent book, evolution began as an alternative to Christianity before it acquired scientific respectability. It was *evolutionism*—a naturalistic worldview that excluded the biblical Creator—before it was science.

The resulting battle between evolutionism and Christian faith has had countless unfortunate consequences. Some Christians resorted to a wooden interpretation of the first pages of Genesis that was no better as science than evolution was as a worldview. More recently, some scientists have reacted with fanatical hostility to the questions that proponents of Intelligent Design ask about evolution.

But perhaps no result of the creation-evolution stalemate is as potentially disastrous as the way it has stymied courageous action on climate change. In May, for a serious article about Intelligent Design that described one proponent's books as "packed with provocative ideas," the editors of *The New Yorker* chose the snippy headline, "Why intelligent design isn't." Rhetoric like that hardly disposes conservative Christians to trust the impeccably researched articles about climate change the magazine published earlier in the year.

All science is ultimately a matter of trust. The tools, methods, and mathematical skills scientists acquire over years of training are beyond the reach of the rest of us, even of scientists in different fields. Thanks to the creation-evolution debate, mistrust between scientists and conservative Christians runs deep. But those scarred by battles with evolutionists might still consider heeding the scientists who are warning us about climate change. As an evangelical scientist said to me recently, the debate over climate change is very much like Pascal's wager, that famous argument for belief in God.

Believe in God though he does not exist, Pascal argued, and you lose nothing in the end. Fail to believe when he does in fact exist, and you lose everything. Likewise, we have little to lose, and much technological progress, energy security, and economic efficiency to gain, if we act on climate change now—even if the worst predictions fail to come to pass. But if we choose inaction and are mistaken, we will leave our descendants a blighted world. As Pascal said, "You must wager. It is not optional. You are embarked. Which will you choose then? Let us see."

Chapter 21

IMAGINING A DIFFERENT
WAY TO LIVE

*Wendell Berry is inspiring a
new generation of Christians
to care for the land.*

Ragan Sutterfield | 2006

Wendell Berry defies easy description. His book jackets call him everything from social critic to farmer to conservationist, and he is all of these, though they do not contain him. He is a writer—poet, essayist, and novelist. Everyone from *The Progressive* to *National Review* has claimed him. Eugene Peterson names Berry one of the seven most important writers on spiritual theology for him, saying that Berry's combination of "prophetic bite and Christian winsomeness ... keeps our identity as followers of Jesus in sharp focus."

Increasingly, his readers are young Christians, particularly evangelicals seeking community life and character transformation. Wheaton College political science professor Ashley

Woodiwiss says, "Students are attracted by the imaginative alternatives and possibilities that Berry sets forth." While some students offer the standard criticism of Berry, that he is a romantic idealist, most see him as a Christian thinker, albeit not an evangelical. Woodiwiss told me that of all the writers that he teaches, including many very "realist" political thinkers, Berry has the most practical impact on students' lives well after college.

Sermon-on-the-Mount Conservationism

For the last four-plus decades, Berry, seventy-two, has been asserting in various ways that we Americans live without much care for the world and our place in it. Berry points out, for example, that most of us consume and adopt new technologies without considering the hidden costs. Berry asks, how many of us think about environmental degradation when we start up our computers, which in many cases depend on electricity from coal gouged out of the mountains of Appalachia?

Berry does not mean that no one should use a computer or technology. Indeed, at the 125-acre farm he calls home at Lane's Landing, near Kentucky's tiny Port Royal (population 116), Berry drives a truck, uses a chainsaw, and has a CD player—though there is no computer. He writes by hand in a treehouse stand on his hillside farm.

"For some," Berry writes, "their involvement in pollution, soil depletion, strip-mining, deforestation, industrial and commercial waste is simply a 'practical' compromise, a necessary 'reality,' the price of modern comfort and convenience. For others, this list of involvements is an agenda for thought and work that will produce remedies."

What Berry advocates is a sort of Sermon-on-the-Mount conservationism. If we are going to care for the world, if we are to walk away from our modern hubris and destruction, then we must "wash the inside of the cup" and "take the log out of our eye." What makes Berry different from so many other conservationists is his argument that we must live with a consistency that finds its roots not in our institutions, but within ourselves.

Berry is a careful reader of the Bible, which I found out during an interview at his home. He quoted easily from the Gospels and Paul's epistles. He is attractive to Christians because he offers a vision of care for creation that is tied up with the sacredness of life. "What Christians offer is an understanding that the world is not ours, that we are not the ones that give things value," he told me in his warm, gentlemanly Southern drawl.

But as Berry's friend, philosophy professor Norman Wirzba, says, he "sees the church as deeply and willingly implicated in an economy that has been unremitting and unrepentant in its destruction." As Berry told me, "The church and all of our institutions have failed to oppose the destruction of the world."

Individual Responsibility

Berry's primary targets are not institutions, but individuals, including himself. He once wrote, "My work has been motivated by a desire to make myself responsibly at home in this world and in my native and chosen place."

In his revolutionary 1977 book, *The Unsettling of America*, Berry describes how several leading environmental organizations "owned stock in the very corporations and industries that have been notorious for their destructiveness and for their indifference to the concerns of conservationists." When discovered, the organizations quickly changed their investment policies and were deeply embarrassed by the oversight. But for Berry, the deeper scandal was that "although the investments were absurd, they were *not* aberrant." The conservation groups "were only doing as organizations what many of their members were, and are, doing as individuals. They were making convenience of enterprises that they knew to be morally, and even practically, indefensible."

For Berry, proxies allow for that possibility. As Berry reminds us, there is nothing inherently wrong with proxies. The problem comes when we do not recognize our proxies and thus abdicate our responsibility for them. A common example for Berry is food production. If we are not able to grow, hunt, or gather our own food, then someone else must do it for us by proxy. In most urban places and increasingly in rural ones as well, food eaters have become "*mere* consumers—passive, uncritical, and dependent."

They have forgotten that "eating is an agricultural act" and that food is tied to the land, ecology, and work of a particular place. Whether that work is good or bad, healthy or destructive, it is beyond the vision of most industrial food eaters. They simply buy what is given to them.

"Eaters ... must understand that eating takes place inescapably in the world, that it is inescapably an agricultural act, and that how we eat determines, to a considerable extent, how the world is used." Berry suggests how to take responsibility for our food proxies: "participate in food production to the extent that you can"; "prepare your own food"; "learn the origins of the food you buy, and buy the food that is produced closest to your home"; "whenever possible, deal directly with a local farmer"; "learn, in selfdefense, as much as you can of the economy and technology of industrial food production"; and "learn what is involved in the *best* farming and gardening."

Berry takes responsibility for his proxies. He has electricity, but the lights remain off because, though it is dim on this overcast day, we can see fine. Berry heats his house using a wood-burning stove with dead wood he has collected from his own forest (a task that becomes more difficult as he moves into his seventies). Behind his house is his garden, where Berry and his wife of nearly fifty years, Tanya, grow much of their own food. Berry's farm is very much a "home economy." It is here that care or destruction begins.

Trading Places

The difficulty, for Berry, is that fewer and fewer of us have a household with the constancy of place and community required for creating a good home economy. We are a transient, moving people who do not stay in places long enough to know local problems. How many of us know how far our watershed extends? Or where our garbage goes? We must be able to readily answer these questions if we are to live with care and responsibility within creation, according to Berry. For Berry, we must put down roots in a local place and community. Both of Berry's parents have at least five generations of farming roots here in Henry County near the Kentucky River.

In a series of novels, Berry has explored these issues through the life of the fictitious community of Port William, Kentucky. It is what Berry calls a "membership," in which all of those who live and take part in the community are remembered—even "horses and mules and milk cows and dogs."

Like Port William, Port Royal is small, with only one store on the main road. There are two churches, Methodist and Baptist (Berry attends the latter). Surrounding the town are many small farms that once mostly grew tobacco, raised lamb, and produced other foods for family and neighbors. Many of the farms are being turned into housing developments for commuters to Louisville and Lexington.

Berry presents the goodness, neighborliness, and struggles of a small community like this one in his fiction. And he bears witness to the destruction of rural places, as his fiction moves from the vibrant Port William of the late 1800s to the present community, which holds a withering, but persistent, "membership." Berry's fiction is best read with his essays. With his poetry, they provide a door to an understanding that makes most dedicated readers of his work want to change their lives.

Evaluating Berry's Vision

Berry has strong words for Christians in his ecological call to repentance. In the essay "Christianity and the Survival of Creation" Berry writes, "Throughout the 500 years since Columbus's first landfall in the Bahamas, the evangelist has walked beside the conqueror and the merchant, too often blandly assuming that his cause was the same as theirs. Christian organizations, to this day, remain largely indifferent to the rape and plunder of the world. ..." But Berry allows that this Christian complicity "comes from an inadequate understanding of the Bible."

Fred Bahnson, a Duke Divinity School graduate who now directs the Anathoth Community Garden at a rural Methodist church in North Carolina, says the evangelical Christianity he grew up with "explicitly and implicitly [sponsored] a dualism between mind and body, religion and economy."

In Wendell Berry, we find a vision of a consistent life, rooted in place and community, a life with limits that offers something deeply missing from this age—humility and closeness to the earth. As Bahnson told me, "We're created to live with our hands in the dirt. Adam from *adamah* [Hebrew for "earth"], human from *humus*—we're made from the dirt and to dirt we return. If we're somehow separated from that by too much asphalt and concrete, something's going to go awry."

Richard Church, a lawyer and farmer with a PhD in theology from Duke, also finds much in Berry's work that resonates with Christians. But Church thinks that many are too uncritical of Berry. Church fears that Berry is "something of a

Constantinian"—a cultural Christian who does not see a difference between the people of God and farmers in rural places.

Ralph Wood, Baylor University professor of theology and literature, also believes Christians should be cautious. Wood finds in Berry a "considerable, kinship ... with the Christian insistence that holy things will always come to us in communal and mediated form." Yet he finds Berry's vision of nature Stoic rather than Christian—"everything fulfills its function by its *physis*, the principle of growth intrinsic to it." According to Wood, Berry misses the "otherness of God" and settles for a deeply natural theology in which God's transcendence is absent.

But Woodiwiss says that Berry is not a theologian. He says we should ask, "What does he have to offer us in terms of imaginative possibilities that Christians can really buy into?"

While Wendell Berry has become the enigmatic subject of both academic and theological inquiry, he doesn't claim to have all the answers. After looking down the long patchwork furrows at his son's farm, Berry drives me back to his house and along the road that stretches through his hillside farm, which Wendell and Tanya have owned for more than four decades. We go past the tree-house stand, through a river-bottom forest, and up to the barn, where he keeps his old draft horse mare. It has begun to rain, and Berry cuts the engine. We sit in silence, watching a small band of chickadees, sparrows, and cardinals in the trees.

"I'm only one voice in all of this," Berry says. "There are many others. What I have written I have written to start a conversation. I don't have the final word."

Chapter 22

ONE-SIZE POLITICS
DOESN'T FIT ALL

*Evangelical social reform is a
many-splendored thing.*

Editorial | 2007

These are anxious days in the trenches of the culture war. The Federal Marriage Amendment is dead. A rollback of President Bush's restrictions on embryonic stem-cell research appears likely after he leaves office. Human cloning looms ominously.

What's more, Christians who speak publicly on these vital causes are called theocrats and worse. This faith-hostile context makes productive debate over contentious issues, such as global warming, ever more difficult among evangelicals.

Little wonder, then, that evangelicals who dispute the cause of and remedy for global warming are critical of fellow evangelicals who signed the Evangelical Climate Initiative (ECI) statement last year. They have three complaints, outlined in a March letter to L. Roy Taylor, chairman of the board of the National Association of Evangelicals (NAE). First, they believe too many evangelicals are uncritically joining the global-warming campaign. Second, they criticize the campaign for adding another priority to our crowded agenda, shifting emphasis away from "the great moral issues of our time." And third, they argue that evangelical leaders lack "the expertise to settle the controversy, and that the issue should be addressed scientifically and not theologically."

The letter, signed by Focus on the Family founder James Dobson, Tony Perkins of the Family Research Council, Don Wildmon of the American Family Association, and more than twenty other conservative Christian leaders, also attacks Richard Cizik, the NAE's vice president for governmental affairs, for his vocal public stance on global warming.

The letter accuses Cizik of orchestrating a "relentless campaign," speaking "without authorization for the entire organization," and advancing "his own political opinions as scientific fact." It concludes, "If he cannot be trusted to articulate the views of American evangelicals on environmental issues, then we respectfully suggest that he be encouraged to resign his position with the NAE."

All Spheres of Life

There are many problems with the letter, not least being that the signatories, as they acknowledge, don't even *belong* to the NAE. Does Dobson think it would be appropriate for members of the NAE to call publicly for his resignation?

But the letter's most troubling assumption is that a conservative approach to social issues represents the sum total of the NAE's mandate and the evangelical political calling. Citing *USA Today*, the letter notes, "We believe that some of [the secular media's] misunderstanding about evangelicalism and its 'conservative views on politics, economics, and biblical morality' can be laid at Richard Cizik's door." Actually, restricting evangelicals to the narrower agenda of "conservative views on politics, economics, and biblical morality" is the bigger problem. This plays into convenient mainstream stereotypes of Christians being obsessed with sexual issues or pawns of the Republican Party.

It also underestimates the scope of modern evangelicalism, as well as Christ's call for us to be salt and light in all spheres of life. Historically, Christian leaders from John Chrysostom to William Wilberforce to Carl F. H. Henry have addressed a broad array of issues. They did not give in to fear of diluting the gospel message, nor did they make common cause with non-Christians uncritically. While some Christians may question global warming, none can doubt our responsibility to be stewards of God's creation.

In response to the letter, the NAE board pointedly reaffirmed its 2004 document, "For the Health of the Nation: An Evangelical Call to Civic Responsibility." This text lists environmental stewardship (although not specifically global warming) among seven key evangelical priorities. The others are religious freedom, the family and children, the sanctity of human life, the poor, human rights, and peace in a violent world.

The NAE, which represents sixty denominations, has not taken the public stand on global warming that Cizik has. While Cizik should practice discretion in his private remarks (as should any public figure), confusion over whom Cizik is representing on this issue is inevitable, no matter how many times he tells reporters he speaks only for himself.

And yes, as the letter notes, evangelicals have not reached a consensus on the magnitude of global warming, its causes, or the remedy. So? Evangelicals don't agree about the Iraq War or the formula for immigration reform or even the best strategy to halt abortion. No evangelical group—Right or Left—can claim to represent all evangelicals. Even the NAE, while formally representing 45,000 churches, does not imagine that all those churches have bent the knee to every item in its "Call to Civic Responsibility." Every evangelical social-political ministry has a unique constituency and a unique calling. Add to this the ambiguous nature of social reform, and it's easy to understand why evangelicals sometimes find themselves in political disagreement.

This diversity—even if it risks misunderstanding in the media—is something we should celebrate. That a wide spectrum of evangelicals feel called to engage in social justice is good for evangelicalism, the nation, and the world. But determining priorities and strategies is a matter of prudential judgment, and anyone who thinks they have the very mind of God on any matter should take heed.

Evangelicals from the Left, Right, and center are wise to heed Paul's words: "If the whole body were an eye, where would the sense of hearing be? If the whole body were an ear, where would the sense of smell be?" (1 Cor. 12:17).

So let's stop questioning each other's evangelical credentials and just do the work we believe God has called us to.

—

Chapter 23

THE GOOD SHEPHERDS

*A small but vigorous movement
believes that in farming is the
preservation of the world.*

Rob Moll | 2007

God had performed miracles for Scott and Donna Lehrer before they began looking for a farm to buy. When their marriage was in crisis, each one had decided, separately, to attend church. They became Christians the same Sunday morning at different congregations.

Over the next couple of years, as their marriage grew stronger, they decided to homeschool their children. Scott faced a difficult work environment as an executive, so they looked to move out of the suburbs. But Scott was skeptical when his wife said that she felt God wanted the family to raise sheep. "Excuse me," Scott replied. "I can't even stand to mow my own yard. What makes you think I'm going to start doing things like that?"

The family took a Sunday drive through Big Rock, Illinois, just a few miles west of their Aurora home in Chicago's sprawling suburbs. They began attending church in Big Rock and let it be known that they were looking to buy a farm.

Soon their pastor put the Lehrers in touch with a family that needed to sell a small plot of land. It was perfect for suburbanites who had never farmed before. It seemed like a miraculous start. Scott continued to commute to work in the suburbs, while the couple began experimenting on their ten acres.

Today, Lamb of God Farm supplies about forty families every week of the summer with fresh fruits and vegetables, and sells produce at farmers' markets around Chicago. Wool from their sheep is sold at a nearby knitting store, owned by their daughter.

During a *CT* editor's visit, Scott bends and grabs a handful of compost. "Smell that," he says, lifting to his nose a mixture of sheep manure and hay. "That'll make some good fertilizer."

It would take a miracle to get him to suit up again for a corporate boardroom, Scott says. "[Farming] is the most satisfying work I've ever done. It's because God's got his hand in it. There's something very elemental about tending this piece of his creation." Like the small but growing number of other Christian families across the US who've left the suburbs to become farmers, the Lehrers now feel closer to God and closer to their family.

Called Christian agrarians, these families are tapping into broader cultural trends: interest in organic and locally produced food, back-to-the-land movements, and conservation and environmental concerns. They are resisting other trends: large-scale conventional agriculture, population flight from rural communities, and fragmented suburban life. Agrarians like the Lehrers also hold faith-fueled convictions that rural life is more wholesome, that families are healthier when they work alongside each other, and that being stewards of creation means both caring for the environment and cultivating it for human benefit.

From Hippies to Homeschoolers

Joel Salatin is a kind of elder statesman of this small movement. He's been working Polyface Farm in Virginia since he was a kid, and he has made a living at it since graduating from college. Though it would be fair to call him an evangelical and an environmentalist, Salatin fights labels. He calls himself a "Christian libertarian environmentalist capitalist." He complains that evangelicals have been inconsistent. "We look at the liberal, who wants to abort babies and hug trees. We say, 'What is it with you?'" he says. "Well they look at you and me and say, 'What is this about you pro-lifers who want to genetically engineer food and eradicate everything?'"

Neither liberals nor traditional evangelicals are flocking to the countryside, but another group is, says Salatin. "Thirty years ago, 80 percent of all visitors to our farm were hippie, cosmic-worshipping, nirvana earth muffins," he says in his typical rambling manner. "Today, 80 percent are Christian homeschoolers."

"Once you opt out of the conventional paradigm [of public schooling] and find it satisfying, then you begin searching for other paradigms to opt out of," Salatin says. Like the Lehrers, families that homeschool often start looking for ways for fathers to leave their office jobs. "How do I leave my *Dilbert* cubicle at the end of an expressway," Salatin says, "and instead invest in my family, my kids, my community?"

Salatin says some homeschooling families not only visit but also choose to farm, because it's a business the entire family participates in and is sustainable for generations. "In our culture today, we've got this mentality that you send your kids off to school to get a good enough education, to get a good enough diploma, to get a good enough job, to pay well enough to work a thousand miles away from home, to accumulate enough money so they can put you in a nursing home when you get old. What I'm looking for is for my grand-kids to argue over who gets to spend the day with grandpa."

Rural Flight

Salatin is getting his wish, something rare among farmers. For decades, farmers have been moving off their land as it takes larger and larger operations to remain profitable. The trend has left rural communities in crisis. For every seven farms that shut down, says Gary Holthaus, author of *From the Farm to the Table*, the rule of thumb is that one business in town closes.

"It's not a sad thing that just farms are going out of business," says Holthaus. "It's a sad thing that small towns in rural America are going out of business." In Big Rock, where the Lehrers live, they may be the only family to have begun farming in years. Half of the downtown shops are closed.

Advanced machinery, technologically developed seed, petroleum-based fertilizers, pesticides, and herbicides are all required on the modern farm, and all are expensive. Traditionally, low commodities prices mean farmers have to till more land to remain profitable. Michael Mangis, professor and director of the Center for Rural Psychology at Wheaton College, says most farming families need jobs off the farm to stay afloat. "They support their family off their jobs," he says. "They keep farming because it's a value of theirs. It's something they believe in."

As rural businesses close, as children leave for jobs in the city, and as fewer resources are directed to rural areas, social problems run rampant. "It used to be urban areas had the highest crime rates, drug-use rates, alcoholism rates, and suicide rates, especially among young people," says Mangis. "Now that's all reversed. Rural rates are higher." Today, Mangis says, rural towns are either being depopulated or are becoming suburbs.

"A significant portion of people who are into organics and agrarianism are basically contemporary hippies," says Mangis. "This is not the kind of people that rural areas are going to welcome." But Christian agrarians reinvigorate rural communities with their traditional approach to agriculture and their entrepreneurial businesses.

Mangis has high hopes for Christians who buy farmland. "Evangelical Christians give a biblical basis for why they're doing what they're doing. I think most rural communities are going to be a lot more open to a Christian family starting a farm and saying we want community, we want a better place for our family, we want better stewardship of the earth because God commanded it. That people can buy."

Expressing "Chickenness"

Every year on his 550-acre farm, 450 acres of which is wooded, Joel Salatin produces 40,000 pounds of beef, 30,000 pounds of pork, 10,000 broiler chickens, 1,200 turkeys, 1,000 rabbits, and 35,000 dozen eggs. In *The Omnivore's Dilemma*, Michael Pollan says the land, despite being used so intensely, "will be in no way diminished by the process—in fact it will be the better for it."

That's partly because Salatin's methods are vastly different from those of most contemporary farmers. In contrast to industrially produced chickens that can't leave their cages, that need to have their beaks cut off so they don't peck at each other, and that are ridden with disease, Salatin allows his chickens to poke freely around his pasture.

Salatin says he is just copying creation. "We use God's design and take it as a template," he says. "Our overriding question is not how do we grow the chicks bigger and faster and cheaper. The goal that we have is how do we ... create a habitat that allows the chicken to fully express her 'chickenness.'"

Every day, Salatin moves his cows to a fresh spot of grass. The cows eat all day. At night, Salatin moves them to another spot. He then moves his chickens to where the cows were. The chickens eat the bugs and larvae growing in the cowpats. This "sanitation crew" cleans up after his cows. "Just like in nature, birds always follow herbivores, like the egret on the rhino's nose," he explains. Chickens' droppings, combined with cows', fertilize the grass, which in two weeks will have regrown enough to be ready for the cows again.

Symbiotic relationships are at work all over Salatin's farm. Without fertilizer, without hormones, and without cows and chickens forced into industrial factories, Salatin produces a healthy amount of food—and it is healthy food, too, for which customers come directly to him and pay top dollar. "What is it worth to have chicken that reduces your cholesterol instead of increasing it?" Salatin says. "We've had our chickens tested. They're twenty-five times cleaner than what's in the supermarket."

"If you raise these animals the way God intended," says Mike Hansen, a farmer in Wisconsin, "you get healthy meat."

The Bottom Line

Hansen can sell organic chickens directly to consumers and charge less than the supermarket. And he receives more money per chicken than if he sold to a wholesaler. Agrarian families like the Hansens are banding together to sell directly to customers through community-supported agriculture programs. "We've now got nine farms working together, trying to create a model for alternative agriculture that's sustainable," he says. 'We've doubled in sales every year."

It's a lot of work to be a full-time farmer and grocer, but Hansen says the payoff goes far beyond profits. A Christian homeschooling family is one of his regular customers. When one of the children became ill, he says, a doctor recommended eating organic food. "They're a relatively poor family," Hansen says. Another family buys his beef, but doesn't need the hamburger. So Hansen sat down with the families and arranged a financial deal. "I do this for our customers all the time," Hansen says. "I do God's work every day."

Donna Lehrer is "tickled pink" when customers ask about Lamb of God Farm. Many young families receive their regular shipments of fruits and vegetables during the summer. "I really feel I have a mentoring role," Donna says. "We do canning classes and processing food. That's what farm families used to do. They'd shuck corn; they'd have a party."

The Lehrers have extended their farm family through their knitting business. The wool from their sheep goes to Esther's Place Fibers, the shop started by the Lehrers' daughter, Natasha. She teaches knitting classes, sells yarn, and demonstrates traditional knitting techniques. It's part of Donna's dream to revive Illinois's sheep industry. Esther's Place purchases as much local wool as they can, and Donna works hard to share her knowledge and strategies with the state's other shepherds.

The Lehrers view their customers as their mission field. Scott points out the growing interest in organic produce. "There are so many people from all walks of life being drawn to healthier foods," Scott says. "It gives us an opportunity to talk about what Christ has done in our lives."

Chapter 24

———

SECOND COMING ECOLOGY

We care for the environment precisely
because God will create a new earth.

David Neff | 2008

Sunday morning, May 18, 1980, my children were leaving the little Presbyterian church in College Place, Washington, where they had been attending a program. They looked up at the sky, and a verse they had read in the Bible leapt to their minds. Jesus said that in the last days, the sun would be darkened, and the moon would not give its light. The sky was so preternaturally dark that my girls thought that the end of the world was upon us. They joined hands and ran the several blocks to our home.

What had happened was the deadliest and most economically destructive volcanic event in US history. Mount St. Helens had blown its dome, killing 57 people and destroying 250 homes, 47 bridges, 15 miles of railway, and 185 miles of highway. The ash cloud darkened our skies, and the nasty stuff settled on our houses and yards and cars, making it impossible to drive without clogging the air intakes and harming the engines.

It was tricky to cope with the event for the next few weeks, but the damage near our home was minor compared with what people in western Washington had to deal with. But for my little girls—for just a moment—it was the end of the world.

Christians have consistently been end-of-the-world people, with at least one eye on matters related to eschatology or "last things"—final judgment, the second coming of Christ, death and the resurrection of the dead, the renewal of Creation, and the coming of God's rule in its fullest and most visible expression. Yet contemporary realities have forced Christians to explore what it means to be an anticipatory people with a strong orientation to these last things when facing environmental degradation, and perhaps even environmental disaster.

Too Future-Minded to Be of Present Good?

It's often said that many Christians—particularly evangelical Christians—don't care for the environment precisely because they are so focused on end times. If God is going to come and destroy all this anyway, why should we invest our energies in preserving it? A frequently cited example is James Watt, an evangelical believer and former Secretary of the Interior during the Reagan administration. Here is one account: "James Watt told the US Congress that protecting natural resources was unimportant in light of the imminent return of Jesus Christ. In public testimony he said, 'After the last tree is felled, Christ will come back.'"

To many minds, this succinct quote effectively sums up the attitudes of evangelicals, except for one crucial fact: James Watt *didn't* say that. This oft-repeated quote comes from a journalist who didn't bother to confirm something that he read on the Internet.

What did James Watt actually say? The only time he gave public testimony about the relationship between his Christian beliefs and care for the environment was in February 1981, in response to Oregon Democrat Jim Weaver, before a House sub-committee on the environment.

> **Mr. Weaver**: I believe very strongly that we should not ... use up all the oil that took nature a billion years to make in one century.
>
> We ought to leave a few drops of it for our children, their children. They are going to need it ... I wonder if you agree, also, in the general statement that we should leave some of our resources—I am not talking about scenic areas or preservation, but scenic resources for our children? Not just gobble them up all at once?

> **Secretary Watt**: Absolutely. That is the delicate balance the Secretary of the Interior must have, to be a steward for the natural resources for this generation as well as future generations.
>
> *I do not know how many future generations we can count on before the Lord returns, whatever it is we have to manage with a skill to leave the resources needed for future generations.* (emphasis added)

That's more like it.

How can a people focused steadily on the last days find the theological motivation and will to steward the natural world "with a skill to leave the resources needed for future generations"?

Creation as Promise to Keep

Theologian John Haught of Georgetown University claims that Christians should not bracket their beliefs about last things when thinking theologically about the environment. There is a fear among theologians who specialize in thinking about the environment that too much talk about the End (for that matter, any talk at all) will undermine care for the Creation. But as the example of James Watt shows us, "It ain't necessarily so."

As the great German theologian Jürgen Moltmann wrote in *Theology of Hope*:

> From first to last, and not merely in the epilogue, Christianity is eschatology, is hope, forward looking and forward moving, and therefore also revolutionizing and transforming the present. The eschatological is not one element of Christianity, but it is the medium of Christian faith as such, the key in which everything in it is set, the glow that suffuses everything here in the dawn of an expected new day. ... Hence eschatology cannot really be only a part of Christian doctrine. Rather, the eschatological outlook is characteristic of all Christian proclamation, of every Christian existence and of the whole Church. There is therefore only one real problem in Christian theology ... the problem of the future.

Haught says we need to think of our doctrine of last things in terms of promise. Of course, the biblical doctrine is a mix of promise and threat, of renewal and destruction, of victory for good and judgment for evil. But the promise of God's kingdom is fundamentally good news, and as a promise it carries within it some importance for the present.

Perhaps an analogy would help illuminate the dynamics of promise. If a young man gives a young woman an engagement ring, this pledge is a carrier of promise, but it is not the wedding band itself—just as the engagement is not the wedding. Similarly, our present existence is like the engagement, and the fullness of the kingdom is like the wedding. Our present environment is God's gift to us. It is not all that it will be when the "wedding" comes, but it is extremely valuable—just like the engagement ring.

I don't think any young woman favorably inclined to her suitor has ever said, "Well *forget that*, it's only an engagement ring. What I wanted was a wedding ring." No, you don't dis an engagement ring.

Or think of a teenager eager to learn to drive, who has just acquired a learner's permit. The learner's permit is not a driver's license. But it is what it is—a bearer of promise. What young man getting his learner's permit doesn't beam with joy? While it's not a driver's license, no teen disrespects a permit.

So an orientation toward that which is to come helps us think in terms of promise and fulfillment. And while promise isn't fulfillment, it is something precious.

Keeping the End in Mind

Framing a discussion of the natural world eschatologically also leads toward other lines of thought we should consider:

First, knowing that the Creation as we have it is promise and not fulfillment means that we will recognize its limits and conserve it. Nature as we know it is bountiful, but not unbounded. As we have been repeatedly reminded, there are limits to fossil fuels. Even the fuels for nuclear power are seriously limited. These facts should not surprise us. The Creation is a limited thing, a provisional thing.

Christians with an eschatological vision do not want to despoil the earth of its resources. Part of being human is learning to live (and consume) within limits. It is liberal Christianity, at least in its classic form with its unbounded optimism about human resourcefulness and technological prowess, that should be readjusting. Christians operating with the End in mind should always have limits in view, but like everyone else in North America, Christians have by and large been co-opted by consumer culture. It is now up to us to live with a theology of limits.

Similarly, seeing Creation as promise prevents us from treating it as mere raw material. If the gift of Creation were simply a commodity, then we could consume it the way we consume a gift box of chocolates. But because it carries promise, it must be conserved until the time of fulfillment.

Second, knowing that Creation is God's promise helps us realize that the Creation is not an ultimate value. The theologians who don't pay attention to this fact end up sliding off into one of any number of views that simply get the world wrong: pantheism, nature mysticism, deep ecology, or re-paganization.

While it is important to reject the mechanical materialism of the seventeenth century (the philosophy that paved the way for industrialization), there is no reason to revert to nature idolatry, paganism, shamanism, or animism. We need to be sure that the core ecological insight—of the complex, weblike interrelatedness of all things animate and inanimate—guides us to a more sophisticated scientific outlook, not an anti-technological mysticism. The technological revolutions that accompanied the rise of capitalism did in fact make life a lot better for many people. They brought health, nutrition, and leisure to the masses for the first time in history. So we are careful to treat nature as a relative good rather than something to be worshiped.

Similarly, seeing nature through eschatological eyes helps us rise above natural cycles. In the ancient world, the pagan view of history was tied to the cycles of fertility and the seasons. The seasonal flooding of the Nile, the early and later rainy seasons in Palestine—these things dominated the pagan view of life. But the Jewish and Christian views were historical. Biblical religion celebrated God's abundance in the annual agricultural cycles. But the more important festivals celebrated historical events: the liberation from slavery in Egypt and the giving of the Torah. This prepared them to understand God and his actions in the framework of world history. What the superpowers of the day—Egypt, Babylon, Persia, Greece, and Rome—did was of significance to God and God's people. And for Christians, what happened at the Cross became the center point of history.

Eschatology is one form of biblical historical consciousness. It helps us see the cosmos in the context of time and history. Such a historical view is a religious perspective that empowers people to take significant action, and not be bound to insignificance by the cycles of time.

Third, an eschatological frame helps us take account of the big picture of salvation. Evangelical forms of Christianity—most notably its pietist and revivalist strands—have tended to focus on the personal experience of present salvation. And there are good historical reasons for that. Think of Luther's struggle for a sense of acceptance with a wrathful God. Or think of John Wesley's famous experience of having his heart strangely warmed when he heard the preface to Luther's Commentary on the Epistle to the Romans read at Aldersgate Chapel: "An assurance was given me that He had taken away my sins, even mine, and saved me from the law of sin and death."

But as the apostle Paul contemplates the end of all things in his epistle to the church in Rome, he talks not just about individuals awaiting their redemption, but about the whole Creation as well.

> The creation was subjected to frustration, not by its own choice, but by the will of the one who subjected it, in hope that the creation itself will be liberated from its bondage to decay and brought into the glorious freedom of the

children of God. We know that the whole creation has been groaning as in the pains of childbirth right up to the present time. Not only so, but we ourselves, who have the firstfruits of the Spirit, groan inwardly as we wait eagerly for our adoption as sons, the redemption of our bodies. For in this hope we were saved. (Rom. 8:20–24)

Christ didn't come to save just you or just me—though his ultimate sacrifice assures us of our individual worth. He came to save Adam's fallen race by becoming the Second Adam, the head of a new humanity that will someday inhabit a new and improved version of the Eden that Adam and Eve were forced to leave. When we remember that a restored humanity in a restored Eden is the crowning vision of Scripture, we come to see ourselves and our responsibilities in a bigger, broader landscape.

That broader landscape will encourage us to engage with the "groanings" of Creation as we are now able to hear them.

Fourth, an eschatological perspective helps us save nature for God's sake, not just for our own benefit. Care for the natural world is not just about a cost-benefit analysis for human welfare, though that must always be done. But if God has a plan for this natural world, has a bright future for it, we do not always need to see the benefit for ourselves before acting to preserve the natural order. It should be enough for us that this is part of God's vision for the future and a carrier of his promises.

Fifth, and finally, an eschatological perspective can help us deepen our relationship to all people and all things. As Christians, we are called to love our neighbors as ourselves, and Jesus defined "neighbor" in extremely broad terms. I find it difficult to love and serve as broadly as Jesus calls me to. In the global community that communication technology and multinational businesses have brought about, I can know about, and feel concern about, needs that I can never hope to address. Geographical and cultural distance can be a real source of frustration when I hear that genocide is going on in one place or starvation in another. Aside from e-mailing my congressional representative and donating a few dollars to disaster response and relief work, it is hard to know how to relate.

There are limitations on my present existence that will no longer exist in the kingdom of God. Yet for now, despite limits of money, time, and energy, as well as cultural, ethnic, and linguistic barriers, relate I must.

The eschatological vision portrays a global community that is no longer divided by tribal and ethnic barriers. Both the Hebrew prophets and the Book of Revelation portray a new humanity drawn from every tribe and nation, language group and people. That vision causes me to care just as much about what rising sea levels do to impoverished people in Bangladesh as about what they do to affluent people living on the isle of Manhattan. That vision causes me to care just as much about what happens when sea erosion causes buildings to collapse on the Alaskan island of Shishmaref as it does when rich people's houses in Malibu slide into the ocean.

Seeing through eschatological eyes pushes me in the direction of relating to desperate people who are at a distance, because God has promised some day to bring them close.

When I was growing up, eschatology meant "end times"—that is, my church focused on the timing and manner of final events.

But Jesus and the apostles played down the time element and even the manner of the End. Instead, they emphasized the inbreaking of God's rule and the way our ability to see his rule helps to transform the present.

If we are given that ability to see God at work, bringing the present into contact with the End, we cannot be indifferent to the way things are. We cannot be deaf to the groanings of Creation. And we can treasure every gift God gives us as a sign of his promises.

Chapter 25

—

NOT ONE SPARROW

*We can be "speciesists" and show
compassion for animals.*

Editorial | 2009

In a recent post on *Her.meneutics*, the *Christianity Today* women's blog, Saddleback Church's Kay Warren shared the story of being emotionally duped, then angered, by a heart-tugging television ad about suffering animals. As someone who has seen Rwandan children orphaned by HIV and surviving on dirt cookies, Warren urged readers to remember the chasm between humans and animals, and the respective dignity that chasm confers. "Only people have a spiritual dimension," she wrote. "Jesus didn't die for animals; he gave his all for human beings."

Warren's post received many thankful "amens." Her frustration resonates with many Christians who are concerned with appeals for animal compassion when so much callousness toward human suffering persists. Such concern is rooted in both Scripture's witness and the intuitive knowledge that, while animals and all of non-human creation are not disposable, neither do they have the same worth as humankind. It was the first human's nostrils into which God, in an embarrassingly intimate act, breathed life; it was the human patriarchs and their families whom God called into covenant relationship; when God chose Mary, a Jewish teenager in a backwater of the Roman Empire, it was human flesh he chose to take on. And though Paul writes in Romans 8 that God will usher the entire creation into freedom in the age to come, he also says that humans alone were chosen "before the creation of the world to be holy and blameless ... to be adopted as his sons through Jesus Christ" (Eph. 1:4–5, NIV84).

Given the highlights of God's story of redemption, Christians cannot help being a bit *speciesist*, a term coined by psychologist Richard D. Ryder for "the widespread discrimination ... practiced by man against other species" and popularized by Princeton philosopher Peter Singer.

But while Christians happily acknowledge the charge, we misstep when we brush off animal cruelty with nonchalance. Showing animal compassion does not *de facto* assign animals the same worth as humans. It merely acknowledges that animals *have* worth and dignity—something plainly assumed in biblical passages like Exodus 21–22:14 and Deuteronomy 25, which outline upright ways to handle livestock, and Proverbs 12:10, which praises the righteous man who "cares for the needs of his animal." The church has traditionally interpreted Isaiah 65's well-known apocalyptic imagery of lions and lambs not as a cozy metaphor of human community, but as a picture of fully restored creation, people and animals. And while Luke 12:6's five sparrows sold for two cents usually refer to God's sovereign care for us in our daily lives, it's remarkable that those five sparrows *aren't* forgotten by God, but are part of his sovereign care as well.

Instead of leading us down dangerous paths toward secular humanism, animal compassion becomes part of our privileged role as custodians of the creatures in which God delights. In fact, C. S. Lewis, who wrestled in many essays with the seeming sense-lessness of animal suffering, argued that it was precisely because humans are higher than animals in creation's hierarchy that they should oppose animal cruelty. Our very superiority to animals, he said, ought to motivate us "to prove ourselves better than the beasts precisely by the fact of acknowledging duties to them which they do not acknowledge to us."

When we hear about dogs being hanged or drowned for not performing well in dogfighting rings, or about legitimate hunting turning into mere slaughter, or when livestock are killed in ways that prolong their suffering, what usually erupts in us is an ada-mant *no!* We do well to pay attention to that *no!*, because it tells us that something has gone horribly wrong with the world, some-thing Christians believe traces back to man's enmity with God. *No!* is also our response, of course, when 8-year-olds are forced to prostitute themselves on Cambodian streets, or a doctor admits to having aborted a child one day before he was due. But we need not worry that our *no!* about cruelty to animals will lessen our response to wrong done to humans.

Compassion is not a zero-sum game. Compassion begets more compassion, though channeled into different responses and for different ends. The most famous evangelical animal activist, William Wilberforce, publicly opposed bull-baiting (a spectator sport where dogs attack bulls) and co-founded the first animal welfare group out of the same vision for Christ's kingdom that led him to support public Sabbath observance, fund evangelism to Indians, and work to overthrow the British slave trade, among countless other initiatives.

It's our recognition of Christ's reign over all things—even the sparrows—that compels us to proclaim our *no!* about animal cruelty in the public square, and to make our *yes!* about the worth and dignity of all God's creatures a joyful witness to his coming kingdom.

Chapter 26

—

A FEAST FIT FOR THE KING

*Returning the growing fields
and kitchen table to God.*

Leslie Leyland Fields | 2010

It's potluck Sunday. I stand near the end of a long line wondering what will be left by the time I get to the front, grateful that I'm not particularly hungry. I have some idea of what the offerings will be: hot dogs wrapped in white buns, cut in half for the more delicate appetites; buckets of drive-through fried chicken anchoring the table. Neon-orange cheese doodles will inevitably show up, somewhere near the salads. The greenest item will be several bowls of lime Jell-O with fruit suspended in it, which, I've decided, is to signal its inobvious function as food.

We pray our thanks over this smorgasbord of chemical wizardry and marketing genius, ask that it would strengthen our bodies (something I believe will take divine intervention), and invite Jesus to be among us as we eat.

When we lift our heads, I consider this last request and wonder, surveying the tables: *What would Jesus put on his plate?* Would Jesus eat lime Jell-O and cheese doodles? Would he care that the chicken in the bucket came from cages where the birds were likely fed their own recycled excrement? Would he eat that barbequed pork that came from massive pig farms that pollute the water, soil, and air? Would he stand, as I do, filled with guilt, dread, and judgment before this culinary minefield?

I think a lot about food these days, and not always charitably. I've been ruminating on the headlines and a recent crop of food books concerning what many are calling "the global food crisis," one that has given rise to a new food movement in the United States and abroad. The movement has taken on the momentum of a religious revival, changing the way Americans eat and how they think about food and the use of the earth. Eric Schlosser's *Fast Food Nation*; Michael Pollan's *The Omnivore's Dilemma*; Nicolette Hahn Niman's *Righteous Porkchop*; Barbara Kingsolver's *Animal, Vegetable, Miracle*; Marion Nestle's *Food Politics*; Jonathan Safran Foer's *Eating Animals*; and many others expose the disturbing state of the nation's food supply and the destructive effects of industrialized food production on the national and global environment.

The most recent confirmation that all is not well on our plates came in August, when 1,500 people were poisoned by eggs contaminated with salmonella, leading to a recall of 550 million eggs. (The chickens at the culprit farms were kept in battery cages, which have been criticized for being both unsanitary and inhumane.) When *The New York Times Magazine* announced its intention to expand its already generous coverage of food this year, it explained that such writing is "perhaps never a more crucial part of what we do than today—a moment when what and how we eat has emerged as a Washington issue and a global-environmental issue as well as a kitchen-table one."

While elements of the new food movement are rarely Christ-centered (more on that soon), I believe the movement has much to teach Christians about stewarding creation, loving our neighbors, and eating and drinking to the glory of God (1 Cor. 10:31).

Manure Lagoons, Superweeds, and GMOs

Where does the news begin? Most of the authors trace our crisis in food conduct and conscience to the events following World War II, when the federal government led a shift from family-operated agrarian economies to corporatized agribusinesses. In agribusiness, efficiency and mass production have, more often than not, overruled fair treatment of farmers, humane treatment of animals, and proper care of the land.

One of the early voices to sound the alarm was social critic and Kentucky farmer Wendell Berry, who has written voluminously about returning integrity to the act of eating. In his essay "The Pleasures of Eating," he describes a typical processed meal, either fast food or cooked at home from packages, so altered from its original form as to be unrecognizable on the plate. "What nature has produced, man has turned into the products of industry," Berry concluded. Two sentences from his famous essay have become rallying cries for the new food revolution: "Eating is an agricultural act"; and "... how we eat determines, to a considerable extent, how the world is used."

Reports on "how the world is used" for food production make up an apocalyptic catalog that leaves no ground untainted. The ills of factory farming begin with the dousing of soil and crops with pesticides, chemical fertilizers, and herbicides, producing foods with measurable levels of contaminants. The runoff from these additives is the primary source of water pollution in the US, more than all other industrial sources combined. Factory hog farms alone, with their massive "manure lagoons," emit seventy thousand tons of hydrogen sulfide gas annually. Herbicides such as Roundup are used in such quantities that "superweeds" resistant to pesticides have sprung up, creating the need for yet more toxic formulas.

Meanwhile, Monsanto, DuPont, and other multinational agricultural corporations are creating a growing number of genetically modified organisms (GMOs), altering the genetic code of one species by inserting genes from another, even animal to plant. (The Grocery Manufacturers of America estimates that seventy-five percent of food on US grocery shelves contains at least one GMO.) There are significant concerns over the long-term safety of such foods, the deep decrease in agricultural biodiversity their use has created, and the monopolizing of patents and seed by corporations. The net result: The nation's food supply is under the dominion of a few conglomerates.

What can we do about such realities? Many books, such as Jane Goodall's *Harvest for Hope: A Guide to Mindful Eating*, include "What You Can Do" lists. While there are notable distinctions between writers, there is general agreement that "mindful eating" (a term borrowed from Buddhist practice) entails the following:

- Educating ourselves on where food comes from (a chemist's lab? a hemisphere away? a local farm?);

- Eating locally as much as possible to support local farmers and to reduce the natural resources it takes to put food on our plate;

- Growing and preparing our own food;

- Eating lower on the food chain, meaning eating less meat and more plants;

- Supporting fair-trade practices that protect rather than exploit workers;

- Supporting organic farms and free-range ranches;

- Advocating for a return to agricultural biodiversity.

Here let me offer full disclosure. I have spent large portions of my life in the New Hampshire woods and Alaskan wilderness, growing, hunting, and harvesting much of my own food. As such, most of the can-do lists read to me as commonsense activities and responses to a real crisis. I would argue a step further: As Christians, under obligation to the God who created our bodies, and as Americans, who continue to lead the industrialized world in obesity rates, we should foster a healthier diet. As believers urged by the apostle Paul to "take captive every thought to the obedience of Christ," we should be more thoughtful about food production and our treatment of God's creatures and his earth.

Yet after reading the literature and listening to the many conversations around me, I have significant concerns and cautions about the new food movement.

Deep-Fried Happiness

My critique begins, paradoxically, with the movement's greatest strengths: its call to an integrated, holistic perspective and the personal moral accountability that integration brings. At the movement's core is the belief that the world is a single, intricate, and interdependent ecosystem. Thus our personal acts have global consequences, for good and for ill, ones we don't often see but that are nonetheless real. The Organic Garden Café in Boston, a raw foods café, exemplifies this sense of unity.

By "embrac[ing] the idea of oneness," the café's mission is to "honor the earth, farmers, and ourselves through our use of pure organic ingredients."

While Christians rightly reject the Eastern and New Age pantheism that often informs "the world as one," we are hard-pressed to ignore the observable fact that what's done upstream has downstream effects—an environmental version of "many parts, one body." Monsanto's controversial pesticide Roundup runs into aquatic systems and kills more than weeds—it also kills amphibians and other animals. The new food movement continues in the footsteps of the environmental movement of the 1960s to counteract the mass reductionism ushered in by industrialization and even the scientific method itself, both of which reduce whole systems to parts and pieces.

Our disconnection from our food and its sources is further fed by our culture's emphasis on personal happiness and moral subjectivity, leading to what author Barbara Kingsolver calls "alimentary alienation." When we pull packages of deep-fried chicken fingers or cans of cheese spray off the grocery shelf—which we are entitled to eat because they make us happy—we don't recognize the source of the food nor consider its cost to workers, farmers, or the environment. We see only the pieced, processed, and packaged final product.

"Whole Foods," then, is not just the name of an upscale grocer. It symbolizes a return to a larger, holistic view of the earth, and a call to moral responsibility within that sphere.

Nowhere are religion and morality more on display—or the voices more hortatory—than in discussions on the killing fields of the factory farms. Several dozen books have appeared recently detailing the horrific cruelties taking place at pens and slaughterhouses. While the authors do not advocate for identical measures, all seek to at least reduce if not outright end animal suffering and/or usage because of its patent immorality. They also believe continuing to raise animals for meat is morally unjustifiable because of its monopoly on resources that could feed the world's hungry. Jonathan Safran Foer, in *Eating Animals*, writes, "So what kind of crime is animal agriculture, which uses 756 million tons of grain and corn per year, much more than enough to adequately feed the 1.4 billion humans who are living in dire poverty?"

The authors are right to reclaim the field, the slaughterhouse, and the kitchen as integrated realms of morality. Is there any activity under the sun beyond the scope of God's goodness, compassion, and righteousness? The attention to the essential unity of creation—all created and sustained by one God, our Father— calls believers into some part of the food movement as well, just as we are called to care for creation and pursue justice on others' behalf. All are inextricably woven together, bearing on our Genesis command to "dress and keep the garden," to exercise caring dominion over its creatures, and to love our neighbors. As Scott Sabin of Plant With Purpose reminds us, "We have little choice as to whether we will interact with creation. But we can choose whether our interactions will be life-giving or death-dealing."

Eating Righteousness

Despite the new food movement's ambitious and commendable goals, however, its core beliefs offer an alternative religious movement, much of it carrying the urgency of an ultimate cause. Its central tenet is that by changing the way we eat, we can save ourselves—and the world. John Robbins's book *The Food Revolution: How Your Diet Can Help Save Your Life and Our World* is just one of many holding out on this explicit promise. One review sums up the book's *raison d'etre* like this: "What can we do to help stop global warming, feed the hungry, prevent cruelty to animals, avoid genetically modified foods, be healthier and live longer? Eat vegetarian." Many books go further, urging a vegan diet that rejects all animal products, including eggs and dairy. (One reason given by Jeffrey Moussaieff Masson, author of *The Face on Your Plate: The Truth about Food*: The animals have not consented to our use of their goods.)

Evangelistic zeal for transforming the world through a restricted diet abounds. Foer reported in a recent interview that 18 percent of college students are vegetarians now, adding, "There are more vegetarians in college than Catholics, there are more vegetarians than any major, except for business ... That's something I feel very good about." Walter Robb, the co-president of Whole Foods, the poster-grocer of the food movement, has described the goals of his company in distinctly religious language: "We're not retailers with a mission, we're missionaries who retail." The "mission" is first: "... to change the way the world eats," a motive that "comes from our soul," Robb says.

In this worldview, *righteousness*, *morality*, *purity*, and *guilt* are common terms applied most often not to people or to actions but to actual foods. The book *Righteous Porkchop* includes a chapter on "Eating the Right Food." Recipes are labeled "righteous" as well: Righteous Tofu Burger, Amanda's Righteous Queso (made without processed cheese), and Righteous Raspberry Lollies (without dairy or refined sugar "so you can suck on them with a clear conscience").

"Pure" is a ubiquitous adjective used to describe a vegetarian or vegan diet and lifestyle. An animal-free diet that also rejects "caffeine, sugar, alcohol, or processed foods" is labeled "ultra-pure."

If you have overindulged, rather than confessing your sins you can undergo a "cleanse," a popular diet or fasting practice that rids the body, and some claim the spirit, of "toxins."

To claim that certain foods lead through the narrow gate to purity and righteousness, and others lead down the wide road to pollution, is nothing new. A popular Hindi website, Food for Life Global ("Uniting the World Through Pure Food"), explains that only "pure vegetarianism" is allowed because what we eat directly affects "our spiritual consciousness" and our "subsequent behaviors." The very purpose of food, it says, "is to give strength to the body and purify the mind." Some strands of Buddhism also require vegetarianism. A woman writes on a food blog, "My desire to be a vegetarian is very tied up to my desire to be a Really Good Person."

Perhaps in no other time has our culture so widely absorbed the largely Eastern concept that physical, mental, and spiritual purity can be derived from food—and that we earn our virtue through vigilance over fork and plate.

Strangely, while these writers offer a global, moral, even theological perspective on food, in practice their approach can lead to myopic self-absorption and legalism. In online social networks, people dish the details of their every meal and bite as if the world hung upon their words and their food choices. Some show signs of *orthorexia*, an eating disorder defined as "an unhealthy obsession with healthy eating." Colorado nutritionist Steven Bratman coined the term after his own journey into obsessively healthy eating while living on a commune and managing an organic farm. In his desire "to eat pure food," he rejected any vegetable plucked from the garden more than fifteen minutes previously. For the sake of mindfulness, he ate alone and chewed each bite fifty times, all of which left him feeling "clear-headed, strong, and self-righteous." He writes, "A day filled with sprouts, umeboshi plums, and amaranth biscuits comes to feel as holy as one spent serving the poor and homeless."

Bratman's goal of achieving "wellness through healthy eating," though, began to take over his life. "I had been seduced by righteous eating. The problem of my life's meaning had been transferred inexorably to food, and I could not reclaim it." Today, Bratman, now restored, sees growing numbers of patients in his clinic with this disorder.

Goodbye, Eden

Part of the devolution from lofty global goals to a crippling personal obsession may simply be our sinful bent toward the self. But I think there is more going on. In a recent essay in *Policy Review*, "Is Food the New Sex?" Mary Eberstadt ponders a cultural reversal in values: We have become mindful and puritanical about food, and mindless and licentious about sex. Perhaps in a world where moral values are subjective and in constant flux, we feel an even greater need for boundaries and stability, at least in some areas of our lives. We may not be able to resist an affair, control our children, prevent sexual abuse in our churches, or restrain Wall Street greed, but we *can* control what we put into our mouths.

In yet one more irony, the save-the-world theology of diet, while seeming to deepen the value of food, paradoxically often reduces food to the function it performs: food as social justice; food as nutrition; food as righteousness. All of these views diminish the fuller meaning of food found in the Scriptures.

On the opening page of the Bible, God announces that all he has made, the fruits and vegetables spoken from his imagination, are "very good." Lush in flavor, exquisite in beauty and fragrance, their value is intrinsic to their God-made-ness. He gives the food to the first man and woman as sustenance. But even in this state of sinlessness, God sets limits on Adam and Eve's diet, that as they obeyed, they would be fed not only physically but spiritually as well. Food was intended to be another expression of their dependence on and communion with their Creator.

The Old Testament dietary laws were given later to God's people not as a means of earning righteousness, but to remind the Israelites that they were set apart from all other nations, and that every activity, even the daily labor of feeding themselves, was to be done within the province and provision of a loving God. The manna God miraculously fed his people in the desert was a foreshadowing of Jesus, who came to give himself as the Bread of Life. In his last hours on earth, Jesus chose to enjoy a dinner with his disciples, where he served homely bread and local wine to mark his death and ongoing life within the disciples and us. While we sup on the bread and wine of Communion now, we hungrily await the marriage supper of the lamb, a coming feast we joyously anticipate through simple daily foods.

Even a cursory reading reveals that food is a major concern in the Scriptures, the locus of both physical and spiritual realities that gesture not solely to one or to the other, but to the essential integration of both. But in the biblical economy, food alone— even the food of the Communion table—can never bestow purity, health, or righteousness. When Christ fed the hungry thousands on the hillside, he fed them not only actual bread but also words of truth and salvation, that he comes as the Bread of Life and the Living Water to help us recognize the deeper needs that he alone can fulfill.

"Every bite of food, given by God himself, is to make God known to man, to make man's life communion with God," Orthodox theologian Alexander Schmemann writes in *For the Life of the World.* But without recognition of the God who has made the earth, our dependence on water and food may move us elsewhere—toward communion with the earth, even communion with food itself. These elements, then, become ends in themselves, and the full integration that the food movement seeks and that God desires for us is lost.

Our attempts to restore the earth and return to Edenic communion with it ultimately cannot succeed. Just as we cannot perfect our bodies or spirits through eating pure foods, so we cannot perfect the earth, no matter how heroic our efforts. Because of our foreparents' appetite for authority and forbidden food, creation has been groaning, subjected to futility and death. Sea lions eat the first fifteen salmon from my family's fishing nets to fill their appetites. They gash and torment thirty more simply for play. One spring I counted ninety deer washed up on our beach line, drowned as they swam across the strait.

Nature will always be "red in tooth and claw." We steward the earth and exercise dominion over its creatures as expressions of love for and obedience to our Creator, who named it all very good, but we cannot take back or re-create the garden. Not until heaven will we see the garden restored, but it will be set not within a wilderness, but within the gates of a massive city, the unavoidable conclusion that the perfected world to come is foremost about proximity and communion with one another and with God.

Cooking Pots to Sacred Bowls

Finally, without a theology rooted in the God of creation and the God of the Scriptures—who alone completes the meaning of creation and its sustenance, and who will someday fully restore it—I worry that the food movement and its calls to action will divert us from our real need: a transformed heart. I worry as well that it may devolve into the very fragmentation it aspires to repair. Without a redeemer, the source of grace, the integration and holism that the movement seeks to easily descend into orthorexia, purer-than-thou-ism, and factionalism.

Such is the case even now. Pollan describes the food movement as a "big, lumpy tent" where "sometimes the various factions beneath it work at cross-purposes." Bratman remembers the splintering and infighting among commune members over whose diet was purer. Tom Billings, a raw-foodist, complains that the raw-foods movement is "split into a number of factions, and it seems that no one agrees with anyone else." The last thing we need inside or outside the church is another brand of factious legalism.

But we in the church have much to answer for ourselves. Here's a question, which I ask myself as well: Why have we ignored food for so long? Why are we not attending more seriously to Paul's injunction to literally "eat or drink … for the glory of God"? Beyond a quick word of thanks before meals, have we seriously considered how our eating and drinking either reveals or suppresses the glory of God? I don't believe we have. Most of us have been living in a kind of self-absorbed somnolence that may be partly rooted in our own lingering dualism that privileges the soul over the body.

Additionally, the Protestants among us have reveled in our dietary freedom and our distinctiveness from more liturgical churches, which follow the church calendar and maintain traditions of feasting and fasting. As Protestants, our food practices have relied far too heavily on a single New Testament passage, I believe: Peter's vision of a sheet full of formerly unclean animals let down from heaven. God's command to "rise, kill and eat" (the supreme-meat-lover's favorite biblical scene), in my opinion, has been used to justify a kind of gustatory free-for-all.

How shall we use our freedom in Christ? Freedom is never given for license or for self-indulgence. If our freedom ends in mindless consumption, abuse of the earth, exploitation of God's gifts, and mistreatment of our bodies, then we have allowed our appetites to enslave us again.

I don't really know what Jesus would have put on his plate at the church potluck that day. I suspect he might have tossed a few cheese doodles on his plate, next to his Jell-O, quietly reminding me that it is not what goes into our bodies that makes us unclean, but what comes out of them, from our mouths and hearts. Even so, I'm pretty sure there will not be junk food in heaven, nor do I think we'll be eating meat. I'm expecting to cook good, slow food there, and I have reason to believe we will.

Zechariah, my new favorite minor prophet, ends his book, which is largely about condemnation and judgment, with a gorgeous culinary image of heaven. When heaven comes down to earth, he writes, "the cooking pots in the LORD's house will be like the sacred bowls in front of the altar. Every pot in Jerusalem and Judah will be holy to the LORD Almighty, and all who come to sacrifice will take some of the pots and cook in them" (Zech. 14:20–21).

Every pot—yours, mine—will be holy to the Lord. And every soup and vegetable and grain and fish and casserole and soufflé and flan and pasta prepared within them will be holy to all who partake.

I believe we're not to wait for this day, that we are to join the food movement thoughtfully and joyously, beginning now to more faithfully give attention to food. I don't pretend to practice or even understand all the ways this is possible, but I am beginning to learn. Many others in the church are already practicing such attention. Some, like Amy Frykholm, are beginning simple fasting practices. Alyssa Herbaly Coons is slowly adding local farm-raised meat to her lifelong vegetarian diet. Green Bay Community Church in Wisconsin has been holding a farmer's market in the church parking lot on Thursday nights, followed by an open-air worship service. The Christian Reformed World Relief Committee has joined a fair trade coffee group, Brew Justice, that buys coffee from small independent farmers. Women in my own church have begun an organic food co-op. And, like most congregations, Fellowship Church in Phillipsburg, New Jersey, has a food pantry open to anyone in need.

So much is possible as we return the growing fields and the kitchen table to God, to whom it all belongs. As we do, we will discover another essential means of divining God's glory in our midst and living out our stewardship of God's earth, ourselves, and our neighbors. May we all take, eat, and be blessed by God's holy, sumptuous foods.

Chapter 27

—

WHOLE EARTH EVANGELISM

*Creation care is part and parcel
of the Great Commission and
the Great Commandment.*

Scott Sabin | 2010

I n the 1960s, the ecology movement was launched with a fundamental insight: Everything is part of a system. If you alter one
thing, it will affect something else—for good or ill. For example,
we discovered back then that using the pesticide DDT to control
mosquitoes and malaria (a good thing) also weakened the shells
of birds' eggs and threatened their ability to reproduce (a bad
thing). Such discoveries helped us think beyond our immediate
actions and anticipate the collateral damage created by the way
we live.

Are evangelization, compassionate justice ministry, and earth
care similarly connected in a spiritual ecology? In this essay for

the Global Conversation, Scott Sabin, author of the newly published *Tending to Eden*, connects those dots.

———

On a precarious slope, Etienne digs in the dusty soil with a small hoe, planting beans in hopeful anticipation of the rains, which have become unpredictable in recent years. Miles away, his wife is returning from the increasingly distant forest with a large bundle of firewood on her head. She was up before dawn carrying water from the spring, nearly an hour's walk away. The infant on her back is sick with intestinal parasites from drinking the water that she has worked so hard to provide.

Though the global context may be lost on Etienne and his family, they live with the consequences of environmental degradation on a daily basis. By contrast, in the United States, frequent headlines warn of the tribulations of the earth and its ecosystems, but because the impact on our daily lives feels minimal, the steady parade of dire predictions is ignored—or worse, fosters despair.

Until I began working with Plant with Purpose (formerly Floresta), I was among those who ignored the signs, occasionally lamenting the loss of a favorite hiking place or noticing that I no longer saw horned lizards in my backyard. Beyond that, the environment was a secondary concern. Those who went before me at Plant with Purpose, however, saw a direct connection between forest health and the health of poor communities. To get beyond treating the symptoms of poverty, we would need to address the health of the ecosystem that supported the poor. Standing on a windswept hillside in Haiti one afternoon, overlooking a panorama of eroded mountains and silt-choked rivers, it dawned on me that we could not give a cup of cold water without restoring the watershed. Over the past eighteen years, I have slowly realized that this observation applies beyond Haiti. We all depend on a healthy world.

As 6.8 billion human beings seek to satisfy their needs and desires on an ever-shrinking planet, it should not surprise us that the issue of environmental stewardship or "creation care" is part of our global conversation.

While climate change dominates the discussion, hundreds of lesser known and less controversial environmental issues are coming to a head.

Marine species we used to think were infinite in number are vanishing at alarming rates. Half of the world's primates are in danger of extinction. Frogs and bees are disappearing. Fresh water is becoming increasingly scarce. Deforestation is reducing rainfall, soil fertility, and water resources in many parts of the world. In light of these realities, what is our role as Christians?

To Serve and Protect

From the very beginning, caring for the earth that God created has been a fundamental part of our role.

In Genesis 2:15, Adam is placed in the garden to serve (*'abad*) and protect (*shamar*) it. Throughout the Old Testament we are reminded that "the Earth is the LORD's" and that our role is one of stewardship—temporary caretakers who will one day be called to account for how well we have discharged our duties. This is reinforced in Revelation 11:18, which says Judgment Day will bring the destruction of those who destroy the earth.

Scripture also indicates a direct correlation between the behavior of humans and the health of the earth. The ground is cursed as a result of Adam's sin. Later, in the story of the Flood, human sin results in the destruction of most life on earth. What is spared is saved through the active participation of Noah. In

Jeremiah 12:4 and many other passages, we see the land and its creatures suffering as a direct result of sin.

"Cursed is the ground because of you; through painful toil you will eat of it all the days of your life" (Gen. 3:17). Much of the world has gone to great ends to mitigate the consequences of the Adamic curse. We have distanced ourselves from the physical labor of producing food (and with that, brought a number of unintended consequences). But for hundreds of millions of subsistence and near-subsistence farmers worldwide, the curse's "painful toil" is a fundamental aspect of life. I clearly remember an afternoon spent planting beans on a rocky mountainside in Haiti, my bloody hands and aching back reminders of the daily reality my brothers and sisters lived.

Yet as the Psalms make clear, creation—even creation broken by sin—gives glory to God. When Job calls God to account, God shows Job his greatness by pointing to his creation and reminds Job of his need for humility in the face of things he doesn't understand (Job 38–41). This passage also gives a glimpse of the delight God takes in the earth. Psalm 104 further emphasizes this, as well as the special relationship God has with his creatures, independent of humanity. Like Job, we need to learn that we are not always the center of the story.

Following in Adam's footsteps, we are still called to be stewards of creation, which still belongs to God. But our role now goes further. Paul tells us in Romans 8:22 that creation is groaning as if in childbirth, anticipating redemption and eagerly waiting for the children of God to be revealed. As God's children, we are a part of this good news for creation—a creation that until now has suffered due to our sin and greed. God's plan of redemption is intended as good news not just for us but for the environment as well. While only God can finally redeem the creation, we are his agents in bringing a foretaste of that redemption. As Christians, our environmental responsibility is awesome and humbling.

The Uninsulated Poor

It is more than an issue of obedience and humility. Environmental stewardship is also a justice issue. There is no need to prioritize between love of neighbor and care for God's creation.

In the United States and Europe, it is easy to forget that the earth is our life-support system. For too many of us, water comes in plastic bottles, and food comes from a supermarket. We see the environment as a luxury.

Yet the poorest people in the world are not so insulated. When the rain doesn't come, people starve. When soil erodes, families go hungry. When water gets polluted, children get intestinal diseases. When all the trees are cut down, women walk hours for firewood. When the land is deforested, watersheds no longer function, causing rivers and streams to dry up. When the rain does come, deadly landslides ensue. For most of the people with whom I have worked over the past fifteen years, their soil and their water are virtually their only assets. Preserving and sustainably using those assets, so as not to further degrade those ecosystems—serving creation as stewards—becomes central to serving those people.

One elitist stream in the secular environmental movement has seen creation solely in terms of its recreational possibilities. From this perspective, humans, and especially the poor, can only be burdens on the land. It has been easy for North Americans to imagine wilderness as something that is best left untouched by human influence.

In truth, there is hardly such a thing as untouched wilderness. The rainforests of the Amazon and the South Pacific and the prairies of North America were all shaped by human influence.

Furthermore, to see creation as something humans should leave untouched is to ignore our stewardship role. God calls us to participate in nature, contributing to and ensuring its fruitfulness. We have little choice as to whether we will interact with creation. But we can choose whether our interactions will be life-giving or death-dealing. Our citizenship in God's kingdom should inform this choice.

The coming of God's kingdom has changed our fundamental reality. We love our enemies and serve our neighbors. Similarly, though we still experience the effects of the curse, we can strive to work with God's natural systems instead of against them. Over and over in our work with sustainable agriculture, we have discovered that we have that choice. Weeds still grow and crops still fail, of course, but we can work in such a way as to give back to creation, mimicking its fertility cycles. The more closely agriculture mimics natural ecosystems, the more sustainable it is. Agroforestry, permaculture, composting latrines, and even recycling are examples in which these principles are put to work.

From Environment to Evangelism

God's ability to work things together for good is obvious in the intricate ways that ecosystems fit together. Nothing is wasted; everything has its niche. Everywhere, life springs forth from death, and resurrection is foreshadowed. Beyond seeking merely to reduce our footprint, we can seek to be restorative in our relationship with the earth.

On a global scale, restoration is a monumental task. We are unlikely to achieve it this side of Christ's return, any more than we are likely to bring about world peace by turning the other cheek. However, kingdom thinking can serve to guide our planning and our individual choices. At Plant with Purpose, we have seen restoration happen. Rivers and streams that had withered have begun to flow again due to upstream solutions. They have become powerful illustrations of God's ability to redeem and restore, both for us and for the farmers with whom we are striving to share Christ's love.

In industrialized countries, where we are shielded from the direct feedback of the land, we have much to learn from our brothers and sisters in subsistence-farming countries. For example, I have understood much more deeply the connection between environmental degradation and misery among Haitian farmers than in biology classes in the US. I have been very impressed with the seriousness with which African, Latin American, and Asian church leaders have embraced creation care. When Care of Creation, an environmental missions agency, hosted a "God and Creation" conference in Kenya, it was filled to capacity with pastors and leaders from all over East Africa. Similar conferences in the US have struggled to get more than a handful to attend.

Furthermore, African conference attendance resulted in action. One Tanzanian pastor encouraged all the churches in his region to establish tree nurseries. They required those going through confirmation classes to plant trees in order to graduate. As a result, over five hundred thousand trees have been planted, and an important water source that had become intermittent now flows steadily.

This is gospel work. Paul reminds us in Romans 1:20 that creation reveals much about God. As such, it is a perfect starting point for a conversation about what we can learn of God's character from his Word. Environmental stewardship can be an integral part of God's story of redemption.

It can also open many doors. Several Plant with Purpose supporters have told me that their involvement has provided opportunities to share Christ with environmentalist friends or colleagues. My colleagues in the creation care community have had countless chances to engage with communities that would otherwise be closed to us.

At the same time, conversations with poor farmers about the land and soil have given us perfect opportunities to integrate the gospel story into our work. After all, the Bible begins the story in the same place, with creation, earth, and soil.

Much of the world is either directly suffering as a result of environmental degradation or reacting in numb despair to gloomy predictions. Both groups desperately need the hope of Jesus Christ. It is the hope they long for, a hope that speaks directly to the redemption of all creation and reminds them that God loves the cosmos.

The gospel is for everyone—from dirt farmers to environmental activists. It is good news that God cares about all that he has created.

Chapter 28

THE JOYFUL
ENVIRONMENTALISTS

*Eugene Peterson and Peter Harris think of
creation care not as an onerous duty but a
natural response to the goodness of God.*

Interview by Andy Crouch | 2011

C reation care is a hot topic among Christians, but it is nothing new for longtime friends Eugene Peterson and Peter
Harris. Peterson's recent memoir *The Pastor* (HarperOne) is sat-
urated with environmental themes and metaphors, grounded in
his annual visits to the family cabin in the highlands of Montana,
where he now resides. In 1983, Peter and Miranda Harris and
a few friends founded a Christian ecological study center in
Portugal called A Rocha (Portuguese for "the rock"). It is now
an international conservation organization that has recently
expanded its work in the United States. *Christianity Today*
editor at large Andy Crouch spoke with Peterson and Harris on

the banks of the Frio River in Texas at a conference on faith and technology at Laity Lodge.

Eugene, how did you come to be so involved in conservation and environmental issues?

I grew up in a very sectarian world. There was no explicit care for creation. My parents were indifferent to it, and my church was indifferent. Hunting was the closest my family or my church ever came to being involved in the world around us. But after they killed their deer or their elk, they were done.

In some ways, that indifference was good for me and for our family, because our kids discovered environmental concerns as we hiked, fished, gardened, harvested, and canned fruits. It was more of a discovery and enjoyment. When I met Peter and saw him at work and listened to him, I realized this really was something significant and biblical.

Peter Harris: It's important to understand that A Rocha, as a movement, is driven by biblical theology. It's not a Christian attempt to "save the planet." It's a response to who God is. Therefore, the role of people like Eugene has been to help us lay that foundation.

Many people—and many Christians—would be happy just to say they are "saving the planet." How would you distinguish a biblically formed movement?

Harris: We may do many of the same things as do secular environmental organizations, but we do them for very different reasons. One question for any kind of activism is, how long are you going to be able to *keep* doing it? If you believe you're going to be able, by technology, by political force, by whatever means, to save the planet, you may well get exhausted and disillusioned and depressed. These are genuine problems within the environmental movement.

If, on the other hand, you do what you do because you believe it pleases the living God, who is the Creator and whose handiwork this is, your perspective is very different. I don't think there is any guarantee we will save the planet. I don't think the Bible gives us much reassurance about that. But I do believe it gives God tremendous pleasure when his people do what they were created to do, which is care for what he made.

There are some obvious biblical texts to which Christians tend to turn when they think about creation—Genesis 1 and 2, and maybe Romans 8:22. Are there any others?

Peterson: The book of Exodus and the Egyptian plagues. Those ten plagues are all exorcisms of specific aspects of Pharaoh's control over the world. For eight months, the whole country of Egypt was turned into a theater of exorcism, item by item by item. Pharaoh was unable to do what he had done to creation, and the evil was exorcised by the command of God.

It's extraordinary, taking away the authority of the powers that be and demonstrating that to the whole nation, maybe most of all to the Hebrews, who themselves had been under Pharaoh's power. Here is a huge wrecking ball: smash, smash, smash, smash, and after eight months there's nothing left of Pharaoh's power.

Then out of this highly technologized world of Egypt—the pyramids, the statuary, the temples—they go into the wilderness, which is supposed to be empty. Yet they are all provided for, and they live by the providence of God in a most unlikely place. You can bet that they gained an appreciation for the fertility of the world they were living in—that they did not need all of Pharaoh's technology to be provided for. That's a great environmental text, even though I don't think it's ever been used that way.

Harris: Our job in reading Scripture is not primarily to find proof texts about creatures with wings or legs. Our job is to discover: Who is God? Who is Jesus Christ? What do they care about? And how does the Spirit enable us to live that life?

Look at Hosea 4. In the first three verses, we have moral problems: adultery and murder, bloodshed following bloodshed. But then, "Therefore the land mourns," and "the beasts of the field and the birds of the heavens, and even the fish of the sea are taken away" (v. 3, ESV). That's a prophecy three millennia before we have the words for a marine crisis. Who would have thought that the fish of the sea would die? Until modern times, the fish of the sea seemed like an inexhaustible resource.

You get those ecological consequences of the broken relationship with God all the way through Scripture. But at the same time, there's the phenomenal hope that as people are restored in Christ to a right relationship with God, there will be a restoration of our relationship to creation and healing for the creation.

How do these themes connect with Americans, who mostly live in either suburban or urban environments?

Harris: That's one distinction between a Christian take on creation and a secular romanticism about wilderness. Think about Psalm 104. In that psalm, which echoes Genesis, you don't just have "the sea and everything in it"; you have ships on it, working. You don't just have the land; you have people, working. There is a radical environmentalism that wishes people were not on the planet. That's not the biblical view at all. A Rocha in the United Kingdom actually works in the most polluted, urban borough of the country, because creation isn't absent just because people are there. The challenge is how to restore a right way of life, rather than escaping to some wilderness paradise. Fifty percent of the planet now lives in cities. That is where we live out our relationship with creation.

As Christian conservationists, do you see urbanization as a good thing, a bad thing, or something neutral?

Harris: My biblical theology means I cannot see it as a bad thing. The ultimate biblical vision is the heavenly city. Our challenge is the redemption of the urban, not the consecration of wilderness.

Peterson: I agree, and I don't think we realize how much of our view of wilderness comes to us through the Romantic movement. Romantic literature was written at the height of the industrial city, with its exploitation, poverty, and child labor. In reaction to all that, they gave us the concept of nature as romantic. But it's not romantic.

Harris: It may not even be natural. Sir Ghillean Prance, who has studied the Amazon rainforest for decades, believes that the very diversity of the rainforest is a result of gardening. The human beings who lived there selectively used it and tended it, and that is the best way to account for its extraordinary botanical diversity.

Even biologically, the idea of a pristine, teeming world without human beings probably isn't accurate. Britain is certainly a case in point. The original British form of vegetation was a pretty monocultural oak forest. It was only as farming came and we had a diversity of habitats that we had the biodiversity that we cherish on the British Isles today.

So we should understand the human presence on the planet in God's purposes as a blessing.

A Rocha focuses on conservation. In a biblical sense, what is it that we are to conserve?

Peterson: For me and for my family, our primary entry point to conservation—to keeping—was keeping the Sabbath. At one point we decided we were going to keep the Sabbath. We kept a regular Monday Sabbath because as a pastor, Sunday was a work day. We're still doing that. Our kids grew up doing that. If you keep the Sabbath, you start to see creation not as somewhere to get away from your ordinary life, but a place to frame an attentiveness to your life. And it doesn't necessarily have to do with seeing birds or foxes or whatever. Sometimes it is your own kids—putting them in a different setting and bringing them home refreshed.

Harris: It's important to recognize that we are losing species on the planet at an unprecedented rate since industrialization. Now, if in Psalm 104 it says, "In wisdom [God] made them all," and if God gave us the work of caring for creation, then clearly, we aren't fulfilling the biblical vision.

But I think the Christian vision of conservation is exactly as Eugene framed it. It's a wider one that has to do with human flourishing, that has to do with recognizing that a ravaged creation has wrecked not just species but God's intention for time, for Sabbath, and that in turn wrecks families and whole societies.

Some Christians believe that prioritizing environmental concerns limits economic growth and consequently the prospects of the poor. Increasingly, one hears the charge that environmentalists care more about birds than people, but more pointedly that they care more about species than about human beings who are poor.

Harris: Every Christian leader I've ever met in poor parts of the world understands that they live in an unmediated relationship with the creation. That means that if there is damage done to the creation, there is damage done to the human community. I would argue that the economic possibilities lie now in the building of a sustainable economy; that's where the smart money is today. In any case, an economy founded on degrading the creation is theologically incoherent. The old model that you can make your money any which way and then give some of it away when you're rich enough is lacking biblical warrant. A much better way is to make money in a way that impacts the poor and the planet beneficially.

Clearly there is a growing enthusiasm among Christians for creation care. But enthusiasm can go wrong. What do you see as the deepest risks in our current interest in environmental concerns?

Harris: I think eco-judgmentalism is a real danger. This is not a matter of finding another five quick rules to keep you on the right side of God. This is not about what we do; this is a change or a development in the depth of our relationship with God himself. It's about everything, not just about a narrow slice of topics. It would be disastrous if we turn the biblical vision into a code that "good" Christians follow—something like, thou shalt eat muesli, wear sandals, and look miserable.

I think the environmental movement has been perceived as judgmental and angry, claiming moral high ground and issuing rules with disapproval. Recently a social scientist at the Cornell Lab of Ornithology told me that studies have shown one of the marker personality traits among environmentalists is anxiety. The Christian approach is very different: it is celebratory and grateful and hopeful.

Chapter 29

———

BACK TO THE GARDEN

*Row by row, urban Christians learn
to bear literal and spiritual fruit.*

Tony Carnes | 2011

On a recent Sunday, Steven Hebbard got stung by a bee. He seemed deliriously happy. "I got stung! I got stung! Whoopee!" Hebbard wasn't crazy. He was just excited that his group of gardeners had put in their first beehive. The day before, Hebbard had trained nineteen students from Gateway Community Church, an Austin megachurch, on how to garden alongside the homeless and impoverished. And earlier this year, Hebbard broke ground on a new garden on an acre of land for the poverty-stricken refugee community living in East Austin. Most of the refugees are Nepalese or Bhutanese. "After looking at the space and realizing they had at least an acre that could be used for community gardening, I contacted the apartment complex manager, and he gave us the go-ahead."

Thirty refugees—about half of them with a Hindu background—came to the kickoff. Christian refugees living nearby joined in, and many of them are now active at the new International Restoration Church.

"After the garden looked amazing in its fully planted form, I fully expected all the refugees to take off," Hebbard told *CT*. "Some did, but most stuck around. The day was an amazing success."

"Back to the garden" is a new way of doing church that adds a missional tweak to traditional gardening. Congregations and ministries are planting sweet corn around their sites, mobilizing gardening networks for the needy, and rediscovering the value of low-tech, high-touch community.

Growing Trend

Several years ago, Hebbard caught a vision for urban gardening and launched the Karpophoreō Project (KP), inspired by the Greek phrase in Colossians 1, "bearing fruit in every good work." His vision is to restore relationships between people and their environment through small-scale gardens.

Across the nation, similar programs are taking root. In Caledonia, Michigan, the sanctuary windows of Redeemer Covenant Church look out not onto headstones but corn, tomatoes, and other vegetable crops.

In New York City, a Bronx Baptist church is reaching out to urban youth by inviting them to an outdoor sanctuary of strawberry plants and watermelon vines at its Righteousness Community Garden.

In Charlottesville, Virginia, Orthodox theologian and author Vigen Guroian mentors students by inviting them to garden on a five-acre plot.

Many Americans consider themselves gardeners, yet researchers have determined that the amount of gardening per US household has been in steady decline. University of Virginia scholar Guroian confirms this. On a recent visit to see his mother in Connecticut, he walked down a residential street that years ago was a gardeners' row. "Now, there are no gardens and at best a little shrubbery."

There is no single cause, Guroian says, yet reliable statistics show that Americans are working longer hours and taking on more jobs outside the traditional workweek.

However, gardening associations say that after the 2008 economic crisis, gardening took off among people seeking to cut their grocery bills. In 2010, there was a 20 percent increase in small gardens. Jung Seed, a large Midwestern seed distributor, says that demand has begun to turn around, and that seed deliveries to churches and community ministries are on the rise.

Calvin DeWitt, co-founder of the Evangelical Environmental Network, told *CT* that he believes many Christians are increasingly motivated to garden as an antidote to high-tech, high-stress living.

"We have moved to the abstract even in the church," says DeWitt. "We praise God for greatness, not the lilies of the field. Hymns with creation-rich verses have been dropped from hymnals in favor of more abstract references."

For Christian gardeners, spiritual motivations typically outrank economic ones. The Christian Cultural Center landscaped an Edenic park around its Brooklyn building that evokes the Ten Commandments, Moses, and African American history. The design also invites the community into the garden as an act of neighborliness. Lead pastor A. R. Bernard says he is inspired when flowers hang through the fence, a kind of invitation to church for neighborhood kids and parents who walk by.

Non-Digital Public Space

Christian gardening, Hebbard believes, creates public space for believers to grow and nonbelievers to begin to grow spiritually.

Part of the appeal is that it is a genuine alternative to the Internet. "I kept getting this call from God: 'Unplug! Back to the soil!'" Hebbard says. Fresh out of Trinity Evangelical Divinity School, Hebbard was working for a federal agency in Austin but uncertain of his career path. Then a friend invited him to a reading group that met in a garden. They studied the writings of Baptist environmentalist Wendell Berry. "He turned my life upside down," Hebbard says. "Berry articulated so many things about our lives that I was feeling but couldn't say."

Hebbard threw himself into several urban farming internships. He realized he desired not farming per se but richer personal relationships through helping the poor and sharing the gospel. After the internships, Hebbard teamed up with Alan Graham, president and founding member of Austin-based Mobile Loaves and Fishes, a group that rehabs trailer homes and rents them to the homeless at low cost.

Hebbard had another big idea: If Christians lived among the homeless, the two groups could garden together and create a Christian community that would be a model to others. This vision evolved into Karpophoreō. Launched in April 2009, KP currently has one hundred volunteers and forty homeless gardeners. It has set up a community center in Austin's Royal Palms Mobile Home Park and is recruiting volunteers.

The approach has caught the imagination of young Austinites, including Jen Ardill. The John Brown University graduate came across KP accidently but responded right away. "I elbowed my way in. I became involved in every way I could."

Ardill, currently on the KP staff, says that communal gardening has helped her address her shyness. "People now knock on my door to see if they can get some of my cilantro," she says.

At first, homeless individuals looked upon Hebbard's ardent gardeners with suspicion. Jimmy Northen, who lived on the streets for nine years, wondered, "Who are these people? What do they want? On the streets, you can't trust just anyone." But after KP started a Thursday night Bible study and a Friday meal called Stone Soup Breakfast, Northen was drawn in.

Or take mobile home resident Theresa Gonzalez. For years, she had been friendless. "I was very isolated," she says. "Then, I heard that they had a Bible study in the trailer across from me. I knew I needed something." She joined the study, made friends, and soon had flowers blooming in front of her home.

Because of her physical limitations, Gonzalez doesn't garden as much as she would like, but she provides cupcakes for birthday celebrations at the Bible studies. She started attending a Baptist church next to KP's garden at the trailer park. "And she stopped drinking," her granddaughter Isabella chimes in.

"Yes," Gonzalez says, "I stopped drinking after I started going to church."

Greater Harvest

Several Austin churches have expanded their outreach programs and seen their faith deepen through their connection to KP.

Last year, churchgoer Amy Hardin was growing restless at home with three boys, and wanted to practice a simpler lifestyle and make more connections with others. Her pastor challenged her to sacrifice something for Lent and to write down one way she could serve the needy. Hardin thought her boys were growing up without any appreciation for nature or compassion for the homeless.

"On a whim, I wrote down 'Garden and help the homeless,' " Hardin says. She typed "gardening for the homeless" into Google and discovered Hebbard's organization. "It was too good to be true."

Hardin spread the word about KP to friends at Austin New Church, and now a half-dozen families from the church work with KP.

Jen and Brandon Hatmaker launched their church plant in a south Austin area known as the "Death Valley of church planting." Some twenty-seven attempts at church planting had failed. But Austin New Church has succeeded and grown to four hundred people.

The Hatmakers call Austin New Church a "missional church," which for them means helping the poor and needy by fostering neighborliness. Over 120 of their new believers came to them by volunteering for church-sponsored outreach, including KP projects.

Another small, new church in Austin, Vox Veniae, has started a community garden and chose a person with disabilities to be chief gardener. While *CT* was visiting, Hebbard was learning beekeeping in order to build a beehive at Vox, which hopes to do more than gardening. Church leader Gideon Tsang says these efforts allow the church and the community to partner authentically with needy individuals.

Citing his own spiritual development, Guroian says this church-community partnership gardening will produce a great spiritual harvest over time.

"We didn't go to church often," Guroian says, recalling his childhood. He didn't have real knowledge of God, but he loved to walk in the woods and experience the sense of wonder. "I was really looking for he who made these wonders."

In college, Guroian continued his search. "My professors didn't realize that they were teaching me the way to God." He concluded that a good work ethic is not enough in life. For him, biblical faith came through powerful images of the garden, the desert, and the harvest.

Lost Discipline

Some see both promise and danger in the current Christian gardening movement. Guroian admits that reverence for creation can become a fetish: "I get nervous when I see people reverently fondling the vegetables and fruits at Whole Foods. Just eat it, please."

On the other hand, he sees younger Christians gardening out of deep spiritual longings. "They have a real sense of a gap between their faith affirmations of the goodness of creation and the way they actually live their lives." The new gardeners also recognize that they have become too busy and self-focused. Gardening is one remedy.

For Guroian, being a gardener has become a vocation on par with his profession as a theologian. He writes in his book *The Fragrance of God*, "When I kneel in my garden, the aromas of the plants may overwhelm me ... God's presence permeates my entire being, though he remains invisible to my eyes."

To go spiritually deeper, suggests Guroian, bring hymns into the garden, especially older hymns such as "In the Garden."

Later this year, Guroian will lead Antiochian Orthodox leaders at a retreat center. His plan is to garden with them while praying the ancient liturgy of the hours.

Chapter 30

THREE REASONS WHY EVANGELICALS STOPPED ADVOCATING FOR THE ENVIRONMENT

It's not theology, it's politics.

Andrew Spencer | 2017

T he recent announcement by the Trump administration that the United States is withdrawing from the Paris Accord, an agreement to limit greenhouse gas emissions signed by President Obama and leaders from 194 other countries in 2016, has produced a flurry of reactions. The legalities of the international pact are debatable, with strong opinions on both sides, but either way there is little clear guidance or precedent for withdrawal from such an agreement by the United States. The continued support among evangelicals for President Trump has caused some to wonder why evangelicals seem to be disinterested in environmental activism.

But there is a clear case to be made for ecological stewardship within the pages of Scripture. In the Garden of Eden, Adam was given the task of tending the garden (Gen. 2:15). God preserved both human and non-human creation while judging the earth through a cataclysmic flood and entered into a covenant with all living creatures not to destroy the earth again by a flood (Gen. 8–9). The Psalms bear witness that creation testifies to God's character (e.g., Ps. 19:1–6). Paul tells us that Jesus came to reconcile "all things" to himself (Col. 1:15–20), which is a state for which creation is eagerly longing (Rom. 8:18–25). There is a biblical case for evangelical Christians to be actively engaged in environmental activism, but political polarization has put creation care among the issues that often divide the right and the left. It has not always been this way.

When the first Earth Day celebration was held in 1970 it was a bipartisan event with over twenty million Americans of various political views participating. The commemoration of this day came under a Republican president, Richard Nixon, who created the Environmental Protection Agency and is still, despite his other public failures, considered to be a "green" president by some environmental ethicists. Earth Day was a response to the obvious environmental issues in the United States and around the world. Famously, in 1969, the Cuyahoga River in Northeast Ohio "caught fire" when a large amount of surface debris and oil ignited, making national news. Acid rain caused a real and obvious threat to lakes and rivers in the Northeast United States, and the Great Lakes were dying. The consensus on these issues was broad and public response was warranted. Although the issues have changed, the greatest shift in environmental concerns has been the division between right and left on this issue, which, in religious communities, has often been driven by factors other than theology.

1. A Misguided Call to Action

One of the first major barriers to theologically conservative Christian engagement in the environment comes from Lynn White Jr.'s infamous essay, "The Historical Roots of Our Ecological Crisis." White's essay was published in *Science* in March 1967 and was based on a lecture given to the American Association for the Advancement of Science. White was a historian who specialized in documenting the cultural influence of technology, including a hotly debated theory about the role of the stirrup in the development of civilization.

White's argument in his essay is that current environmental problems have been caused by the rise and abusive use of technology, and that technology was developed in the West because of Christian de-paganization of nature. Consequently, Western Christianity is at fault for the ecological crisis. White recommended modifying Christian orthodoxy to accommodate environmental concerns.

Sociologist Sabrina Danielson, in a study of conservative Christian responses to the ecological crisis, notes that the debate over the Lynn White thesis has held back legitimate engagement by conservative Christians on the environment as they attempt to defend Christianity from his accusations. Nearly every major Christian discussion of environmental ethics written since that essay introduced White's thesis and reacted to it within the first few pages. Responses to White's proposal of renovating Christian doctrine have been predictable. Theological conservatives have rejected White's claims that Christianity has been responsible; more liberal commentators have tended to accept White's claims and encourage doctrinal adaptations or, at least, a shift in emphasis.

In reality, however, White's essay has been promoted beyond its value. Critiques of "The Historical Roots of Our Ecological Crisis" tend to focus on the ends of White's essay and miss the weakness, which resides at the heart of his accusation. White's argument fails because he places blame for the loss of wonder at nature on Christianity. As Alister McGrath argues in *The Reenchantment of Nature*, however, it was naturalistic influences of modernist philosophies that reduced the universe to its instrumental value for humans and encouraged the abuse of nature. Some Christians went along with that shift, but it was a result of their adaptation to prevailing ideas of their time, not a biblical theology of stewardship. The appropriate answer is not to revise orthodox Christianity, but to restore a Christian vision of the inherent value of creation.

White's essay was intended to inspire Christians to become environmentalists by changing their doctrines. There is little he could have said that would have more strongly increased resistance to his cause. Unfortunately, his call for revision of orthodox theology was based on a misdiagnosis of the cause of the environmental crisis. His error still impedes reasonable environmental engagement among some conservative Christians today.

2. Aligning Abortion with Environment

The second wedge driven between many conservative Christians and environmental activism is the explicitly misanthropic emphasis of some forms of environmentalism. Concerns about overpopulation are not unique to the twentieth and twenty-first centuries. In the eighteenth century, Anglican clergyman Thomas Malthus published a volume, *First Essay on Population*, predicting the population would grow beyond the means of agricultural production, which would in turn result in mass starvation of the poor. His proposed solution included delaying marriage and voluntarily limiting family size, both reasonable solutions for a faithful Christian. His predictions turned out to be vastly wrong.

In the mid-twentieth century, Paul Ehrlich, a biologist from Stanford, wrote a contemporary Malthusian proposal in his book *The Population Bomb*. Unlike Malthus, however, Ehrlich links population control with the legalization of abortion and distribution of birth control. Population control was also a significant plank in the syncretistic philosophy of Deep Ecology, with some advocates of Deep Ecology advocating abortion as a means of reducing the impact of humans on the earth.

The connection was made clearer between abortion and environmentalism in the mind of the American public upon the release of the Rockefeller Commission report, "Population and the American Future." That report, commissioned by Nixon in 1969, was based on public concern for the environment and overpopulation, driven by Ehrlich and others. It was released in 1972 and openly recommended the legalization of abortion and government-funded contraceptive distribution. Political tensions were high as Nixon was running for a second term. The contentious *Roe v. Wade* case was already at the US Supreme Court, making abortion a hot button issue. Although he had founded the EPA and endorsed Earth Day, Nixon was compelled by politics, if not by conviction, to undermine the Rockefeller Commission through a public statement rejecting the findings in the report before it was issued, in addition to behind-the-scenes efforts to ensure none of the recommendations ever made it to the legislative process.

The link between abortion and environmentalism is one that the environmental movement has been unable to shake because some groups continue to reinforce it, which biases some evangelicals against environmental activism. In reality, there is no necessary connection between environmental concern and abortion. A beautifully orthodox evangelicalism should have room for opposing abortion and caring for creation.

3. Leftward Drift of Environmentalist Evangelicals

A third factor in the resistance of some conservative Christians to environmental activism is the apparent leftward drift of Christians who are also environmentalists. As Mark Stoll notes in his recent volume, *Inherit the Holy Mountain*, "A high proportion of leading figures in environmental history had religious childhoods. A surprisingly large contingent had ministers or preachers as close relatives or had even considered the ministry themselves. Curiously, few (and after 1900, hardly any) were churchgoers as adults." This apparent pattern, combined with fears of young Christians abandoning their faith, tends to raise resistance to environmentalism as a perceived cause of the decay of faith.

Adding fuel to the fire, popular pleas for the environment often use explicitly religious, often Christianesque language. John Muir, who was raised in the Disciples of Christ movement, used language about conversion and religious experience, and wrote of experiencing God in nature. In Muir's apologetics for national parks and environmental preservation, the religious language served to raise concerns of paganization among many conservative Christians. At a time when fundamentalism and evangelicalism were developing in response to the modernist controversy, Muir's choice of language may have alienated otherwise sympathetic Christians.

The pattern of leftward drift among evangelicals who engage in environmental activism still continues, with some notable figures who argued for evangelical engagement with the environment also becoming proponents of sexual revisionism. The recent popularity of ecotheology, a brand of highly revisionist liberation theology that focuses on freeing the oppressed environment, also contributes to the association of liberalism with environmentalism.

Additionally, many well-intentioned environmentalists, in part because of their acceptance of the Lynn White thesis, insist that revision of orthodox Christianity is necessary for environmental engagement. For example, in a 2015 article in the *Bulletin of the Atomic Scientists*, Bernard Zaleha and Andrew Szasz argue that the best hope for conservative Christian belief in climate change is to have theological liberals take over denominational structures and incorporate panentheism (the belief that God is greater than the universe and all of reality exists within and as a part of God) into Christianity. Statements like this increase resistance to the issue of environmental concern because of legitimate theological concerns.

The tendency of environmentalists drifting leftward is worth noting, but a robust theological framework should be able to support both a love of God and a concern to care for creation without compromise. If Scripture does call for environmental activism, evangelicals have an obligation to balance the two.

As Katherine Wilkinson shows in her 2012 volume, *Between God and Green: How Evangelicals are Cultivating a Middle Ground on Climate Change*, there have been recent efforts among evangelicals to work for the common good through environmental activism. However, many of those actions were met with resistance from other conservatives, often followed by the accusation of theological compromise. In some key cases, time has shown some of those criticisms to be warranted, though the continued association of environmentalism with theological liberalism is both unwarranted and unhelpful.

The financial crisis of 2008 and the rise of concern over sexual revisionism within Christianity has largely pushed environmentalism to the backburner of conservative Christian social concern. However, the path for an orthodox environmental ethics has been laid by Francis Schaeffer. Whatever imperfections in his cultural analysis, his 1970 volume, *Pollution and the Death of Man*, makes a compelling case for a robust environmental ethic while holding tight to the fundamentals of the faith. The same man was a vocal opponent of abortion, which later dominated his discourse and crowded out other themes like the environment. Schaeffer's theology provides an exemplary foundation for evangelical environmental activism.

Vitriolic rhetoric about the environment increases the difficulty in getting some concerned Christians engaged. The all-or-nothing approach to party platforms by both sides continues the association between abortion and the environment. The common cause of stewarding creation for future generations requires coalition building and acceptance of a middle ground, while the current political climate seems to have people on both sides interested in domination of the opposition.

Although there are some proposals from environmentalists that Christians must oppose if they are to remain consistent with historical Christian ethics, the basis of the instinctive resistance of some conservative Christians to environmental activism is often rooted in historical, political concerns rather than theological concerns. Conservative Christians would do better to argue about the theological basis for concern for God's creation and the ethics that flow from that rather than making economic concerns or political associations the primary influence in environmental decision-making.

Chapter 31

———

OIL IS A GIFT FROM GOD.
ARE WE SQUANDERING IT?

*What the church can do when the
world's had too much of a good thing.*

Ken Baake | 2019

By August 27, 1859, New England railroad conductor Edwin L. Drake had been spending borrowed money for months, and it was running out. His steam-powered drill had bored sixty-nine feet into the rock near Titusville, Pennsylvania, at the rate of three feet a day, and he had yet to strike oil. His employer, America's first petroleum exploration company, had given up on him. When Drake and his crew went home for the night, they were already accustomed to being the punchline of local jokes.

The next day, one of Drake's men spotted black liquid bubbling up in their well, and they began pumping it by hand into a washtub. What followed was arguably the most rapid economic and cultural transformation of the world.

The oil boom Drake triggered was accompanied by a flood of superlatives about the wonders, mysteries, and splendor of what was known at first as "rock oil." Most immediately, Drake's discovery offered America and the world affordable light. Kerosene—which could be made from petroleum—rapidly became the low-cost choice for lamp oil (its main competitor was pricey whale oil). Within two decades, kerosene had brought artificial lighting to city streets and to nearly every home in America.

Celebratory language continued into the early twentieth century, as petroleum products found revolutionary new uses as lubricant and, eventually, as fuel for motor vehicles. Geologists, businessmen, politicians, poets, and songwriters speculated on what this new discovery meant for America and humankind.

Pastors and theologians weighed in, too. For Presbyterian minister S.J.M. Eaton of Franklin, Pennsylvania, the sudden profusion of drilling sites along nearby Oil Creek was not the result of chance. In Eaton's view, God put vast pools of oil in the ground but kept it from man until just when we needed it to lift us out of the sin and trauma of the Civil War. In his 1866 book, *Petroleum: A History of the Oil Region of Venango County Pennsylvania*, Eaton wrote: "Who can doubt but that in the wise operations of God's Providence, the immense oil resources of the country have been developed at this particular time, to aid in the solution of the mighty problem of the nation's destiny?"

The year after Drake's discovery, another historian named Thomas A. Gale published a book on oil that opened with a quotation from the Book of Job, where the tormented Job was longing for the return of God's blessings, "when my steps were washed with milk, and the rock poured out for me streams of oil" (29:6, RSV). The verse probably references olive oil, but for early celebrants of petroleum, it seemed to apply far more directly to their divine gift from the ground. Historian Darren Dochuk, whose new book *Anointed With Oil* chronicles the intertwining paths of Christianity and crude, has noted that "many of the aspiring men who moved to the oil region of Western Pennsylvania after the Civil War did so armed with a certainty that they were chasing something from God."[1]

Nineteenth- and early twentieth-century adults in Chautauqua assemblies, the era's equivalent of TED Talks, learned from Alexander Winchell's 1890 geology text that coal—the fossil fuel that launched the industrial revolution—was also a gift from God. It was laid down, according to Winchell's *Walks and Talks in the Geologic Field*, for the benefit of man, who "is the fulfillment of the prophecy of the ages."

Within a century of Drake's discovery, America had powered itself to world dominance—with oil fueling the engine of its growth and prosperity. Of course, the blessings of oil have never been equitably enjoyed. In an economy as diverse as that of the United States, extractable fossil fuels and minerals have generally been a boon for most of the population. In countries with less diverse economies or with more authoritarian leaders—think the Democratic Republic of the Congo or Iraq—abundant natural resources have more often been linked to conflict and widespread poverty, a phenomenon economists call the "resource curse."

Nonetheless it is difficult to fault early optimism about the potential of fossil fuels to lift mankind to new heights of flourishing, because they did. After biblical times, the earth's population edged slowly upward to around a billion until the late eighteenth century, when economic and technological advancements,

---

[1] Darren Dochuk, "Anointed with Oil: God and Black Gold in Modern America," https://nanopdf.com/download/dochuk-darren-anointed-with-oil-god-and-black-gold-in-modern_pdf.

enabled by coal and then oil, lengthened life expectancies and sent the population soaring on a near vertical trajectory to 7.7 billion today.

Unquestionably, for our forebears and for so many of us, oil indeed has been a gift from God. Why then, in the public square today, are oil and other fossil fuels increasingly spoken of as the source of looming catastrophe, like an addictive substance from which we are anxious to wean ourselves?

Last year, thirteen government agencies from NASA to the Department of Commerce endorsed a report with dire warnings that the carbon dioxide byproduct of burning fossil fuels is layering the earth with a heat-trapping blanket, raising temperatures and sea levels.[2] In 2016, United Nations member countries ratified a new approach to fighting poverty that, in part, prioritized helping the poor in countries without the resources to adapt to a warming earth.

Americans are far from unified on our views of climate change. Yet various surveys show a growing majority are both worried about the trend and see human activity as its likely cause.[3] Evangelical Christians, on the whole, remain skeptical but are becoming less so; half say that global warming is happening and a quarter say humans are partially to blame, according to 2015 research by Pew. (A 2013 LifeWay study found that more than four in ten Protestant pastors "believe global warming is real and man made.") And in a 2015 encyclical letter both lauded and criticized by Christian communities, Pope Francis suggested that ignoring climate change is tantamount to ignoring the poor.

---

[2] "Third National Climate Assessment," https://nca2014.globalchange.gov/report.

[3] Megan Jula, "Where American Communities Agree and Disagree on Climate Change," American Communities Project, December 5, 2018, https://www.americancommunities.org/where-american-communities-agree -and-disagree-on-climate-change/.

Concerns about climate change aside, our consumption of oil products in particular has had a host of other less-disputed consequences. Plastic waste from our packaging-laden economies is filling our oceans to the tune of between 5.3 million and 14 million tons a year by some estimates—most of it from trash dumped on the ground and in rivers in developing countries. Researchers are only beginning to glimpse the impacts of microplastics, barely visible particles that are swirling in the oceans and that researchers this year found raining from the air in France.

Even our well-intended efforts at recycling—the fallback creation care practice for so many of us ("At least I recycle")—appear to be failing. China, where we sent most of our recyclables until now, announced major restrictions last year on how much paper and mixed plastics it would accept. The move has left much of America with almost no market for recyclables, prompting some cities to stop recycling altogether.

If we take a step back from our daily dependence on oil and our partisan views toward its place in our lives, the larger story arc is difficult to miss: As the God-appointed stewards of creation, we were handed one of the most priceless treasures from the depths of the earth and we fell in love with it. In ways deliberate and unwitting, we placed more and more of our hopes in its potential, until our union with oil became so intimate that it stretched our technological, theological, and social imaginations to think we could ever exist otherwise.

Oil in Our Blood

Every one of us is a child of oil and its material offspring. The moment we are born in a modern hospital, we are wrapped not in swaddling clothes, as Jesus was, but in oil, notes environmental scholar Vaclav Smil in his book, *Oil*. The first things we likely encounter as newborns are surgical gloves, flexible tubing, catheters, IV containers, and other trappings of sanitary health care—all made of oil-based plastics, as is the housing of the many computers and electronic instruments that monitor our well-being.

Our trip from the hospital to a well-lit and heated home will likely be in a car fueled by gasoline on roads paved with asphalt. Unless we are organic and local-food movement devotees, what we eat will have come from crops fertilized with fossil fuel derivatives and delivered to our homes on trucks or giant cargo ships from distant lands.

There is no denying oil's awesome power, harnessed from solar energy sequestered in simple ocean organisms that sank over eons to the sea floor. Under intense pressure, this dead carbon formed deposits that when mined and refined have such pent-up strength—as petroleum engineers like to tell it—that a mere teacup of gasoline can move a one-thousand-pound vehicle a mile up a mountain road.

But as the twentieth century brought population growth, technological and agricultural wonders, and wars on unprecedented scale, oil became less of a marvel and more of a "given" in our society. If anything, we lost sight of its miraculous and gift-like nature and came to take it for granted.

Instead, Americans celebrated the automobile and the freedom and mobility it brought. Popular songs lauding the "Merry Oldsmobile" of the early twentieth century and the "Little GTO" of the postwar baby boom sounded almost like psalms of praise for the almighty car. Such hymns persist today in musical worship of the iconic truck. "Thank God for the red words Jesus said," sings Kyle Thomas Nunn in a hard-driving country anthem. "Thank God for trucks."

Iconic images of the oil industry itself have become fundamental parts of American identity. "They don't wash out with the mud," asserts Montana country music singer-songwriter Eli Hundley, proclaiming his love for oilfield work. "It's in our American blood."

And yet that oil-rich "blood" is no longer reserved for the developed world. Beijing, New Delhi, Bangkok, and many other Asian cities are choked with dangerous smog as the region's growing middle class plays catch-up with the West in consumption. The Asia Pacific region has already overtaken the West in carbon dioxide emissions, which many experts see as a tipping point of sorts toward inevitable sea-level rise, droughts, and what Texas Tech climate scientist Katharine Hayhoe and others refer to as "weather on steroids."

Hayhoe and her husband, Andrew Farley, are evangelicals whose book *A Climate for Change* argues that God's gift was in creating a planet whose atmosphere was perfectly suited to human life. But by pouring greenhouse gasses into that atmosphere, we have upset the balance, essentially defiling the gift.

Fruit of the Spirit, Fruit of the Earth

Assuming, for argument's sake, that the vast majority of climate scientists[4] are correct in their view that humans are warming the world, it's difficult then not to ask: Could we have done anything differently up to this point? After all, serious research into atmospheric warming didn't begin until the mid-1900s, so it would be uncharitable to accuse 19th-century industrialized nations of willfully disregarding the global consequences of carbon emissions.

---

[4] https://climate.nasa.gov/scientific-consensus/.

Humans were polluting the air for hundreds of years before the Industrial Revolution, and history suggests we have long had an intuitive—if unscientific—sense that it was bad for us. The dangers of dirty air were contemplated as early as AD 61, when Seneca wrote about the "oppressive atmosphere" of smoke shrouding ancient Rome.[5] The Romans allowed smoke pollution lawsuits, and more than a thousand years later, England made modest attempts to limit the burning of coal under Queen Elizabeth I. Large-scale organized campaigns to curb air pollution eventually materialized in the mid-1800s, when the coal-hungry steam engine was supercharging the world's economy and coating neighborhoods in London, Chicago, and St. Louis with black soot.

Still, clean air concerns were almost entirely localized until recent decades. The notion that emissions could threaten the entire planet has only recently gone mainstream. But even if science and popular perception failed to raise sufficient alarms about climate change, was there nothing else to check our consumption of fossil fuels—and in particular our consumption of them as Christians?

There probably was. In the throes of the energy crisis in 1980, a man named George Sweeting, then president of Moody Bible Institute, sat down to write an essay for this magazine urging Christians to consume less.[6] Like many Americans, Sweeting was worried that the world would soon run out of oil. Advances in oil extraction technology have deferred such concerns today, but his call feels just as timely as climate change and mounting waste dominate conversations.

---

[5] Jim Morrison, "Air Pollution Goes Back Way Further Than You Think," *Smithsonian Magazine*, January 11, 2016, https://www.smithsonianmag.com/science-nature/air-pollution-goes-back-way-further-you-think-180957716/.

[6] George Sweeting, "Entering the Twilight Age," *Christianity Today* 24.12 (June 27, 1980): 28–29.

"We buy things that are convenient. We eat more than we need. Expensive packages and containers become trash," Sweeting wrote. "As victims of an easy lifestyle we have unthinkingly perpetuated a problem that is fast becoming a crisis. Somehow, we have to convince ourselves that even though things seem right, something is very wrong."

Whether intentional or not, Sweeting's essay was informed by the apostle Paul's list of the fruit of the Spirit in Galatians 5:22–23, arguably the simplest and most all-encompassing description of true Christian character. Paul not only makes the case that a life of love, joy, peace, patience, kindness, goodness, faithfulness, gentleness, and self-control is the ultimate goal of the Christian but also that such a life is only fully possible through the inner work of the Spirit. These postures are to govern our every relationship—with one another, with God himself, with our resources, and with the created world around us. And when our behaviors stem from these postures, Paul says, we'll have no need for laws to tell us what to do because we'll already be outperforming the law.

If Paul is correct, then the fruit of the Spirit may be the gold standard governing how we consume God's most precious natural gifts, such as fossil fuels and metals—or how we use any treasure, for that matter, such as an unexpected inheritance or a suddenly valuable piece of land on which a church building sits.

A loving posture toward our neighbors, for instance, would among other things certainly rule out binging on precious resources for our own benefit at the expense of others. "Wasting energy is as much an act of violence against the poor as refusing to feed the hungry," Sweeting wrote. Along the lines of self-control, Sweeting argued that Christians must be examples of those "who restrain our self-desires." Seeming to make the case for patience, Sweeting argued that exploitation is the natural result of "greed and haste" when we "take too much too fast." In an essay accompanying Sweeting's in the same 1980 issue, evangelical philosophy professor Loren Wilkinson seemed to also have an attitude of patience in mind, writing:

> Good stewardship does not place on the future greater debts than it inherited from the past. This principle is particularly important in considering our use of nonrenewable resources like metals and fossil fuels. It suggests that if we use those things, part of their use should be diverted to establishing a substitute the future can use.

One could probably extend Sweeting's and Wilkinson's logic today and argue, for example, that an outlook of joy and contentment would ask whether we really need that jet-fueled international vacation this year, whether we really need quite so large a house to heat and cool, or whether we really need the latest cellphone.

Acts of the Flesh

Whether or not we have individually demonstrated the fruit of the Spirit in our consumption of fossil fuels over the past two centuries, the story of the oil industry itself is replete with "the acts of the flesh"—what Paul posed as the opposite of Christian living. History echoes Old Testament accounts of gold and other treasure that, in the service of corrupt kings and ordinary human greed, became idols that eventually invited God's wrath.

The first oil king was John D. Rockefeller. Born 1839 in upstate New York to a pious mother and an unscrupulous cad of a father, Rockefeller was a devout Baptist. He launched and quickly dominated the oil refining and transportation businesses. But Rockefeller was a flawed godly king, accused by critics of poor labor practices and cutthroat and deceptive business dealings. He consumed everything in his path like the giant octopus portraying him in newspaper cartoons of the day, and eventually his

Standard Oil Co. was dismantled by the US Supreme Court as an illegal monopoly.

Many others were overcome with "oil fever" and turned away from God. Tales of stock swindles, oil field murders, and boom-and-bust town chicanery reveal a people embracing false idols, bewitched by the promise of wealth. Only six years after Drake's discovery, William Wright was lamenting in an 1865 book, *The Oil Regions of Pennsylvania*, that "in Petrolia, the church universally believed in is an engine-house, with a derrick for its tower, a well for its Bible, and a two-inch tube for its preacher."

As with our stewardship of most of God's good gifts, of course, our relationship with oil is a complex mix of vice and virtue. The oil industry has been exploited by some but, at the same time, it birthed a new era of philanthropy in the United States. Rockefeller's charitable giving to public health, higher educa-tion, and Baptist missions helped transform entire segments of American society. So too did the philanthropy of other oil barons, including J. Howard Pew, whose contributions supported semi-naries and Billy Graham's ministry and subsidized the founding of *CT*.

That the oil industry has done so much good may explain, in part, why calls for environmental stewardship are often met with claims that to leave fossil fuels in the ground is tantamount to rejecting the bounty that a divine creator put there for our use. Energy writer Alex Epstein argues in *The Moral Case for Fossil Fuels* that turning away from oil would deny people in the developing world the same gifts that built and succored the West. The Cornwall Alliance, a right-of-center network of Christian scholars in diverse fields, affirms on its website that "one way of exercising godly dominion is by transforming raw materials into resources and using them to meet human needs." To leave such bounty in the earth, the group asserts, is as wrong as it was for the laborer in the Gospel of Matthew who hid his wages in the ground rather than investing them in a quest for abundance (25:14–30).

Greener Idols

The Cornwall Alliance's arguments are persuasive in many ways: There's no denying that the gifts of oil and other fossil fuels have enabled countless other "good and perfect" gifts that, as Scripture points out, came in some way or another from God. Their critique of carbon haters is that to suddenly change the rules of the energy game and deprive the rest of the world the quality of life that Americans enjoy is not especially loving.

Outside some extreme voices, however, the green energy crowd isn't exactly preaching a message of privation. Their rhetoric often rings with almost the same blessing-for-all euphoria as nineteenth- and twentieth-century celebrations of oil. The Sierra Club's summary of a congressional proposal for a "Green New Deal" is an example. The excited rhetoric with which Eaton described oil in 1866—marshaling words like "bounty," "immense," and "mighty"—can be heard echoing in an online Sierra Club explainer titled "What is a Green New Deal?"[7] The plan is "a big, bold transformation of the economy to tackle the twin crises of inequality and climate change," the group writes. "It would mobilize vast public resources to help us transition from an economy built on exploitation and fossil fuels to one driven by dignified work and clean energy."

Green New Deal evangelists root their hope less in a particular resource than in human ingenuity. In this, many climate activists and climate skeptics share a common belief: Whether mankind must act now to save the planet or whether, guided by

---

[7] Sierra Club, "What Is a Green New Deal?" https://www.sierraclub.org/trade/what-green-new-deal, accessed June 7, 2021.

market forces, mankind will eventually adapt to whatever the earth serves up, human progress will prevail.

But even if we do someday innovate a door to a distant, carbon-lite future, we'll be just as prone to turn whatever miraculous new gifts it holds into idols. In truth, while wind turbines and solar panels and electric cars are also good gifts from God, our excited anticipation of such technologies is often as much about dodging the need for self-constraint as it is about caring for creation. We are eager for anything that doesn't disrupt our consumer lifestyles.

Economic analysts suggest that at least some greater transition to alternative fuels is increasingly viable. Renewable energy has finally become cost-competitive with conventional fuels, and even oil giant British Petroleum is in what its CEO calls "a race to lower greenhouse gas emissions" as its own scientists expect renewable energy to overtake traditional sources within two decades.[8]

But as Christians debate the risks of climate change and the need for action, we must be careful not to replace adulation of oil and the progress it fueled with adulation for new technological innovations. Alternative energy certainly is an important tool in the creation care toolbox, but the hope that yesterday's technology will easily be replaced with acres of solar panels and wind farms may lead to disappointment and missed opportunities to adopt a more prudent lifestyle.

Baptist Theological Seminary Bible professor Mark Biddle offers perhaps the best warning for those who would substitute temples to oil with temples to new technology: "Christianity

---

[8] Adam Vaughan, "BP Aims to Invest More in Renewables and Clean Energy," *The Guardian*, February 6, 2018, https://www.theguardian.com/business/2018/feb/06/bp-aims-to-invest-more-in-renewables-and-clean-energy.

does not offer a utopian vision of perfected human society," Biddle writes in his 2005 book, *Missing the Mark: Sin and Its Consequences in Biblical Theology*. "It issues a call to the kingdom of God." For Biddle, progress is the myth of a society "marked by arrogant overconfidence in human capabilities."

Human overconfidence is not just a religious concern but also a technological one. Manufacturing wind turbines takes massive amounts of energy, and transporting the blades, steel, and concrete to building sites requires large, diesel-fueled trucks. Likewise, the manufacture of alternative transportation sources, such as electric and hybrid cars, demands staggering amounts of energy and rare earth metals whose production has particularly nasty environmental side effects. And many forms of green energy and transportation remain expensive and out of reach for low- and middle-income Americans.

Clearly, we will not be given solutions to climate change or to the global trash epidemic absent hard choices and sacrifices. And no sacrifice from the church alone will be enough to turn the tide without significant efforts from industry and the massive global supply chains that are only responding to current consumer habits and even government regulations. (Who has ever bought supermarket blueberries in anything other than those clear clam shells that, in fact, aren't very recyclable but do deliver a healthy and fresh product?)

But Sweeting, the former Moody president, argued that the church is God's "living, small-scale demonstration of the world as it should be." He felt that Christians did not have to be alarmist because "our confidence is in the Lord," and rather than try to solve every problem, we should seek "God's help to be examples to the world."

Confidence in God will be as necessary for any changes we make today as it was for the Israelites during the Exodus from

Egypt. This is something Evangelical Environmental Network president Mitchell Hescox knows, having come from a family of Pennsylvania coal miners. People of faith understand that climate change is real and dangerous, he says. But he adds in his book with meteorologist Paul Douglas: "We know how life was in Egypt, but we're scared of the future going into the Promised Land."[9]

Is it possible that the very process of choosing to live more simply could free us, through acts of humility, to lay hold of something better than ourselves? To paraphrase Paul in his letter to the Philippians, we must not look to our own interests but instead suffer the loss of things in exchange for the knowledge of Christ.

Slaves to One Another, Not to Our Stuff

When the prophet Isaiah foretold the breakup of Israel and Judea, he referenced their abundant wealth and even their transportation, whose "land is full of silver and gold," where "there is no end to their treasures," and where "there is no end to their chariots" (Isa. 2:7–8).

Writers paint similar pictures of American society. In 1996, environmental writer Bill McKibben wrote a *CT* cover story subtitled "Why spending less and turning off TV should be part of the church's mission to the world." McKibben proclaimed that our consumer ethos was like "a tree whose canopy spreads so wide that it blots out the sun, that it blots out the quiet word of God. ... We are led daily, hourly, into temptation."

Five years later, John de Graaf and his co-authors reported in their book, *Affluenza: The All-Consuming Epidemic*, that four million pounds of raw material such as mined metals and oil are necessary to provide for one average American family's annual

---

[9] *Caring for Creation: The Evangelical's Guide to Climate Change and a Healthy Environment* (Bloomington, MN: Bethany House, 2016).

consumption. Americans spend more on trash bags in a year than 90 of the world's 210 countries spend for everything.

While consumption is a major component of the hallowed gross domestic product by which many politicians and economists measure goodness, it seems undeniable that Americans, including Christians, will eventually have to learn to live with less. We will have to treat our gifts from God—whether natural resources, material well-being, or personal and societal freedoms—with reverence rather than abandon.

We may need to turn again to Paul. When he wrote to the Galatians and made his case for the fruit of the Spirit, he set up his argument just a few sentences earlier with an admonition that surely was not written with our modern levels of material consumption in mind but whose application rings eerily prescient in our day:

> You, my brothers and sisters, were called to be free. But do not use your freedom to indulge the flesh; rather, serve one another humbly in love. For the entire law is fulfilled in keeping this one command: "Love your neighbor as yourself." If you bite and devour each other, watch out or you will be destroyed by each other. (5:13–15)

SOURCES

1   Editors, "Fulfilling God's Cultural Mandate," *Christianity Today* 14.11 (February 27, 1970): 24–25.

2   Editors, "Ecologism: A New Paganism?" *Christianity Today* 14.14 (April 10, 1970): 33–34.

3   Editors, "Terracide," *Christianity Today* 14.15 (April 23, 1971): 26–27.

4   Carl H. Reidel, "Christianity and the Environmental Crisis," *Christianity Today* 15.15 (April 23, 1971): 4–8.

5   James M. Houston, "The Environmental Movement—Five Causes of Confusion," *Christianity Today* 16.24 (September 15, 1972): 8–10.

6   Martin Labar, "A Message to Polluters from the Bible," *Christianity Today* 18.21 (July 26, 1974): 8–12.

7   Loren Wilkinson, "Global Housekeeping: Lords or Servants?," *Christianity Today* 24.12 (June 27, 1980): 26–30.

8   Paul Brand, "A Handful of Mud," *Christianity Today* 29.7 (April 19, 1985): 25–31.

9   Kim A. Lawton, "Environment: Is There Room for Prolife Environmentalists?," *Christianity Today* 34.13 (September 13, 1990): 46–47.

10 William A. Dyrness, "Are We Our Planet's Keeper?: Our Problems with the Environment Are Not Merely Technical, They Are Spiritual," *Christianity Today* 35.4 (April 8, 1991): 40–42.

11   Loren Wilkinson, "Earth Summit: Searching for a Spiritual Foundation," *Christianity Today* 36.8 (July 20, 1992), 48.

12   Ronald J. Sider, "Redeeming the Environmentalists," *Christianity Today* 37.7 (June 21, 1993): 26–29.

13   Loren Wilkinson, "How Christian Is the Green Agenda?," *Christianity Today* 37.1 (January 11, 1993): 16–20.

14   Tod Connor, "Is the Earth Alive?," *Christianity Today* 37.1 (January 11, 1993): 22–25.

15   David N. Livingstone, Calvin B. DeWitt, and Loren Wilkinson, "Eco-Myths," *Christianity Today* 38.4 (April 4, 1994): 22–33.

16   Bill McKibben, "Christmas Unplugged," *Christianity Today* 40.14 (December 9, 1996): 19–23.

17   Randy Frame, "Greening of the Gospel?," *Christianity Today* 40.13 (November 11, 1996): 82–84.

18   Tim Stafford, "God's Green Acres," *Christianity Today* 42.7 (June 15, 1998): 32–37.

19   Editors, "Heat Stroke," *Christianity Today* 48.10 (October 2004): 26–27.

20   Andy Crouch, "Environmental Wager," *Christianity Today* 49.8 (August 2005): 66.

21   Ragan Sutterfield, "Imagining a Different Way to Live," *Christianity Today* 50.11 (November 2006): 61–63.

22   Editors, "One-Size Politics Doesn't Fit All," *Christianity Today* 51.5 (May 2007): 22–23.

23   Rob Moll, "The Good Shepherds," *Christianity Today* 51.10 (October 2007): 64–69.

24   David Neff, "Second Coming Ecology," *Christianity Today* 52.7 (July 2008): 34–37.

25   Editors, "Not One Sparrow," *Christianity Today* 53.7 (July 2009): 19.

26   Leslie Leyland Fields, "A Feast Fit for the King," *Christianity Today* 54.11 (November 2010): 22–28.

27 Scott Sabin, "Whole Earth Evangelism," *Christianity Today* 54.7 (July 2010): 27–29.

28 Andy Crouch, Eugene Peterson, and Peter Harris, "The Joyful Environmentalists," *Christianity Today* 55.6 (June 2011), 30–32.

29 Tony Carnes, "Back to the Garden," *Christianity Today* 55.7 (July 2011): 56–58.

30 Andrew Spencer, "Three Reasons Why Evangelicals Stopped Advocating for the Environment," *Christianity Today* online, June 14, 2017, https://www.christianitytoday.com/ct/2017/june-web-only/three-reasons-evangelicals-dont-advocate-for-environment.html.

31 Ken Baake, "Oil Is a Gift from God. Are We Squandering It?" *Christianity Today* 63.5 (June 2019).

SCRIPTURE INDEX

Old Testament

New Testament